THE PRIZE
of the
HIGH CALLING

being
an exposition of the epistle to the
PHILIPPIANS

By

Charles H. Welch

Author of

Dispensational Truth
The Apostle of the Reconciliation
The Testimony of the Lord's Prisoner
Parable, Miracle and Sign
The Form of Sound Words
Just and the Justifier
In Heavenly Places

THE BEREAN PUBLISHING TRUST
52A, Wilson Street, London, EC2A 2ER
ENGLAND
Study Shelf
by *Pilkington & Sons*
1-800-784-6010
www.StudyShelf.com

© THE BEREAN PUBLISHING TRUST

ISBN   0 85156 148 9

First Edition	1950
Reset and reprinted	1992
Reprinted	1999

CONTENTS

ii

PREFACE

It was very gracious of the Author to invite me to write the Preface to the present volume for I possess no special qualification for such service. True I have known the Author for many years and that is probably the reason for the invitation, for there has been a joyful fellowship from the beginning until now.

The subject-matter of this book is a very necessary exhortation for the present day, namely, service that follows on identification with the Risen Lord and is stimulated by the 'mind that is in Christ Jesus', as the highest example, and then of those who follow – Paul, Timothy, Epaphroditus.

Perfection is progressive, and we are urged to 'go on unto' perfection. That suggests a resolute and determined pilgrimage. Paul said he did not speak as one that had attained, but, forgetting the things that were behind, he pressed on towards the mark of the prize of the high calling of God in Christ Jesus. That should be a salutary warning to us all.

God is our Counsellor and He gives us the best instruction necessary to know His will by 'rightly dividing the Word of Truth' (2 Tim. 2:15). Let no would-be student turn a deaf ear to this gracious instruction and thereby go his own way and do that which seems right in his own eyes. God has a purpose beyond John 3:16. All Scripture is surely profitable – thank God for its preservation – yet it is needful to give special attention to the Epistles of the apostle to the Gentiles, of whom we are.

Bible students should be much indebted to the Author who has gone to such lengths to place so full an exposition in the hands of present-day seekers after truth and any apparent repetition but emphasizes the completeness of presentation.

With these thoughts – that the book will be helpful to many who are seeking to follow on to 'serve The Lord' with all humility of mind as did the apostle to the Gentiles – our prayer is that this book will be graciously used to the exaltation of Him in the hearts of all whom He has redeemed.

W. H.
152, Astwood Road,
Worcester
1950.

INTRODUCTION

The Prison Epistles

The Acts of the Apostles records the ministry of two servants of Christ – Peter and Paul. Both have a special enduement of the Spirit (Acts 2 and 13) and both conclude their ministries, so far as the Acts is concerned, with imprisonment (Acts 12 and 28). The conversion and commission of Paul is first recorded in chapter 9, but certain features of it are not mentioned until his earlier ministry came to an end (Acts 26:16-18). Paul is found speaking in a Jewish synagogue for the last time in Acts 19:8, and in chapter 20 we find him assuring the Ephesian elders that they would see his face no more. Paul had arranged for these elders to meet him at the sea-port Miletus because he hasted, if it were possible for him, to be at Jerusalem on the day of Pentecost. As we listen to his words to these elders we are quite certain that he is summing up a ministry that has finished, and his subsequent words show that he has in view a ministry soon to begin. Let us hear the apostle:

> ' ... Ye know, from the first day that I came into Asia, after what manner I have been with you at all seasons, serving the Lord with all humility of mind, and with many tears, and temptations, which befell me by the lying in wait of the Jews: And how I kept back nothing that was profitable unto you, but have shewed you, and have taught you publickly, and from house to house, testifying both to the Jews, and also to the Greeks, repentance toward God, and faith toward our Lord Jesus Christ' (Acts 20:18-21).

It is very evident that Paul is about to bid the Ephesians farewell and he seeks to impress upon them the nature of the ministry they had received. In verses 25-27, he continues :

> 'And now, behold, I know that ye all, among whom I have gone preaching the kingdom of God, shall see my face no more. Wherefore I take you to record this day, that I am pure from the blood of all men. For I have not shunned to declare unto you all the counsel of God'.

In this second statement the apostle not only declares that he did not keep back anything that was profitable, but adds that he did not shun to declare all the counsel of God.

In Acts 26:22,23 we have a further statement which has a bearing upon Acts 20:27 :

'Having therefore obtained help of God, I continue unto this day, witnessing both to small and great, saying none other things than those which the prophets and Moses did say should come: That Christ should suffer, and that He should be the first that should rise from the dead, and should shew light unto the people, and to the Gentiles'.

It is evident from these words that when Paul declared all the counsel of God, he made no mention of the dispensation of the mystery, for that was never revealed either to Moses or to the prophets, but was 'hid in God' until the time came for its manifestation, and that, not until Israel had been set aside.

What was it that had come into the apostle's life to make him realize so definitely this change of ministry? Let him speak once more for himself :

'And now, behold, I go bound in the spirit unto Jerusalem, not knowing the things that shall befall me there: save that the Holy Ghost witnesseth in every city, saying that bonds and afflictions abide me. But none of these things move me, neither count I my life dear unto myself, so that I might finish my course with joy, and the ministry, which I have received of the Lord Jesus, to testify the gospel of the grace of God' (Acts 20:22-24).

The reader will recognize the Holy Spirit's sign of a change in the words 'and now', which are found in other important contexts. It appears quite clear that the apostle was contemplating a ministry closely associated with imprisonment; he was prepared by grace not only for prison but death itself so long as he might finish his course. This he was most graciously enabled to do, for in his last prison epistle, and in view of approaching martyrdom, he could say, 'I have finished my course'.

He summarizes his future ministry in the words: 'to testify the gospel of the grace of God' – a fitting gospel for that 'dispensation of the grace of God' which Ephesians 3:1,2 declares was entrusted to him as the prisoner of Jesus Christ.

What the apostle anticipated in Acts 20 he declares as an established fact in Acts 26, so we will turn to his statement before king Agrippa for further light upon his prison ministry. Standing before king Agrippa the apostle gives a rapid summary of his early life, his antipathy to the name of Jesus of Nazareth, and to his persecution of believers even to strange cities. This brings him to the Damascus road and the revelation of the ascended Christ. He hears from heaven that he is persecuting the Lord Jesus, and the Lord says to him :

'But rise, and stand upon thy feet: for I have appeared unto thee for this purpose, to make thee a minister and a witness both of these things which thou hast seen, and of those things in the which I will appear unto thee; delivering thee from the people, and from the Gentiles, unto whom now I send thee. To open their eyes, and to turn them from darkness to light, and from the power of Satan unto God, that they may receive forgiveness of sins, and inheritance among them which are sanctified by faith that is in Me' (Acts 26:16-18).

Here is a twofold witness and commission revealed by the employment of the word 'both' – 'the things which thou hast seen' and 'those things in the which I will appear unto thee'. Christ not only appeared to Paul on the road to Damascus and commissioned him to bear His name before Gentiles and kings and the children of Israel; He appeared, also, according to His promise at some time subsequent to Acts 9, commissioning the apostle as the prisoner of Jesus Christ to the Gentiles and entrusting to him that dispensation of the mystery whose terms are faintly foreshadowed in Acts 26:18. A further confirmation is found in Acts 22:15, where Paul records the words of Ananias :

'For thou shalt be His witness unto all men of what thou hast SEEN and HEARD'.

It is a matter beyond dispute that Acts 20 sees the close of one ministry, and the dawn of another. It is beyond dispute on the evidence both of Acts 20 and 26, that the new ministry was a prison ministry, that it was the subject of a special revelation from the Lord, and that it had the Gentiles specially in view :

'The Gentiles, unto whom now I send thee'.

From this imprisoned minister went forth the message :

'The salvation of God is sent unto the Gentiles' (Acts 28:28).

To find that word of truth which includes the gospel of our salvation (Eph. 1:13), we must study those epistles written by Paul after Acts 28 which bear the mark of prison upon them. What are these prison epistles? Can we discover them?

There are five epistles written from prison after the setting aside of Israel, and we have but to read these epistles to discover the fact for ourselves.

EPHESIANS IS A PRISON EPISTLE.

'For this cause I Paul, the prisoner of Jesus Christ for you Gentiles' (3:1).

'I, therefore, the prisoner of the Lord, beseech you' (4:1).

'The mystery of the gospel, for which I am an ambassador in bonds' (6:19,20).

PHILIPPIANS IS A PRISON EPISTLE.

'Both in my bonds, and in the defence and confirmation of the gospel' (1:7).

'My bonds in Christ are manifest in all the palace' (1:13).

'Many of the brethren ... waxing confident by my
    bonds' (1:14).

'Supposing to add affliction to my bonds' (1:16).

'All the saints salute you, chiefly they that are of
    Caesar's household' (4:22).

COLOSSIANS IS A PRISON EPISTLE.

'The mystery of Christ, for which I am also in bonds'
    (4:3).

'Aristarchus my fellowprisoner saluteth you' (4:10).

'Remember my bonds' (4:18).

2 TIMOTHY IS A PRISON EPISTLE.

'Be not thou therefore ashamed of the testimony of
    our Lord, nor of me His prisoner' (1:8).

'Wherein I suffer trouble ... even unto bonds' (2:9).

'At my first answer no man stood with me' (4:16).

PHILEMON IS A PRISON EPISTLE.

'Paul a prisoner of Jesus Christ' (1).

'Now also a prisoner of Jesus Christ' (9).

'Onesimus, whom I have begotten in my bonds' (10).

'He might have ministered unto me in the bonds of
    the gospel' (13).

'There salute thee Epaphras, my fellowprisoner in
    Christ Jesus' (23).

Here then are five epistles, each one unmistakably
written from prison. The epistle to Philemon is somewhat
of a private nature. Philemon was host to the church at
Colosse, and the epistle shows something of the home life
at the time of writing. We feel there is not sufficient
evidence given us in these epistles to decide in what order
they were written, but – and this is far more important to

us – they have a most definite inter-relation that is of the utmost importance for us to observe, for a true realization of the scope of each epistle is essential to the correct interpretation of smaller passages.

Before we set out this intimate inter-relationship, it will be necessary to discuss the presence of a principle that is found throughout the pages of revealed truth. Truth is balanced, not arbitrarily but morally and essentially. The truth revealed in Scripture concerning the Lord's people deals with their *standing* and with their *state*. Not standing only, for all privilege without some responsibility is fatal to growth. Not state only, for the burden of responsibility, with the knowledge of so much failure, would depress and render salvation fruitless. These two sides of the Christian life, standing and state, are expressed in a variety of ways. These are some of them:

Standing	State
SALVATION.	SERVICE.
FREE GIFT.	REWARD OR PRIZE.
NOT OF WORKS.	UNTO GOOD WORKS.
IF WE BE DEAD WITH HIM, WE SHALL ALSO LIVE WITH HIM.	IF WE SUFFER, WE SHALL ALSO REIGN WITH HIM.

Two passages from the epistles may be studied here with profit. The first is from Corinthians :

'According to the grace of God which is given unto me, as a wise master-builder, I have laid the foundation, and another buildeth thereon. But let every man take heed how he buildeth thereupon. For other foundation can no man lay than that is laid, which is Jesus Christ. Now if any man build upon this foundation gold, silver, precious stones, wood, hay, stubble; every man's work shall be made manifest: for the day shall declare it, because it shall be revealed by fire; and the fire shall try every man's work of what sort it is. If any man's work abide which he hath built thereupon, he shall receive a reward. If any man's work shall be burned, he shall suffer loss: but he himself shall be saved; yet so as by fire' (1 Cor. 3:10-15).

Standing and state are here represented in the figure of foundation and building. The foundation is not in question: 'he shall be saved' even though he be saved 'so as by fire'. 'He shall be saved' even though 'he shall suffer loss'. There is the greatest difference between 'he shall *suffer* loss', and 'he shall *be* lost'. The test, the reward, and the loss relate only to the subsequent 'work'. Notice the repeated reference to a man's work: 'every man's *work* shall be made manifest'; 'every man's *work* of what sort it is'; 'if any man's *work* abide'; 'if any man's *work* shall be burned'.

Before we turn to the second reference, we ought perhaps to anticipate an objection. Some have said that the whole atmosphere of the revelation of the mystery is of such grace as to rule out all idea of reward or loss. Of course this is perfectly true if we confine ourselves to the revelation of doctrine, the revelation of our perfect standing in Christ. But even the Epistle to Ephesians, with its wondrous acceptance in the Beloved, warns its readers against some terrible sins, and in the practical section the apostle writes :

'Knowing that whatsoever good thing any man doeth, the same shall he receive of the Lord, whether he be bond or free' (Eph. 6:8).

Colossians is even more to the point :

'And whatsoever ye do, do it heartily, as to the Lord, and not unto men; knowing that of the Lord ye shall receive the reward of the inheritance: for ye serve the Lord Christ. But he that doeth wrong shall receive for the wrong which he hath done: and there is no respect of persons' (Col. 3:23-25).

To those who bow before the authority of Scripture, these two citations are the end of all argument, and as we are not writing to persuade others, we can now pass on to our second illustrative passage in 2 Timothy :

'... if we be dead with Him, we shall also live with Him: if we suffer, we shall also reign with Him: if we deny Him, He also will deny us: If we believe not, yet He abideth faithful: He cannot deny Himself' (2 Tim. 2:11-13).

Here are two statements which, if not divided aright, appear contradictory – 'He will deny us'; 'He cannot deny Himself'. But the first deals with *living*, and the second with *reigning*. Now living is one thing; receiving a throne, a dominion and a crown is another. Both attainments have the necessary qualifications prefixed.

How may we hope to 'live with Him'? This is settled once and for ever by the fact that all who believe in Christ are reckoned by God to have 'died with Him'. This cannot be altered. It can neither be won nor lost. It stands entirely in grace. It is God's free gift, and even though one thus saved should become unfaithful, nevertheless, He will abide faithful to His work and promise. He cannot deny Himself; such shall be saved, just as surely as the man of 1 Corinthians 3.

How may we hope to 'reign with Him'? This does not depend upon being reckoned to have died with Christ. It is connected with a voluntary fellowship with His sufferings. If we endure, we shall reign; if we do not endure, then we shall not reign. No cross, no crown. If in the realm of suffering and reigning we draw back, we cannot lose our life, for that is not in question, but we can forfeit the reward; in that sphere, and that only, 'if we deny Him, He also will deny us'.

The reader may well ask why we have digressed from our main theme and entered into this discussion. The reason is that we desire to show these five great epistles of the mystery give balanced truth. We have not five epistles written about privilege; neither have we five epistles written about responsibility. We have a pair that lays the foundation, and a pair that deals with the building and one that sets forth the atmosphere of this calling; the first pair reveals our standing and acceptance, and the second pair, our state and our acceptableness. They are related as follows :

A   EPHESIANS.   *Standing.*   Accepted in the Beloved.
   B   PHILIPPIANS.   *State.*   Work out your own salvation
                                      A prize in view.
      C   PHILEMON.   The truth seen in daily living.
A   COLOSSIANS.   *Standing.*   Presented unblameable.
   B   2 TIMOTHY.   *State.*   Not crowned except he
                                        strive lawfully.

The above is merely to focus the attention and display the arrangement of the epistles. It is no proof, however, that the arrangement is true. The reader will rightly demand something more than a few random texts, and so we will now show the scriptural reasons provided by these epistles themselves to justify the above correspondence.

The correspondence between Philippians and 2 Timothy may not be obvious at this stage, but an examination of the parallels, and particularly the last two which we give, should be enough for the most exacting.

THE PRISON EPISTLES

Structure showing their distinctive doctrines and their interrelation

A EPHESIANS
Seated
together.

The dispensation (3:2 and 9 R.V.). Mystery (3:3). The church which is His body (1:22,23). The fulness (1:23; 4:10). Christ the Head (1:22). Principalities and powers (1:21).*

B PHILIPPIANS
The Prize.

Try the things that differ (1:10 margin). Strive (1:27). Press toward the mark (3:14). Prize (3:14). *Depart†* (1:23). *Offered†* (2:17).

C PHILEMON.

A COLOSSIANS
Complete
in Him.

Dispensation (1:25). Mystery (1:26). The church which is His body (1:24). Fulness (1:19). Christ the Head (2:19). Principalities and powers (1:16; 2:10).*

B 2 TIMOTHY
The Crown.

Rightly dividing the Word (2:15). Strive (2:5). Course finished (4:7). Crown (4:8). *Depart†* (4:6). *Offered†* (4:6).

---

* *None of these expressions occurs in Philippians or 2 Timothy.*
† *Only occurrences in Paul's epistles.*

In its own place we must give attention to the various interpretations that have been given of Paul's desire 'to depart', but the reader will expect, with this evident parallel between Philippians and 2 Timothy in view, that we shall reject any interpretation that runs counter to the Spirit's own explanation as given here.

For the moment we are not discussing the interpretation of details, but seeking to establish the fact that the revelation of the mystery, though unique, and revealing a calling, a standing, a sphere and a constitution hitherto unknown, is no exception to the rule that we have been considering. The wondrous revelation of grace calls for a walk that is worthy, and unless we embrace the truth of these epistles together, we shall fail to grow and our knowledge will be barren and unfruitful. The *high calling* will be ours, but we shall miss *the prize* of the high calling. The *inheritance* will be ours, but we shall miss *the reward* of the inheritance. We shall have nothing to lay at His feet in the crowning day that is coming.

Our special study in this volume is the epistle of 'the prize' and of 'the out-resurrection' and of those who go on unto 'perfection'; we shall not meet with such terms as 'the Mystery', 'principalities and powers' or 'dispensation' for these belong to the hope and to Ephesians, rather than with the prize and to Philippians.

Special attention has been given to the meaning of the words 'depart and be with Christ', and we commend that section of the exposition that attempts to understand what is involved in the 'mind that was in Christ Jesus' as set out in Philippians 2:6-9.

A fairly comprehensive structure of the epistle is provided, and every effort has been made to let the Scripture speak for itself. Greek words are represented by italic type thus, *lego*, but no attempt has been made to indicate the omega (or the long o); the reader who is familiar with the Greek does not need it, the reader who cannot read Greek does not want it and the appearance of the type page, to say nothing of the proof corrector's feelings, will be improved by their omission.

Now may the Lord bless us all as we consider the prize of our high calling, and the spiritual qualities that are called into play as we seek to emulate the apostle who said :

'... This one thing I do, forgetting those things which are behind, and reaching forth unto those things which are before, I press toward the mark for the prize of the high calling of God in Christ Jesus' (Phil. 3:13,14).

CHAPTER 1

The Scope of the Epistle

Philippians is a 'prison epistle', containing four references to the apostle's 'bonds' (Phil. 1:7,13,14,16), and the statement that these bonds in Christ were manifest to the whole Praetorium, and to all the rest (1:13). A special salutation is sent to the Philippians from the saints that were in 'Caesar's household' (Phil. 4:22). The imprisonment which the apostle had suffered at Caesarea was at any time terminable by him by an appeal unto Caesar, which we know was actually the case (Acts 25:10-12). In the imprisonment referred to in the epistle he was 'in a strait' betwixt life and death, but became confident that his release would be granted, and that he would see the Philippians once more (Phil. 1:24-26; 2:24). Not only must the epistle have been written during the two years detention in Rome, it must also have been written toward the end of that period. There are certain events recorded that demand a period of time for their accomplishment. The Philippians had learned of Paul's imprisonment in Rome, and had had time to make a collection on his account and to send Epaphroditus as their messenger (Phil. 2:25); Epaphroditus had in the meantime fallen dangerously ill, but sufficient time had elapsed, not only for his recovery, but for the news to have travelled as far as Philippi (Phil. 2:26). Epaphroditus moreover is the bearer of this epistle back to the Philippians. The apostle expressed the wish to send Timothy *shortly* to Philippi (Phil. 2:19) 'as soon as I shall see how it will go with me' (Phil. 2:23). It is therefore fairly obvious that his trial is drawing to an end. It is indeed probable that the epistle was written after his case had been heard by the Emperor, and before the public declaration that set him at liberty. This would account for all the allusions made to both his confinement and his expectation of immediate release. A considerable length of time moreover must be allowed for reasons that while not actually mentioned in the epistle,

were matters of well known historic fact. On similar
occasions, the testimony of historians helps us to see that
the Jews would adopt delaying tactics, for if they could not
succeed in accomplishing the apostle's death, the next best
thing for their own cause, would be to keep him bound.
According to the law, Paul's accusers could apply for an
adjournment while they summoned witnesses (Tac. An. 13.
52), especially as Paul was charged with exciting sedition
throughout 'the world' (Acts 24:5). Paul himself had
referred to this law when he stood before Felix saying that
the Jews of Asia ought to have been summoned to the trial
(Acts 24:19). Tacitus mentions a case in the time of Nero,
when a year was allowed for the obtaining of necessary
evidence. We can be fairly certain therefore   that
Ephesians, Colossians and Philemon had been written
before Philippians was penned, Philemon being the epistle
immediately before Philippians, for in that very gracious
and personal letter to Philemon Paul wrote 'but withal
prepare me also a lodging: for I trust that through your
prayers I shall be given unto you' (Philem. 22).

Ephesians appears to have been written earlier in the
period, for, although Tychicus was to make known to the
believer all Paul's affairs, there is not the slightest hint that
his trial was imminent or that he expected release.   If
Ephesians had already been written then Philippians must
have been written in the full light of the revelation of the
mystery. Philippians therefore takes its place as one of the
prison epistles, and demands from every member of the
One Body a patient hearing and a ready response.

The analogy between Philippians and Hebrews

Ephesians may be looked upon as holding the same
position in the Dispensation of the Mystery, that Romans
occupies in the earlier ministry of the Reconciliation. Both
are basic. The same basic teaching that is found *in extenso*
in Romans is found in a more controversial form in
Galatians and this finds its parallel in Colossians where
the basic doctrines of Ephesians are repeated, but

supplemented and intertwined with warning and exhortation. Philippians finds its parallel in such an epistle as that to the Hebrews, which presents an exhortation 'to go unto perfection', with a warning about drawing back to perdition which is equally true of the Philippian epistle.

Perfection and Perdition are the focal points of Hebrews :

'Let us go on unto perfection' (Heb. 6:1).

'We are not of them who draw back unto perdition' (Heb. 10:39).

'Perfection' is the Greek word *teleiotes*, 'perdition' is *apoleia*. In Philippians we read :

'Not as though I ... were already perfect' (Phil. 3:12).

'Whose end is destruction' (Phil. 3:19).

'Perfect' here is the Greek word *teleioo*, 'destruction' is *apoleia*.

From this parallel it will be seen that Philippians will not be giving basic doctrine as to what constitutes the high calling, so much as exhorting the believer to walk worthy of the calling he has already received.

In both epistles, a prize, or a reward is in view, enforced by the figure of a race course and by the example of Christ Himself.

PRIZE. 'I press toward the mark for the prize of the high calling of God in Christ Jesus' (Phil. 3:14).

REWARD. 'Cast not away therefore your confidence, which hath great recompence of reward' (Heb. 10:35).

THE RACE. 'I press toward the mark'. 'Striving together' (Phil. 3:14; 1:27).

'Let us run with patience the race that is set before us' (Heb. 12:1).

In this going on unto perfection, some things must necessarily be left behind.

LEAVING. 'Leaving the principles of the doctrine (*margin* leaving the word of the beginning) of Christ let us go on' (Heb. 6:1).

FORGETTING. 'Forgetting those things which are behind' (Phil. 3:13).

This pressing forward had in view a special resurrection. In Philippians it is called the out-resurrection (Phil. 3:11), while in Hebrews the equivalent is found in chapter 11:35, where it speaks of those who obtained a 'better resurrection'. In both epistles there is the guarantee of grace for the exercised believer.

'It is God which *worketh in* you both *to will and to do* of His good pleasure' (Phil. 2:13).

'Make you perfect in every good work *to do* His *will, working in* you that which is well pleasing in His sight, through Jesus Christ' (Heb. 13:21).

In both epistles there are references to the Cross that are parallel. In Hebrews 12:1,2 the Cross is endured for the joy that was set before the Lord, and the example of Christ is brought forward to encourage the believer. In Philippians 2:5-9 the Cross is endured with the consequent exaltation by the Father, and this is recorded to enforce the exhortation 'Let this mind be in you'.

Moreover, the strange reference in Hebrews 6:6, to those who 'crucify to themselves the Son of God afresh', is echoed by the equally strange reference in Philippians 3:18 that certain ones constituted themselves 'enemies of the cross of Christ'.

The 'one morsel of meat' of Hebrews 12:16, that made Esau lose his birthright is balanced in Philippians by those 'whose God is their belly' (Phil. 3:19).

Both the Hebrews and the Philippians are reminded of the blessing of 'contentment' (Heb. 13:5 and Phil. 4:11) and of 'communicating' (Heb. 13:16 and Phil. 4:14,15). In both the ministry of the saints is likened to a 'sacrifice' (Heb. 13:16 and Phil. 4:18), and in both the apostle speaks of 'fruits of righteousness' (Heb. 12:11 and Phil. 1:11).

The murmurings of Israel in the wilderness provided a background for the exhortations of Hebrews 3 and 4, and 'murmurings' and a reference to a 'perverse nation', literally generation, in Philippians 2:14,15 show that much the same teaching is intended. In both epistles there is the exhortation to 'follow', in Hebrews 13:7 the Greek word being *mimeomai*, while in Philippians 3:17 it is *summimetes*. Again the Hebrews are told that they had in heaven an enduring substance (Heb. 10:34), the word 'substance' being a translation of *huparxis*, and the Philippians are told 'our citizenship (*huparcho*) is in heaven' (Phil. 3:20). Finally, the salutation of the epistle to the Hebrews contains greetings from 'they of Italy' (Heb. 13:24), while Philippians concludes with the salutation from the saints in 'Caesar's household' (Phil. 4:22).

Reverting to the analogy instituted on page 2, we draw attention to the fact that Romans, Galatians and Hebrews quote the words of Habakkuk 2:3,4, 'the just shall live by faith'. In Romans it is cited in connection with the basic position of the epistle, in Galatians it is cited in much the same way, but in Hebrews, *the doctrine* of justification by faith is not in view, it is 'living' by faith as one of the essential things that 'accompany salvation' that is stressed.

So Ephesians and Colossians give the great basic teaching of the dispensation of the mystery, whereas Philippians, assuming that revelation, leads the matter forward into the realm of experimental living. It is only too easy to become 'doctrinaire' in our acceptance of the high glory of the mystery, and to avoid the essential and practical accompaniments of so high a calling. It is to serve these most important ends that the Philippian epistle takes its place in the Testimony of the Lord's prisoner, and should commend itself to all who realize the moral issues that are involved in redemption and faith.

We believe that the unbiased reader will be ready to admit that the items that have been brought forward from the epistles to the Philippians and Hebrews are too many and too close to allow for mere coincidence, and as we cannot hope to convince any who are ruled by prejudice, we pass from these introductory studies to the main task of expounding the epistle to the Philippians itself.

We pray that the added light which such a study must throw upon our pathway may be so gladly accepted and readily followed, that as a result of this examination many more may find themselves following the examples put before them, both in the most wonderful condescension of the Lord Himself and of His humblest followers, whose faith and courage adorn the doctrine of the Lord and encourage us also 'one thing' to do.

The scope of the Epistle, exhibited in the structure

The scope of any book of the Bible can be discovered in two ways. By finding its literary structure and by comparing its key words with those of another book belonging to the same group. We would here present the reader with the results of this twofold process.

The opening salutation of the Epistle is addressed to 'the Saints in Christ Jesus' (Phil. 1:1); the closing salutation is sent from 'the saints' who form part 'of Caesar's household' (Phil. 4:22). The body of the epistle lies between these two members, and occupies Philippians 1:3 to 4:20. While the opening member of the epistle deals with a variety of subjects, there is one item that reappears at the close, and constitutes the first link in structural correspondence.

In Philippians 1:3-5 the apostle opens the epistle with thanksgiving 'for your *fellowship* in the gospel from the first day until now'.

After the main argument of the epistle is presented, the apostle returns to this personal theme as he brings the epistle to a close 'now ye Philippians know also, that in the beginning of the gospel, when I departed from Macedonia, no church *communicated* (same Greek word as is translated fellowship) with me as concerning giving and receiving but ye only. For even in Thessalonica ye sent once and again unto my necessity' (Phil. 4:15,16). In the opening section he speaks of 'gain', even though in a context of much loss for Christ's sake (Phil. 1:21), so also in the closing section he speaks of abounding, of having all, of being full, even though at the same time he admits a state of necessity which was relieved by the gifts sent by the Philippians. In like manner he speaks in the first chapter of being 'filled' with the fruits of righteousness, and in chapter 4 of not only being 'full' himself but having the assurance that God would 'supply' (*pleroo* – same root word) all the needs of His people. It is evident by these few scattered phrases, that the opening section of chapter 1 is in structural correspondence with the closing section of chapter 4.

When we consider the next member of the epistle we are put on the track of the truth by remembering that the word *politeuo* 'conversation' (Phil. 1:27) is echoed by *politeuma* 'conversation' in Philippians 3:20,21. In addition we discover that the word *steko* 'stand fast' occurs in Philippians 1:27 and again in 4:1. It appears therefore that we are discovering evidence for the next pair of corresponding members in the structure. We read on and observe that the words 'with one spirit and one soul' of 1:27 find their corresponding member in 4:2 'the same mind', and we find moreover, the words 'striving together' of 1:27 and 'laboured with' of 4:3 are translations of the Greek *sunathleo*, which word occurs nowhere else in the New Testament.

This brings us to the central member of the epistle, and we find the sevenfold humiliation of Christ (Phil. 2:6-11), balanced by the sevenfold loss of Paul (Phil. 3:4-19).

With the material already to hand we can now set out the epistle as a whole :

PHILIPPIANS

(*Introversion*)

A 1:1,2.   Salutation.
            Saints in Christ Jesus.
  B 1:3-26.   Fellowship in gospel
               from the first day.
    C 1:27 to 2:5. Conversation here.   *Mind of*
                    Stand fast   *Christ.*
      D 2:6-11.   Sevenfold humiliation   *Example.*
                   of Christ.
        E 2:12-17.   Exhortation. Work out.
          F 2:17-30.   Example of Paul,
                          Timothy and
                          Epaphroditus.
        E 3: 1-3.   Exhortation. Beware.
      D 3:4-19.   Sevenfold loss of Paul. *Example.*
    C 3:20 to 4:10. Conversation there.   *Body of*
                      Stand fast   *Christ.*
  B 4:10-20.   Fellowship in beginning
                  of gospel.
A 4:21-23.   Salutation. Saints of
               Caesar's household.

It will be a useful appendix to this *opening study*, if we indicate some of the essential differences that are observable between the epistle to the Philippians and that to the Ephesians. With this comparison and that already instituted between Philippians and Hebrews, we shall then have both positive and negative testimony to the real purpose of the Philippian epistle.

Some differences between Ephesians and Philippians

(1) *Fulness*. Ephesians is an epistle of fulness, the word *pleroma* occurring four times, namely in 1:10,23; 3:19 and 4:13. In contrast with this, Philippians places great stress on the *kenosis* or 'self emptying of the Lord' ('no reputation' Phil. 2:7) but never uses the word 'fulness'.

(2) *Boldness.* This is insisted on in Ephesians 3:12. Not only has the believer access, but access with boldness. Fear and trembling, however, is the attitude of the believer in Philippians 2:12, for there 'service' not 'access' is in view.

(3) *Ascension.* The Lord's ascension is stressed in Ephesians. The believer's hopes are all centred there, where Christ sits at the right hand of God. In Philippians, the Lord's descent is emphasized. His original equality with God being veiled while He humbled Himself to the death of the cross. His exaltation being a sequel, parallel to 'the joy that was set before Him' in Hebrews 12:1,2.

(4) *Remember.* The Ephesian believer is urged to remember that he was once an alien, a stranger, hopeless and Christless (Eph. 2:12). Conversely, the Philippian believer is urged to forget the things that are behind, lest they hinder him in running the race set before him.

(5) *The Hope of the calling.* Ephesians deals with the 'Hope' of the calling, Philippians with the 'Prize' of the calling, which 'prize' is associated with the figure of running a race and the possibility of failing to attain the goal.

(6) *Fellowship.* Fellowship expressed by the use of the preposition *sun* 'together with' in combination follows two lines of teaching characteristic of the two epistles. There are eight distinctive words used in Ephesians which have the affix *sun*, that give a fairly comprehensive view of the distinctive teaching of that epistle – all of them, moreover, deal with basic position, none with experimental teaching. These we will here set out :

Fellow citizens (Eph. 2:19); fitly framed together (Eph. 2:21); fellow heirs, the same body, partakers (Eph. 3:6); the bond of peace (Eph. 4:3) and fitly joined together (Eph. 4:16).

When we turn to Philippians we find the affix *sun* associated with a completely different set of words, indicating a completely different line of teaching. 'Partakers of my grace' (Phil. 1:7). This refers to suffering for the Gospel. 'Striving together' and 'fellow labourers' (Phil. 1:27 and 4:3); 'fellow soldier' (Phil. 2:25); 'followers together' (Phil. 3:17); 'fashioned like unto' (Phil. 3:21). This last occurrence is the only reference that approaches a line of teaching similar to that of Ephesians. The similarity however is superficial. When we examine the passage we shall see that Philippians 3:21 is continuing the teaching given concerning the 'out resurrection' and 'the prize' which occupies the chapter from verse 10. The fellowship that is stressed in Philippians is not that of being *seated* together, but of *striving* together, and can be summed up in the words of Philippians 3:10, where 'the (voluntary) fellowship of His sufferings', which has the out-resurrection in view, is in order that 'if by any means I might attain unto' the prize of the high calling. In Ephesians we meet the word *teleios* 'perfect' but once, as the goal of the church 'the perfect man'. In Philippians we meet the word *teleios* but once, with one occurrence also of *teleioo* (Phil. 3:12,15), where the context speaks of running with a prize in view. Having seen the parallels that exist between Philippians and Hebrews and the contrasts with Ephesians, together with the structure of the epistle as a whole, we can now take up the study of the epistle, feeling that we have done what is necessary in clearing the way for its examination.

We insert the accompanying diagram as a supplement to the literary structure of the epistle.

BEREAN **PHILIPPIANS** CHARTS

Perfection iii. 12. NO. II. Perdition iii. 19.

Wherefore God hath HIGHLY EXALTED HIM. ii.9.

The Out-Resurrection out from among the dead. iii.11.

The PRIZE of the HIGH CALLING of GOD. iii.14.

Christ's Example

Paul's Example

I press toward the mark iii. 14.

Even the Death of the Cross. ii. 8.

Conformable unto His Death. iii. 10.

Timothy's Example

NO REPUTATION ii.7.

Epaphroditus' Example

He did not seek his own. ii.20.21.

Not regarding his own life. ii.30.

ALL THINGS BUT LOSS. iii. 8.

ii.12. Work out your own salvation.

ii.13. God worketh in you.

C.H.W.   1933

CHAPTER 2

Things that are more Excellent

Philippians 1:1-18

Upon reading the opening words of the epistle, one or two questions immediately present themselves.

'Paul and Timotheus the servants of Jesus Christ, to all the saints in Christ Jesus which are at Philippi, with the bishops and deacons' (Phil. 1:1).

(1) Why does Paul omit the title 'apostle'?
(2) Why does he include the title 'servants'?
(3) Why does he mention 'the bishops and deacons'?

Four of the epistles of Paul omit the title 'apostle' in the opening salutation.   These are 1 and 2 Thessalonians, Philippians and Philemon.   As 1 and 2 Thessalonians are addressed by 'Paul and Sylvanus and Timotheus', the title 'apostle' could hardly be included without lowering its distinctive meaning when used elsewhere by the apostle Paul of himself.   In the body of the first epistle to the Thessalonians, there is a reference to 'apostles' with whom the apostle Paul associates himself.

'We might have been burdensome as the apostles of Christ' (1 Thess. 2:6).

It is not so generally known as it should be that there were 'apostles' other than 'the Twelve' and of another order than that of the apostleship of Paul himself.

For example, when we read in Acts 14:4 that part held with the Jews 'and part with the apostles', it is evident that Barnabas as well as Paul is so named.   Another passage that should be pondered is Romans 16:7, 'salute Andronicus and Junia, my kinsmen and my fellow prisoners, who are of note among the apostles, who also were in Christ before me'.   Commentators are divided in their opinion concerning this passage.   Some hold that Paul means that these fellow prisoners of his were held in great esteem by the other apostles, some hold that Paul means that these fellow prisoners were also of note among the apostles, thereby giving to them the title 'apostle' also. There was not that close working together of Paul and the twelve for such a remark to refer to them and the added clause, introduced by the word 'also', lends weight to the opinion expressed by Alford and endorsed by the *Companion Bible*, that this title was used in a wider sense in the early days of the Church than we are in the habit of using it now. In the epistle to the Corinthians, the apostle Paul says that God has set in the Church 'first apostles' and asks 'are all apostles?', using the word in the plural (1 Cor. 12:28,29), yet in 1 Corinthians 15:1-9 he uses the title in the highest and more restricted sense. Again in 1 Corinthians 4:9 he speaks of 'us the apostles' in a context where it is difficult to include the twelve. In the second epistle to the Corinthians it is most evident that the word *apostolos* was used with a wider significance than can be contained by the apostolate of the twelve or of Paul.

'Whether any do enquire of Titus, he is my partner and fellow helper concerning you: or our brethren be inquired of, they are the messengers (apostles) of the churches, and the glory of Christ' (2 Cor. 8:23).

Paul could never be designated 'the apostle of the churches', neither could any one of the twelve. Again, if the number of those who could rightly use the title 'apostle' was limited to Paul or the twelve, it does not seem possible for the agents of Satan to transform themselves into 'apostles of Christ' (2 Cor. 11:13). Again, the comparison which Paul makes of himself with 'the very chiefest apostles' (2 Cor. 12:11), seems rather strong language if no others than the twelve could ever be called apostles.

In Philippians 2:25, Epaphroditus is called 'your apostle', and while the A.V. rendering 'your messenger' is possible, yet a more appropriate word was at hand for messenger', namely *angelos*, which is used in seven passages in the New Testament. If there were 'apostles of the Church' (2 Cor. 8:23) Epaphroditus might well be one of them. Theodoret, an ecclesiastical historian who was born at Antioch about the year A.D. 386, maintained that in the apostolic age the same persons were called by the two names *presbuteroi* 'elders' and *episkopoi* 'bishops', and that those who were called in his own time *episkopoi* were formerly called *apostoloi* or apostles. 'Thus' (concludes Theodoret) 'Epaphroditus was the apostle of the Philippians'.

Finally Ephesians 4:11 declares that the *ascended* Christ gave 'some apostles'. Now as none of the 'Twelve', except Matthias, were appointed after the Lord ascended we must be prepared to discover that there was another group that had a right to the title apostle.

We have digressed somewhat and must now return to the opening verse of Philippians to examine more carefully the titles of service that are actually there employed. Paul and Timothy are called 'servants' and the salutation is sent not only to the saints, but to 'the bishops and deacons'. There *must* be a reason for this somewhat unusual introduction, and the acquaintance we have already made with the general trend of the teaching of this epistle enables us to appreciate the way in which the apostle has linked himself at once with its great theme, namely, that of service.

Paul and Timothy are not the only 'servants' to be noted in this epistle. They sink into nothingness at the great condescension of chapter 2:6-8, where we read of Him, Who though equal with God 'took upon Him the form of a servant'. Timothy figures in this same chapter serving 'as a son with the father', and the apostle himself speaks of being 'offered on the sacrifice and service' of faith. Further, the Philippians were enjoined 'to work out' their own salvation, and God Himself is seen 'working in' them, and finishing the work which He had begun (Phil. 2:22, see also 12,13 and 1:6). It has been objected by some that 'bishops and deacons' can have no place in the Church of the One Body. This however is fallacious, for if the fact that in this Body every member is equal rules out the ministry of bishops and deacons, it would at the same time rule out apostles, prophets, evangelists, pastors and teachers, but as this ministry is directly given by the ascended Christ to the Church of the mystery, it will be seen that the objection is not valid.

The word translated 'bishop' is *episkopos*, and is retained in the English *episcopalian*. The word is a compound of *epi* 'upon' or 'over' and *skopeo* 'to look', as in 'telescope', hence in Acts 20:28, the word is translated 'overseers'. There is nothing officious about the original meaning of the word, the first occurrence of *episkeptomai* being Matthew 25:36, 'sick and ye *visited* Me'. So *episkopeo* is translated 'to look diligently' (Heb. 12:15) and 'take oversight' (1 Pet. 5:2). The word has become 'bishop' in English by the softening process which is characteristic of the Anglo Saxon. The P becomes B and the sk becomes sh, *episkop* becoming 'bishop'. As the title 'Apostle' belongs to Christ (Heb. 3:1), so does the title 'Bishop'.

'For ye were as sheep going astray; but are now returned unto the Shepherd and Bishop of your souls' (1 Pet. 2:25).

At the conclusion of the list of characteristics of a true bishop in 1 Timothy 3, the apostle asks :

'For if a man know not how to *rule* his own house, how shall he *take care* of the church of God?' (1 Tim. 3:5).

So long as the redeemed still gather together for worship or for witness, there will be a call for those who are gifted and qualified in the task of gracious guidance and tender care.

The word translated deacon is *diakonos*. The derivation of this word is uncertain, but it is possible that it is from *dieko* 'to run to serve'. Certainly service is the uppermost idea, and it is sanctified to us for ever by the fact that Christ Himself is set forth as 'a *minister* of the circumcision' (Rom. 15:8). Paul also uses the word when he said 'I magnify mine *office*' (Rom. 11:13), using the same word that is translated '*the office of a deacon*' in 1 Timothy 3:10. This ministry is fairly comprehensive. It may be the lowly work of the house (Luke 10:40), it might be the daily ministry that could be spoken of as 'serving tables' (Acts 6:1,2); on the other hand it may be the very ministry of angels (Matt. 4:11). This 'ministry' is not confined to one sex, for Phoebe is called a 'deacon' in Romans 16:1.

Returning to the objection that such ministry does not fit in with the conception of the church as the Body of Christ, let us remember that the gifts of Ephesians 4:11 are 'for the work of the *ministry*' (Eph. 4:12), and that Paul himself when contemplating the high honour given him in connection with the mystery said 'whereof I am made a *minister*' (Eph. 3:7).

Instead therefore of setting aside Philippians because of this reference to bishops and deacons, we should rather pray most earnestly that such gifts of ministry may ever remain with us, however far we may now have departed from the order of the primitive church.

The comment of Wordsworth on the absence of the title 'apostle' from Philippians 1:1 is suggestive :

'This was the last epistle that he wrote to a Gentile Church, he was now Paul the aged, and had almost run his apostolic race. He was still an apostle to Timothy and Titus (1 Tim. 1:1; Tit. 1:1; 2 Tim. 1:1), and had an apostolic charge for them. But he had done his work for the *churches* of Asia and Greece. He was now like Aaron before his death, laying aside his sacred garments, in order that others might wear them (Num. 20:28). He would not magnify himself, but the nearer he was to heaven the more lowly he would be. He would divest himself of his official dignity, and leave behind him an example of self-abasement after a life of self denial and self sacrifice for Christ'.

We conclude this introductory study by giving in outline the seven epistles of Paul written after Acts 28, showing the way in which the introduction of 'bishops and deacons' in Philippians 1:1 is balanced by the commands concerning them in the Pastoral Epistles.

A Ephesians   The Mystery.
B Philippians   a Bishops and Deacons.
                               b The Prize.
C Philemon   Truth in daily life.
A Colossians   The Mystery.
B 1 and 2 Timothy   a Bishops and Deacons.
   and Titus   b The Crown.

Confidence and continuance, with special attention to the word
epiteleo

Paul opens the epistle proper with thanksgiving 'upon every remembrance' of the Philippians, and that with particular reference to their 'fellowship in the gospel from the first day until now' (Phil. 1:3-5).

Two very characteristic words appear in this opening, namely, *eucharisteo* 'I give thanks' and *mneia* 'remembrance'. *Eucharisteo* is for ever rendered sacred by the fact that it was used by the Lord when He took the cup of wine that set forth in type the very shedding of His life's blood and yet 'gave thanks' (Matt. 26:27). It has also been rendered odious by the Pharasaic self complacency of the man who stood and prayed 'God, I thank thee, that I am not as other men are' (Luke 18:11). This expression 'I thank' or 'we thank' marks the introduction of seven of the epistles of Paul (Rom. 1:8; 1 Cor. 1:4; Phil. 1:3; Col. 1:3; 1 Thess. 1:2; 2 Thess. 1:3 and Philemon 4). Not only so, but the companion word *mneia* 'remembrance' occurs but seven times in the New Testament and every occurrence is found in Paul's epistles (Rom. 1:9; Eph. 1:16; Phil. 1:3; 1 Thess. 1:2; 3:6; 2 Tim. 1:3 and Philemon 4). The reader will be aware that as age creeps on memory becomes fickle, yet we note that 'remembrance' (*mneia*), 'be mindful' (*mnaomai*), 'call to remembrance' (*hupomnesis*), and 'put in remembrance' (*anamimnesko*), are found together in the opening verses of Paul's last epistle, 2 Timothy.

If the use of the word *eucharisteo* is laden with precious thoughts as we think of its use at the Last Supper, the use of 'remembrance' in connection with thanksgiving is likewise sanctified by the Lord's saying at that same feast, 'this do in *remembrance* of Me' (Luke 22:19; 1 Cor. 11:24).

When writing these epistles, Paul is not only recording doctrine by Divine revelation, he is also recording certain characteristics of his own by grace. It is certainly no accident that 'the giving of thanks' and the word for 'remembrance' are each used seven times by him in his epistles as already indicated, which makes us aware that some of his success as a preacher of the gospel, must be ascribed to this very lovely trait of thankful remembrance. In Philippians this thankful remembrance is linked with the Philippians' continual fellowship in the gospel from the first day. Perhaps an examination of the other epistles that use this expression will deepen the suggestion we have made, that there exists a relationship between the thankful remembrance of the preacher, and the growth in grace of his hearer.

In Romans 1:8 Paul thanks God that the faith of the saints at Rome is spoken of throughout the whole world, and to this he adds the solemn assertion 'for God is my witness, Whom I serve with my spirit in the gospel of His Son, that without ceasing *I make mention* of you always in my prayers'.

How far was the faithful stand of the Roman Christians connected with the thankful and unceasing remembrance of them by the apostle?

If the Roman believers' faith was spoken of throughout the whole world, the Thessalonians were likewise thankfully remembered (1 Thess. 1:2,3), for he wrote there 'from you sounded out the word of the Lord not only in

Macedonia and Achaia, but also in every place your faith to God-ward is spread abroad: so that we need not to speak anything' (1 Thess. 1:8).

This thanksgiving of the apostle was continuous and comprehensive. 'Every' remembrance; 'always' in 'every' prayer for you 'all'. Where the apostle in the Philippian epistle assures the believer that on 'every' remembrance he gave thanks, in Romans, 1 Thessalonians and 2 Timothy he substitutes the words 'without ceasing', which is but another way of saying that he remembered continually.

It appears therefore that there is this vital link of thankful remembrance between the teacher and the taught, that the responsibility and privilege of ministry does not end at the class room or the meeting, but is a remembrance 'without ceasing' before the throne of grace.

Paul not only assured the Philippians that he made 'request' on their behalf but he made it 'with joy', and this joy was because of the continuous and unbroken fellowship that they had had with him in the gospel 'from the first day until now'.

When the apostle uses the word 'joy' again in this chapter, it is in close association with similar thoughts that are found connected with the first usage. In Philippians 1:25 there is 'confidence' and 'furtherance', even as in Philippians 1:3-18 there is 'confidence' and 'furtherance'. 'Being confident of this very thing', *auto touto*.

The reader's attention is especially drawn to the fact that these words form a logical link between the two statements that flank it in Philippians 1:5,6.

A   Subject of thanksgiving with joy.

B   *Continual, unbroken fellowship from*
the first day until now.

A   Subject of confidence 'this very thing'.

B   *Continual, unbroken performance by God*
until the day of Jesus Christ.

'Until now' is in the original *achri tou nun*. 'Until the day' of Jesus Christ is *achris hemeras*.

The reason why we break into our exposition in order to draw the reader's attention to these facts, is that an interpretation has been put forward of Philippians 1:6, that teaches Paul's meaning here is that something which God had commenced, was now about to be discontinued (*epiteleo*). The discontinuance being necessary because it is taught the dispensation of the mystery was imminent.

It will be seen that Paul's argument would lead in the other direction. He rejoices that the fellowship of the Philippians had never been discontinued, but had remained constant 'until now'. He is thereby the more 'confident' that the good work already commenced in them by God would continue unbroken 'until the day of Jesus Christ'. One does not need even to be spiritually minded to be able to follow a simple argument, and it is contrary to all reasonable discourse for Paul to rejoice in the *unbroken* fellowship of the *believer*, and receive from the contemplation of this faithfulness 'confidence' that God was going to *discontinue* a work which *He* had begun!

The words 'until now' and 'until the day of Jesus Christ' cannot have opposite meanings in such a context, what one means the other means, and to attempt a rendering that reads 'God will discontinue *until* the day of Jesus Christ', does not even make sense.

The true force of the apostle's argument however lies in the word *epiteleo* translated 'perform', set over against the word *enarchomai* 'begun'. Now happily we have these two words brought together in another epistle of Paul, where his meaning is unchallenged.

'Are ye so foolish? having begun (*enarchomai*) in the Spirit, are ye now made perfect (*epiteleo*) by the flesh?' (Gal. 3:3).

If *epiteleo* here means 'discontinue' Paul would have said 'how wise you are', instead of 'are ye so foolish'. Let us observe the way in which Paul uses *epiteleo* in other contexts.

'But now I go unto Jerusalem to minister unto the saints .... When therefore *I have performed* this, and have sealed to them this fruit, I will come by you into Spain' (Rom. 15:25-28).

It is a matter of New Testament history that Paul did convey the offering of the Gentile Churches to Jerusalem, and he could speak of this offering as a 'seal' in consequence, just as surely as he could in Ephesians 1:13 and 4:30.

His own use of the figure of a 'seal' in Romans itself shows that it referred to something accomplished.

'A seal of the righteousness of the faith which he had yet being uncircumcised' (Rom. 4:11).

In 2 Corinthians 8, Paul refers to the collection for the saints again, and again uses the word *epiteleo* in the sense of 'performing'. Here moreover is found a similar word to that used in Galatians 3, *proenarchomai*.

'Insomuch that we desired Titus, that as he had *begun*, so he would also *finish* in you the same grace also' (2 Cor. 8:6).

'This is expedient for you, who have *begun* before, not only to do, but also to be forward a year ago. Now therefore *perform* the doing of it; that as there was a readiness to will, so there may be a *performance* also out of that which ye have' (2 Cor. 8:10,11).

It is impossible to substitute the idea of 'discontinuance' for 'finish' or 'perform' in these verses without reducing the earnest appeal of the apostle to nonsense. If we will now turn back to chapter 7 of this same epistle we shall see that 'discontinuance' if introduced there becomes a positive menace to truth.

'Having therefore these promises, dearly beloved, let us cleanse ourselves from all filthiness of the flesh and spirit, *perfecting* holiness in the fear of God' (2 Cor. 7:1).

Paul may not have been sure that he, himself, would 'attain' (Phil. 3:11), but he was blessedly certain of the faithful performance of his God.

Paul had very much before his mind 'the day of Jesus Christ' (Phil. 1:6), 'the day of Christ' (Phil. 1:10; 2:16). 'The day' he tells us which shall declare the character of all our service (1 Cor. 3:13), and he placed that day over against 'man's day' (1 Cor. 4:3, margin), even as he looked to 'that day' for the crown of righteousness and for the recognition of the faithful ministry of Onesiphorus (2 Tim. 1:18; 4:8).

This consciousness of 'that day' is in complete harmony with the general theme of the epistle, which is the practical outworking of the truth, the running of a race, the attaining unto perfection, the winning of a prize.

The apostle rounds off the first section of Philippians by telling the believers at Philippi that it was meet for him to think 'this' of them all, the word 'this' referring to their blessedly assured 'performance' or 'continuance' because of the mutual regard that the apostle and the Philippians had for each other in the defence and confirmation of the gospel; by which words the apostle brings the subject round to that with which he had started, namely thanksgiving for their fellowship in the gospel from the first day until now.

We shall appreciate this persistence the better as we proceed with the study of this epistle of race and prize.

Approving things that are more excellent

When in the preceding section we entered into the exposition of Philippians 1:3-26, the importance of Paul's intention in using the two words 'begun' and 'perform' appeared so great that we did not stay to consider the section as a whole. This omission we must now remedy before going further.

Omitting much detail which will be exhibited in the process of exposition, Philippians 1:3-26 can be set out as follows :

Philippians 1:3-26

FELLOWSHIP IN THE GOSPEL

(*Corresponding with Philippians* 4 : 11-20)

A 3-5.   Thanksgiving.
                  Fellowship and defence of gospel.
    B 6-8.   CONFIDENCE. *Pepoitha* (6).
A 9-12.   Prayer (Paul's). Furtherance of gospel.
    B 13-18.   CONFIDENCE. *Pepoitha* (14).
A 19-21.   Prayer (Philippians').
                  Furtherance of faith.
    B 22-26.   CONFIDENCE. *Pepoitha* (25).

We must now give attention to the second pair of members in this structure, which occupies verses Phil. 9-18. The first member is devoted to the prayer of verses 9-11 and to the examination of this we now devote ourselves. This prayer is an alternation and may be exhibited as follows :

A 9   That (*hina*) your love may abound.
    B 10   Unto (*eis*) the approving of things.
A 10   That (*hina*) ye may be sincere.
    B 10,11   Unto (*eis*) the day of Christ.

This alternation hinges upon two Greek words *hina* 'in order that' and *eis* 'unto', as unto a goal – the second pair arising out of the first. *Hina* is 'a causal conjunction' which is translated 'that' in the A.V. 542 times, and rightly so, the only problem that such a translation introduces lies in the fact that twenty-four other words are also translated 'that' with equal propriety! We must remember that in English, the word 'that' stands for an adjective, a pronoun, a conjunction, and an adverb. As a conjunction 'that' is used to introduce a clause, a reason, a purpose, a consequence, or a supposed fact. For the sake of clearness therefore it is well to adopt some such rendering as 'in order that', so that we shall know that 'a purpose' is in view.

Eis is a preposition, and like most prepositions it can be conceived of in the terms of direction, it suggests a movement toward and attainment of a goal. In the passage before us (Phil. 1:9-11), we find *eis* translated 'that' 'till' and 'unto'; *'that* ye may approve', *'till* the day of Christ', *'unto* the glory'.

We see that Paul's prayer was *in order that* the love of the Philippians may abound, and that this abounding love should lead to the approving of things that are excellent, this in its turn being *in order that* they may be sincere and without offence with a view to the day of Christ.

It is characteristic of the apostle, that where he emphasizes the most his sufferings, there he stresses with corresponding emphasis abounding grace. If he says in 2 Corinthians 'in labours more *abundant'*, 'in prisons more *frequent'*, he can also speak of consolations that *'abound'* (2 Cor. 11:23, see also 1:5). If Paul was compelled to speak of 'sin' abounding he could through the mercy of God immediately follow with superabounding grace (Rom. 5:20). So in this epistle wherein he reveals that he had suffered the loss of all things for Christ, he tells us that he knew also 'how to abound' (Phil. 1:9; 4:18). While we may readily think of 'love' abounding, we do not so readily think of abounding love leading to most practical discrimination, yet that is the goal of the apostle's prayer.

'And this I pray, that your love may abound yet more and more in knowledge and in all judgment' (Phil. 1:9).

Out of this abounding love, the apostle expected to see knowledge, judgment, approval, testing and sincerity. Later when writing to Timothy, the apostle brought together 'love and a sound mind'. Peter places 'love' at the end of a long list adding 'if these things be in you and abound, they make you that ye shall neither be barren nor unfruitful in the knowledge of our Lord Jesus Christ' (2 Pet. 1:8). While Peter uses a different word for 'abound' than is used by Paul in Philippians 1:9, the sentiment is the same. 'Abounding love' leads to knowledge. Here, the two apostles agree in word as well as in sentiment, for they both use the Greek word *epignosis*. This word is translated in four places by 'acknowledge' (Col. 2:2; 2 Tim. 2:25; Tit. 1:1 and Philem. 6). In the verbal form it is translated 'acknowledge' five times (1 Cor. 14:37; 16:18; 2 Cor. 1:13 (twice), 14), and in most places, if not in all, acknowledgment rather than knowledge is seen to be the intention of the writers. Acknowledgment after having received the truth, is as necessary to growth and enlightenment as confession is to the experience of the forgiveness of sins.

Where the Authorised Version reads 'increasing in the knowledge of God' (Col. 1:10), the meaning of the apostle seems to demand the rendering 'increasing *by the acknowledgment* of God', even as the rendering of Ephesians 1:17 'may give unto you the spirit of wisdom and revelation in the knowledge of Him', should be altered to read 'in the acknowledgment of Him'. That is to say, the coveted illumination is not given in order that knowledge of Him may increase, but rather that this wise and revealing spirit is itself the product under grace of the acknowledgment of the Lord. As we acknowledge, we receive illumination, says Ephesians 1:17. As we acknowledge, we receive increase, says Colossians 1:10. As we acknowledge, we shall discern, says Philippians 1:9.

'And in all judgment' (Phil. 1:9). This word judgment is used in the New Testament to translate nine different Greek words, and is often so associated in the mind of the reader, with the figures of judge, law and penalty as to exclude the legitimate concepts of reason and perception. In ordinary language judgment is either the act of judging, as in the administration of justice, and the awarding of a sentence, *or* it is the act or process of the mind in ascertaining the truth by comparison of ideas, facts or propositions.

Now the word so rendered in Philippians 1:9 is the Greek *aisthesis*. This word occurs in but three forms in the

New Testament and in three passages. Let us record these occurrences before we proceed further.

Aisthesis. 'In knowledge and in all judgment' (Phil. 1:9).

Aistheterion. 'Having the *senses* exercised to discern both good and evil' (Heb. 5:14).

Aisthanomai. 'They understood not this saying, and it was hid from them, that they *perceived* it not' (Luke 9:45).

In the LXX version, this word *aisthesis* apart from one reference in the law, is found only in the book of Proverbs.

'And speak thou to all those who are wise in understanding, whom I have filled with the spirit of wisdom and *perception*' (Exod. 28:3).

'The fear of the Lord is the beginning of wisdom, and there is good *understanding* to all that practise it, and piety toward God is the beginning of *discernment*' (Prov. 1:7).

'Judgment is the comparing together in the mind two of the notions, or ideas, which are the objects of apprehension, whether complex or incomplex, and pronouncing that they agree or disagree with each other .... Judgment is therefore affirmative or negative: as, Snow is white; All white men are not Europeans' (*Lloyd's Encl. Dict.*).

In the two passages where Paul has used the word *aisthesis* or *aistheterion*, he has actually expanded the idea of discriminating by saying either 'to discern both good and evil' (Heb. 5:14) where the word 'discern' is *diakrisis* 'discriminate, divide up, make a distinction' between two things – or as in Philippians 1:10, he continues 'that ye may approve things that are excellent'. The Authorised Version gives as an alternative rendering 'that ye may try the things that differ'. The original reads *eis to dokimazein humas ta diapheronta.* 'Approval' is rather the result (*dokimos*) than the process (*dokimazo*) and always implies some sort of test or trial, being derived from the root *dokeo*, 'to think' in the sense of concluding that anything 'is what it seems to be'. 'It seemed good' (Luke 1:3); 'it seemed to me unreasonable' (Acts 25:27); 'these who seemed to be somewhat' (Gal. 2:6). *Dokimazo* is used for 'discerning' the face of the sky (Luke 12:56); 'trying' anything by fire (1 Cor. 3:13), like 'gold' (1 Pet. 1:7); and then of 'examining' self (1 Cor. 11:28); 'proving' all things (1 Thess. 5:21), and so finally 'approving' things that are excellent (Phil. 1:10).

The word translated 'excellent' is *diapheronta*, and refers to things that are discrepant, or that differ, things that must be distinguished one from another, the word 'distinguished' in English having this double meaning, first of the marks of distinction that separate things, and then of the mark of approval that such 'distinction' indicates. This dual meaning can be seen in such translations of *diaphero* as 'better than' 'of more value than' (Matt. 6:26; Matt. 10:31), and 'one star differeth from another'; 'differeth nothing from a servant' (1 Cor. 15:41; Gal. 4:1). The process of this discrimination is expressed by the Authorised Version margin 'that ye may *try* things that *differ*'. The result of this discrimination is found in the text 'that ye may *approve* things that are *excellent*'.

We have already indicated that there is a close connection in theme between Philippians and 2 Timothy (see p. xiv), and the process and result of discrimination here expressed in Philippians 1:9,10 is repeated in a different form in 2 Timothy 2:15, where 'approval' is used of the workman before God, and 'trying things that differ' is restated in the words 'rightly dividing the word of truth'.

One more connection is seen between these two passages when we continue in Philippians 1, 'that ye may be sincere and without offence till the day of Christ'. This is a similar extension of the subject to 'a workman that needeth not to be ashamed'. 'Sincere' is *eilikrines* 'to be judged in and by sun light'; 'without offence' is *aproskopos*, which is the negative of *proskopto* 'to dash', as the foot against a stone (Matt. 4:6) and so 'to stumble' (John 11:9,10), and *proskomma* 'a stumbling stone' or a 'stumbling block' (Rom. 9:32; 14:13). A warning is uttered in 1 Corinthians 8:9, 'but take heed lest by any means this liberty of yours become a *stumbling block*, to them that are weak'. If we compare 1 Corinthians 8:1, 'knowledge puffeth up but love edifieth', with 1 Corinthians 13:4 'love ... is not puffed up' and Romans 14:1 'not to doubtful *disputations*' (*diakrisis*), we shall see that there can be a discrimination, a 'trying of things that differ' that can be offensive and cause stumbling, but both Philippians 1 and Romans 14 link the true discrimination with two great governing influences.

(1) The originating cause 'love' 'abounding love' in Philippians 1:9, and 'walking in love' in Romans 14:15.

(2) The Day of Christ. 'We shall all stand before the judgment seat of Christ' (Rom. 14:10), and 'till the day of Christ' (Phil. 1:10).

The Jew is represented as approving 'the things that are more excellent' (Rom. 2:18) where the same words are used as are found in Philippians 1:10, but in the second chapter of Romans it is manifest that such discrimination did not proceed from abounding love. It arose rather out of abounding pride, and instead of being tempered by the consciousness that the motives that prompted this discrimination must be brought to the trial of the judgment seat of Christ, they were exercised by those who believed that there was a respect of persons with God, and that they would 'escape the judgment of God'. From all such harmful manifestation of the flesh the apostle prayed that the Philippians should be spared.

The last clause of this prayer is suggestive 'being filled with the fruits of righteousness' (Phil. 1:11). The apostle looked for fruit, both in himself and in others (Phil. 1:22; 4:17), and 'by the fruits' would the believer's walk and work be recognized.

'The fruit of righteousness is sown in peace of them that make peace' (Jas. 3:18).

The prayers that lie at the opening of these great prison epistles, are directed particularly to the theme and purpose of the epistle in question.

In Ephesians, which opens up the glory and grace of the new dispensation, a spirit of wisdom and revelation in the acknowledgment of Him, is sought in order that they may know what is the hope of His calling. In Colossians, wisdom and spiritual understanding are sought, that they might walk worthy, and that they might increase by the acknowledgment of God. In Philippians, where the theme is the practical outworking of the truth, and service in view of the prize, the prayer concentrates upon the faculty of discrimination, abounding love and the day of Christ.

As members of this high calling, we need these three prayers continually. We need to know, we need to discern, we need to walk worthy. May an abundant answer be granted to us all 'until the day of Christ'.

'A mind at leisure from itself'

A very gracious characteristic of the apostle Paul is, that after he has made some claim upon the believer, some exhortation to high faith, great endurance, or self effacing love, he follows such exhortation with a reference to his own example. This reference to himself does not intrude, it flows naturally in the course of his writing and is so evidently a part of himself that he is entirely free from any suspicion of pose. In his prayer which we have just been studying he directed the Philippians' thoughts to the day of Christ, suggesting that with that day in view mean and unedifying things would fade and die, and abounding love produce the fruits of righteousness which are by Jesus Christ unto the glory and praise of God (Phil. 1:9-11). The new section occupies verses 12-18, and balances the section which occupies verses 6-8; both sections can be headed with the word 'confidence' which occurs in each.

In this new passage, the selfless, Christ exalting nature of this man in bondage is manifested, revealing how it is possible by grace to rise above all the circumstances of this life and realize to the full the fact that we are 'more than conquerors' through Him that loved us.

This man of God was about to refer to 'the things which had happened' unto him. He was going to speak of 'his bonds', and of the very grievous fact that some by their factious preaching were intentionally adding to his affliction. How was all this variety of circumstance and pressure met by him? He says that the things that had happened unto him had fallen out rather 'unto the furtherance of the gospel'. His bonds he calls his 'bonds in Christ', and the only reply he makes to the sad attitude of those who preached Christ out of envy and strife was 'what then? notwithstanding, every way, whether in pretence or in truth, CHRIST IS PREACHED; and I therein do rejoice, yea, and will rejoice' (Phil. 1:18).

It is this spirit which he is about to urge upon the Philippians themselves (Phil. 2:1-4), being stimulated by a greater example than his own (Phil. 2:5-11), that is exemplified at every turn in the section now before us.

The analysis of the passage before us is simple. 'Confidence' and 'rejoicing' are pivoted on the altruistic and challenging interrogation 'what then?' of verse 18. This we set out in structure form as follows :

Philippians 1:12-18

A 12-17. CONFIDENCE   **a** Furtherance of gospel.
                                  b Bonds manifested.
                                        c Confidence by bonds.
                                  b Bonds, afflictions added to.
                                  a Defence of the gospel.

B 18.   WHAT THEN?   Notwithstanding every way.

A 18.   REJOICING   **d** Whether in pretence.
                                  e Or in truth.
                                       f Christ is preached.
                                 d Herein I do rejoice.
                                   e And will rejoice.

The apostle introduces this new section of his epistle with the words :

'But I would ye should understand, brethren' (Phil. 1:12).

On a number of occasions Paul prefaces an important feature of an epistle by some such phrase as 'I would not have you to be ignorant', or 'I would that ye knew', 'I would have you know'. Ignorance of facts plays into the hand of the enemy. Paul would have his hearers understand, so that they may see all and frame all their judgments in the clear light of truth. In the particular case before us, Paul is concerned that the Philippians should not feel that after all their long and continued fellowship in the Gospel, that by any lack of faithfulness, wisdom or power, on the part of the Lord Who had the disposing of all events and all lives, that the gospel and preaching were in any sense adversely influenced.

> 'Now I would have you know, brethren, that what I have gone through has turned out to the furtherance of the Good News rather than otherwise. And thus it has become notorious among the Imperial Guards, and everywhere, that it is for the sake of Christ that I am a prisoner: and the greater part of the brethren, made confident in the Lord through my imprisonment, now speak of God's message without fear, more boldly than ever. Some indeed actually preach Christ out of envy and contentiousness, but there are also others who do it from good will. These latter preach Him from love to me, knowing that I am here for the defence of the Good News; while the others proclaim Him from motives of rivalry, and insincerely, supposing that by this they are embittering my imprisonment. What does it matter, however? In any case Christ is preached – either perversely or in honest truth; and in that I rejoice, yes, and will rejoice' (Phil. 1:12-18, Weymouth).

The word chosen by the apostle to speak of 'the furtherance' of the Gospel indicates a progress that could not be accomplished without considerable effort and trial, the word employed being *prokopto*, a compound of *kopto* 'to strike'. This word supplies the word 'offence' in verse ten. The word *kopto*, when used in a literal sense, means 'to cut down' as branches (Matt. 21:8), and *kopiao*, a kindred word, means to toil or to labour (Matt. 6:28; Matt. 11:28) and is found in Philippians 2:16.

There is, however, a deeper reason for using *prokopto* than merely to indicate the toil and labour involved. Paul had used this selfsame word in Galatians 1:14 when he had described his manner of life as a bigoted Pharisee, saying that he had 'profited' or 'forged ahead' above many of his equals in the Jews' religion. Now the same zeal is consecrated to the furtherance of the gospel.

With what grief must the apostle have penned the words in 2 Timothy 'they will *increase* unto more ungodliness', 'evil men and seducers *shall wax* worse and worse' (2 Tim. 2:16; 3:13), where *prokopto* is used of the 'furtherance' of evil.

The furtherance of the Gospel is not an isolated effort. The reader may remember that in a published statement concerning the work of the Berean Forward Movement, it was stated that our purpose was to 'foster and to further' the claim of Dispensational Truth. If the Gospel is to be furthered, it must also be fostered. Paul does not use this term in Philippians, but he does speak of being set for 'the defence and confirmation of the gospel' (Phil. 1:7) which is equivalent.

The word translated 'defence' is *apologia* and originally meant 'to talk oneself out of a difficulty', even as the word apology has this lower meaning in our own tongue. The word is used both in the New Testament Greek and in English in a higher sense, being employed by the early 'fathers' for the 'defence of Christianity'. Today we have a department of theology entitled 'Apologetics' from this same word. The word *apologia* is used of or by Paul seven times.

'Hear ye my *defence*' (Acts 22:1). To his Hebrew accusers.

'And have licence *to answer* for himself' (Acts 25:16). Festus to the Chief Priests.

'At my first answer (*defence*)' (2 Tim. 4:16). Paul before Nero.

And in 1 Corinthians 9:3 it is translated 'answer' and in 2 Corinthians 7:11 'clearing'.

In Acts 19 to 26 *apologeomai* is translated 'make defence', 'answer for' or 'speak for', in relation to Paul's trial. In only two references out of eighteen is the secondary and lower meaning 'make excuse' intended, namely in Romans 2:15 and 2 Corinthians 12:19.

Paul was blessedly conscious that his very imprisonment would be overruled and provide a testimony to the integrity of the gospel. It should not and must not be allowed to pass unobserved, that whereas in Acts 19 to 26 Paul is concerned with his own defence, now that he is at Rome and in prison he is far more concerned with the defence of the gospel, even as, when writing to the Colossians at the selfsame time that he had said 'remember my bonds', he had prayed for an 'opened door', yet not so that he might be set free from prison but that 'God would open unto us a door of utterance, to speak the mystery of Christ, for which I am also in bonds' (Col. 4:3).

Not only was Paul 'set' for the defence, but also for the 'confirmation' of the Gospel. Here he uses the word *bebaiosis*, and anyone who had been a zealot for the law as he had been, would know that this word occurs once in the LXX, namely at Leviticus 25:23, in the law concerning the sale of land in Israel. The Hebrew reads 'the land shall not be sold for a *cutting off*', which the LXX translates 'the land shall not be sold *for a permanence*'.

Paul would also remember that the verb is found in Psalm 119:28, where we read '*strengthen* Thou me according unto Thy Word'. *Bebaios* is translated 'sure', 'stedfast' and 'firm' (Rom. 4:16; Heb. 6:19 and 3:6). *Bebaioo* is rendered 'confirm' and 'establish' (Mark 16:20; Rom. 15:8; 1 Cor. 1:6,8; 2 Cor. 1:21).

In the background, yet nevertheless 'behind' all this defence and furtherance, was the loving and constant 'fellowship in the gospel from the first day until now' (Phil. 1:5), the human side; and the confidence that 'He Which had begun a good work' would perform it (Phil. 1:6), the Divine side of the same blessed story.

The bonds of the apostle were manifest as 'bonds in Christ' and this had been made known throughout the praetorian guard. The very fact that his imprisonment necessitated that one of the guard should always be with him, chained by the wrist, ensured that in time the doctrine and principles for which Paul was imprisoned would be widely circulated. The apostle was so whole-heartedly devoted to the Gospel he served with such selfless singleness of eye, that he could look beyond the faction that preached Christ of envy and strife and meet it with the challenging 'what then?'; Christ was preached, that sufficed. Christ was all in all in Colossians 3:11, Christ is as surely all in Philippians, and it is this thread that binds the sections of this epistle together, linking Paul's choice in Philippians 1:21-24, with Christ's example (Phil. 2:5-11), providing the attitude of mind that attains unto the out-resurrection (Phil. 3:10-14) and giving true contentment in all circumstances (Phil. 4:11,12). Here we have indeed, what the hymn writer later desired :

'A mind at leisure from itself',

because so fully occupied with Christ.

CHAPTER 3

Far Better

Philippians 1:19-26

The section that now opens before us is one that has provoked much thought and has been the battle ground of conflicting interpretations. The centre of the argument being the apostle's words 'to depart, and to be with Christ' (Phil. 1:23).

> 'To be a saint in paradise dwelling in the light of Christ's countenance, though not the perfect state, because the body was not redeemed and raised up in the likeness of Christ's glorious body, was indeed "far better"' (Sadler).

These words, quoted from a popular commentary, give a fair presentation of the view held by orthodox Christians.

> 'Paul believed that the soul of the Christian would be immediately with the Saviour at death. It was evidently his expectation that he would at once pass to His presence, and not that he would remain in an intermediate state to some far distant period. The soul does not *sleep* at death. Paul expected to be *with* Christ, and to be conscious of the fact – to see Him, and to partake of His glory' (Barnes).

Here again is a very popular view, held by many who in other doctrines may be far apart.

In the scholarly exposition of Bishop Lightfoot, the popular view is tempered. He says :

> 'The faithful immediately after death are similarly represented as in the presence and keeping of the Lord (2 Cor. 5:6,8) ... on the other hand their state after death is elsewhere described as a sleep from which they will arise (1 Cor. 15:51,52; 1 Thess. 4:14,16). The one mode of representation must qualify the other'.

Bishop Lightfoot does not explain how the one mode can qualify the other. How a person can at the same time be represented as 'in the presence' of the Lord 'immediately after death' and at the same time be 'asleep' from which there will be no awakening until the resurrection, is not explained and is possibly unexplainable. It is noteworthy, nevertheless, that the problem is honestly recorded, even if it be not solved.

Another interpretation has been widely accepted by many who hold scriptural views concerning the state of the dead. This is expressed in the interpretation given by some writers (Hudson, Roberts, Ellis and Read) 'having a desire for the RETURNING and being with Christ', supposing it to refer to Christ's second coming.

Between these two extreme views, of course, there is a variety of interpretations that shade off from pure annihilation to the doctrine of 'sudden death – sudden glory'.

It would serve no good purpose for us to fill our pages with further quotations; we are Bereans, in the true sense of the word, and we must 'search and see' whether these things are so, but not only so, we must above all things search the Scriptures at first hand in order to discover truth at the fountain head.

In the first place, let us exhibit the structure of the section before us.

Philippians 1:21-26

A 21   TO ME (*emoi*) to live.   Christ.

  B 22,23   **a** Live in flesh. Fruit.
     THE   **b** Paul's choice.   Not made known.
    STRAIT.   **c** Paul's desire. With Christ.

  B 24,25   *a* Abide in flesh. Needful.
     THE   *b* Paul's confidence. I know.
  CONFIDENCE.   *c* Paul's continuance. With you all.

A 26   BY ME (*emoi*) my presence.   Glorying in Christ.

While the heart of this controversial passage is verse 23, it is essential that the spirit in which this passage was approached by Paul shall be appreciated by us, and therefore our first inquiry must be into the intention of the apostle when he wrote :

'For to me to live is Christ, and to die is gain' (Phil. 1:21).

It will be seen at once that the presence of the argumentative 'for', with which this resolution is prefaced, compels us to go back into verses 19 and 20. When we do we discover that these verses, too, open with the logical conjunction 'for' and so link the new section on to the selfless rejoicing of the apostle when he said 'what then?' The 'furtherance' of the gospel is still in view and plays an essential part in the right understanding of the whole passage :

> 'For I know that this shall turn to my salvation through your prayer, and the supply of the Spirit of Jesus Christ, according to my earnest expectation and my hope, that in nothing I shall be ashamed, but that with all boldness, as always, so now also Christ shall be magnified in my body, whether it be by life or by death. For to me to live is Christ, and to die is gain' (Phil. 1:19-21).

What does the apostle mean here by 'salvation'? Some refer it to deliverance from prison, some to salvation in the highest sense. First we must give heed to the fact that he uses the word once more in the first chapter in a similar context, the only difference being that on the first occasion he is speaking of himself, whereas on the second occasion he speaks of the Philippians :

> ' … in nothing terrified by your adversaries: which is to them an evident token of perdition, but *to you of salvation* and that of God. For unto you it is given in the behalf of Christ, not only to believe on Him, but also to suffer for His sake' (Phil. 1:28,29).

Here we have something that is an advance upon 'believing on Him', it is the added 'suffering for His sake'. This indicates that salvation is not used here in its purely evangelical sense. It is, moreover, set in a context of 'striving' for the faith of the gospel and the false judgment of 'adversaries'.

Most important of all is the fact that 'salvation' is used over against 'perdition', and a true understanding of this word will place the salvation which Paul has in mind in its true light.

Apoleia, 'perdition', is used again in Philippians 3:19, where it is translated 'destruction' and there it is in contrast with 'perfection'. Now this association is proved to be intentional, because in Hebrews – which we have already demonstrated is parallel with Philippians – these two words 'perfection' or 'perdition' present the two focal points of the theme. The Hebrew believers were either 'going on unto perfection' or they would 'draw back unto perdition'. Now the primitive meaning of *apoleia* is 'waste', as seen in Matthew 26:8. 'Salvation', therefore, in Philippians is equated with 'perfection', the goal that was before both the apostle and the Philippians and closely associated with 'the fellowship of His sufferings' (Phil. 3:10-12).

Salvation – and the Supply of the Spirit of Jesus Christ

It is this aspect of salvation that Paul had in mind when he urged the Philippians to 'work out' their own salvation with fear and trembling (Phil. 2:12). The apostle had earlier used the word 'salvation' in a context of suffering and triumph (2 Cor. 1:6), a context which employs the word 'tribulation' (2 Cor. 1:4; Phil. 1:16); 'partakers' in reference to suffering (2 Cor. 1:7; Phil. 1:7); 'pressed out of measure' (2 Cor. 1:8; Phil. 1:23); the 'helping together by prayer' (2 Cor. 1:11; Phil. 1:19); 'sincerity' (2 Cor. 1:12; Phil. 1:10), and 'conversation' (2 Cor. 1:12; Phil. 1:27); where, even though different Greek words are used, the things indicated are similar.

There is, however, another Scripture which will throw light upon the apostle's meaning here, for the words of Philippians 1:19 contain a word for word quotation of the LXX version of Job 13:16, which in the Authorized Version reads 'He also shall be my salvation'.

The Greek version of Job 13:16 reads :

– *kai touto moi apobesetai eis soterian.*

The Greek of Philippians 1:19 reads :

– *hoti touto moi apobesetai eis soterian.*

In what way does the fact that Paul quotes from the book of Job illuminate the meaning of Philippians 1:19? Let another apostle supply the answer. James, in his epistle speaks of the trial of faith, its perfect work, and the issue 'the crown of life' (Jas. 1:2,3,4,12). In the closing chapter of his epistle he says 'Ye have heard of the patience of Job, and have seen the end of the Lord' (Jas. 5:11).

To the apostle in his imprisonment, and in all his sufferings for Christ's sake, the story of Job would come as a real 'word in season'. As surely as Job could say 'this shall turn to my salvation' so also could Paul. 'Though He slay me', said Job, 'yet will I trust Him'; 'for me to live is Christ, and to die, gain', said Paul.

The expression 'this shall turn' to my salvation, should be compared with 'and it shall turn to you for a testimony' (Luke 21:13), where persecution and betrayal are in the context. To this should be added Mark 13:9 'for a testimony against them', with which we should compare Philippians 1:28. This 'turning out' of adverse circumstances to the furtherance of the gospel, and to the 'salvation' of the apostle, is related to the Philippians' fellowship with him in prayer.

'Through your prayer, and the supply of the Spirit of Jesus Christ' (Phil. 1:19).

The apostle employs a very colourful word to speak of the 'supply' of the spirit of Jesus Christ here.

Epichoregia goes back to the Greek chorus, and the custom of appointing a wealthy patron to cover the expenses of the theatrical entertainment, called *choregos*. The word is used with special significance in the prison epistles. It is used of the members of the body 'that which every joint *supplieth*' (Eph. 4:16) and *'having nourishment ministered'* (Col. 2:19).

In Philippians the church is never called 'the body', neither are fellow believers called 'members'. Here in this epistle the practical outworking of that truth is seen. Paul acknowledges by the use of the word *epichoregia* the fellowship of fellow members. It should be unnecessary for us to observe, that unless 'members' do thus 'supply' or at least mediate the needed supply (Eph. 4:16), such members will suffer atrophy.

Paul was supplied 'with the Spirit of Jesus Christ'. This should be no difficulty, it is on the same level as the desire for the mind that was in Christ Jesus (Phil. 2:5). Paul met adversity, prison, misrepresentation, suffering in 'the spirit' of his Lord. It is this that he expands into 'fellowship with His sufferings' and 'conformity unto His death' in chapter 3.

All that we have seen in this nineteenth verse is preparatory to the claim of verses twenty and twenty-one, and these in their turn lead on to the great dilemma of verse twenty-three. The examination of these verses must now receive attention.

The salvation here in view is not the initial salvation from sin, nor is it exhausted by referring it to deliverance from prison, it is rather 'the salvation which is in Christ Jesus with age-abiding glory' (2 Tim. 2:10), a salvation that is associated with 'suffering and reigning', even as in Philippians it is associated with 'the prize'.

In this, the apostle gladly acknowledged that the prayer of the Philippians played a part. Nevertheless he himself was not inactive, for he continued :

'According to my earnest expectation and my hope, that in nothing I shall be ashamed, but that with all boldness, as always, so now also Christ shall be magnified in my body, whether it be by life, or by death. For to me to live is Christ, and to die is gain' (Phil. 1:20,21).

These words fill out the meaning of the apostle's reference 'salvation', a salvation manifested by either life or death. That we are still dealing with the same theme that was started in verse 19, the word 'according' bears witness. Whatever it was that the apostle had before his mind, he looked forward to it with intense eagerness. The word translated 'earnest expectation' is *apokaradokia*, a word which occurs once more in Romans 8:19. This is a word compounded of *apo* 'away', *kara* 'head', *dokein* 'to expect' and so 'to look forward with outstretched neck'. *Karadokeo* does not occur in the New Testament, but Aquilla uses it in his version of Psalm 37:7 'wait patiently for Him'. The apostle seems to have been led to the choice of this word by the fact that he represents himself in this epistle, as an athlete 'forgetting' the things that are behind, 'reaching forth' or 'stretching forth' unto the things which are before, while he 'pressed' to the mark for the prize of the high calling.

What was this earnest expectation and hope that so gripped the apostle? It had nothing to do with his deliverance from prison, or even with the hope of future glory. One overwhelming desire possessed him, which he immediately proceeds to announce and which was related to present service in view of the day of Christ.

'In nothing' *en oudeni*, verse 20. 'In nothing' *en medeni*, verse 28. *Oudeis*, is an independent unconditional negative, *medeis* is a conditional negative. *Oudeis* deals with a matter of fact, *medeis* with a matter of supposition. The apostle uses each of these words three times in this epistle. It will help us to observe the contexts of each reference.

Oudeis. The unconditional negative :

' In *nothing* I shall be ashamed' (1:20).

' I have *no* man likeminded' (2:20).

' *No* church communicated with me' (4:15).

Medeis. The conditional negative :

' In *nothing* terrificd by your adversaries' (1:28).

' Let *nothing* be done through strife' (2:3).

' Be careful for *nothing*' (4:6).

For himself the apostle can speak positively; for others he allows a certain amount of relativity and supposition. We may not be able to explain every passage satisfactorily and show why the one word was chosen rather than the other, but we can see that the choice of *oudeis* in Philippians 1:20, is all of a piece with fixedness of purpose that is so manifest through the entire epistle.

'In nothing I shall be ashamed'. Here again his earnest expectation is seen to be concerned with faithful service rather than with the blessed hope. Paul seems to have had a special sensitiveness to being 'ashamed' and uses the word on more than one occasion in connection with ministry.

The root of the word employed by Paul is *aischros*, 'vile'. The following samples of the way in which this word is found in his writings will supply sufficient reason for his shrinking from any approach to anything so despicable.

Aischros, 'filthy lucre's sake' (Tit. 1:11).
Aischrotes, 'neither *filthiness*' (Eph. 5:4).
Aischrokerdes, 'filthy lucre' (1 Tim. 3:8).
Aischunomai, 'ashamed' (Phil. 1:20).
Aischune, 'despising the *shame*' (Heb. 12:2).
Kataischuno, 'hope maketh not *ashamed*' (Rom. 5:5).
Epaischunomai, 'nevertheless I am not *ashamed*' (2 Tim. 1:12).
Anepaischuntos, 'a workman that needeth not *to be ashamed*' (2 Tim. 2:15).

In Mark 8:38, the Saviour is recorded as saying 'whosoever therefore shall be ashamed of Me and of My words in this adulterous and sinful generation: of him also shall the Son of Man be ashamed, when He cometh in the glory of His Father with the holy angels'.

In Matthew 10:33, the word 'deny' is used as a synonym of 'be ashamed', and this leads us to the words of 2 Timothy 2:12, where in view of the 'prize' or 'crown' and as a direct outcome of 'the salvation' which is 'with eternal glory', the apostle uses the word 'deny' in the same sense and context that the Saviour used the word 'ashamed' in Mark 8.

'If we suffer, we shall also reign with Him:
If we deny Him, He also will deny us' (2 Tim. 2:12).

In contrast with being 'ashamed', the apostle places 'boldness'. 'Boldness' in the New Testament is expressed by three different words.

Tharreo, 'so that we may boldly say, The Lord is my helper' (Heb. 13:6).

This word being associated with the idea of 'warmth' (*thero*, hence the word 'therm' heat) indicates 'courage'.

Tolmao, 'many ... are much more *bold* to speak' (Phil. 1:14). This word has the sense of 'daring' 'would even dare to die' (Rom. 5:7), 'they durst not ask' (Luke 20:40).

Parrhesia, 'that I may open my mouth *boldly*' (Eph. 6:19). This word demands a little fuller examination, as it is the one used by Paul in the passage before us, and chosen rather than *tolmao* already employed in Philippians 1:14. *Parrhesia* is a compound of *pan* 'all' and a derivative of the verb *rheo* 'to flow', which is translated many times 'to speak' (Matt. 1:22). This root word is seen in the English word 'rhetoric' and in the word *rhetor*, 'orator' (Acts 24:1); and in *rhema*, 'word' (John 17:8).

The idea of 'flowing' can be seen in such words as 'issue of blood', *rhusis* (Luke 8:44), 'the prow or bow of a ship' *prora* (Acts 27:30), 'let slip' *pararrheo* (Heb. 2:1).

The boldness which the apostle speaks of in Philippians 1:20 is not so much that of courage or daring, though it involves both, but is especially concerned with frank, fearless declaration, neither being intimidated nor bribed into silence. This meaning can be seen in the following examples of the way *parrhesia* is translated in the Authorized Version.

'Great *plainness* of speech' (2 Cor. 3:12); 'with all *confidence*, no man forbidding him' (Acts 28:31); 'tell us *plainly*' (John 10:24); 'let me *freely* speak unto you' (Acts 2:29). For this the apostle sought the Ephesians' fellowship in prayer 'that I may open my mouth *boldly*' (Eph. 6:19), and it was this fearless plain speaking that he had in mind in Philippians 1:20.

Paul had so spoken in earlier days (Acts 9:27; Acts 13:46; Acts 19:8); and he had asked prayer that this may continue. Here, writing to the Philippians, he confidently links the past with the future, saying 'as always, so now also', and then by a change of terms speaks of his boldness and eagerness under another figure.

'Christ shall be magnified in my body, whether it be by life or by death' (Phil. 1:20).

To the Hebrew, the idea of 'magnifying' the Lord would be a familiar as well as very sacred form of worship. The word comes naturally in the Virgin's song (Luke 1:46); in the praise of those who were of the circumcision (Acts 10:45,46), and in the thanksgiving of David (2 Sam. 7:26). Paul knew, moreover, that the word was used synonymously with 'exalt' in the translation of the LXX, and there may have been an anticipation of the glorious exaltation of the Lord, of which he speaks in Philippians chapter 2, for the word *megaluno*, 'to magnify', is akin to *megalosune*, 'majesty' (Heb. 1:3; Heb. 8:1), a word closely associated with the Saviour's exaltation. It is as though Paul said 'I know and have taught that the Saviour has been highly exalted, and that in a future day, this exaltation will be acknowledged and acclaimed. I count it a privilege to anticipate that day, for Christ shall be magnified *now*, not only in the future, in my body and not only in glory'.

Anticipation is the very life of faith, for faith is the substance of things hoped for. Paul would have the Philippians 'like Christ' now, at least so far as the 'mind' is concerned (Phil. 2:5), in anticipation of the future day when they shall be like Him in body also (Phil. 3:21). Paul would have the Philippians' 'conversation' here and now (Phil. 1:27) anticipate their glorious 'conversation' which is in heaven (Phil. 3:20). This is a blessed and fruitful theme, and the reader might profitably pursue it further.

It is one thing to 'believe in the second advent'; it is another 'to live ... looking for that blessed hope'. The crown of righteousness is not held out to all who have 'believed the *doctrine* of His appearing', but to all those 'who have *loved* His appearing'. Paul did not simply say 'let the Lord be magnified', he did not say 'Christ shall be magnified in my spirit' or 'in my ministry' or 'in my private worship'. He went to the extreme length of saying 'Christ shall be magnified in my body', a statement that is fuller, more reaching and more intensely personal than them all. Why did he stress the 'body' here? In some of his writings the body is completely set at nought. It is called 'the body of sin', or 'the mortal body'; but these statements occur in the great doctrinal portion of Romans. Even so, it is in Romans that we read 'present your bodies a living sacrifice'. He speaks of bearing about in the body the dying of the Lord Jesus, that the life also of Jesus might be made manifest in the body. At the close of the epistle to the Galatians Paul cried 'I bear in my body the marks of the Lord Jesus'.

In Philippians Paul contrasts the present 'vile body', or, better, 'this body of our humiliation', with the future resurrection body which will be changed like unto His glorious body (Phil. 3:21). In this body of humiliation, said the apostle, I would exalt and magnify the Lord, in blessed anticipation of that day without tears when suffering for Him will have for ever passed.

Even so, we have not yet descended to the depths with Paul, for he goes on to say 'Christ shall be magnified in my body, whether it be by life or by death'. In some contexts, life and death are in opposition, but here they are united. In this passage they are united in a common category, they are modes of service, and hence, it is a matter of indifference to such an one as Paul, whether the Lord should elect to be manifested in the continuance of his life, or whether He should elect to be magnified by a martyr's death. He who exhibited indifference as it concerned others so long as 'Christ is preached', and brushed aside as of no account any extra hardship which the preaching of some might add to his bonds, exhibits the same blessed disregard here.

To the apostle, Christ was Lord both of the dead and of the living. Redemption and resurrection were such realities that the natural fear of death or clinging to life had been exchanged for a mind like that which characterized Christ (Phil. 2:4,5), a mind indeed 'at leisure from itself', as we have already observed.

The apostle sums up his attitude and motive in the words :

'For me to live is Christ, and to die is gain' (Phil. 1:21),

the implications of which shall now occupy our attention.

Christ shall be magnified in my body

These words of the apostle have so great a challenge and indicate so important a line of teaching that we must continue our study and consider their bearing upon doctrine and practice a little more particularly.

In the first place we must be on our guard against a false spirituality, which would ignore the rightful place of the body, and secondly we must be clear in our understanding as to the place that the body is intended to occupy in the disciplinary pilgrimage of the believer as he presses on to the glory of the future day.

We might at first have felt that the apostle would have said 'Christ shall be magnified in my spirit', leaving the body out of the question as being too advanced as an instrument of evil, to be considered in such a context.

However, a moment's consideration will enable us to perceive that it should be comparatively easy for a believer to magnify Christ in his 'spirit', for the spirit belongs to the new creation. It is the first fruits of complete emancipation :

'For the law of the spirit of life in Christ Jesus, hath made me free from the law of sin and death' (Rom. 8:2).

'They that are after the spirit (do mind) the things of the spirit' (Rom. 8:5).

Those who have risen with Christ to walk in 'newness of life' find that they can also serve in 'newness of spirit'. We have been given 'the earnest of the spirit', and the believer who walks in the spirit will not fulfil the lusts of the flesh (Gal. 5:16). The reader, however, knows that we could continue to add reference to reference that teach the believer's emancipation and new power in the realm of the spirit.

The apostle prefaces his reference to 'the body' by a reference to 'the supply of the spirit of Jesus Christ' (Phil. 1:19); and this supply was an all sufficient justification for his triumphant and challenging claim 'Christ shall be magnified in my body', for 'the spirit of Jesus Christ' which he here refers to, is exemplified in Philippians 2:6-10, and is set before the believer as an example, 'let this mind be in you, which was also in Christ Jesus'.

To the Philippians the apostle addressed the hope that they would 'stand fast in one spirit' and with 'one soul' ('mind' in A.V.) (Phil. 1:27). The apostle lovingly reasoned with the Philippians that 'if' there were 'any fellowship of the spirit', that they would be 'one soul' ('accord' A.V.) and mind one thing (Phil. 2:1,2). The mind, the spirit, the soul seem accounted for in regard to others, but Paul does not merely contemplate the triumph of the spirit, he says of himself 'Christ shall be magnified in my BODY'.

From one point of view 'the body' is entirely repudiated. Writing to the Colossians Paul said :

'In Whom ye were also circumcised with a circumcision not made with hands, in the putting off of the body of the flesh, in the circumcision of Christ' (Col. 2:11 R.V.).

The Greek texts that are considered most authoritative omit the words found in the Authorized Version 'the sins of'; it is not 'sin' that is in question so much as the 'flesh', and the influence of the flesh as manifested by the 'body'. What that influence means can be understood best in the light of all that spiritual circumcision portends.

This 'body of flesh' which is here 'put off' is further indicated in Colossians 3:5, 'mortify therefore your members which are upon the earth', a counsel which is followed by a list of fleshly defilement and evil. Again in Colossians 3:9 when we read 'ye have put off the old man with his deeds', the 'body of the flesh' is in view.

From these passages it might be inferred that 'the body' must be repudiated as an instrument of righteousness, that though it must needs be suffered, it should be 'neglected' in fact, and all our spiritual activities, prayers and watchfulness, be concentrated upon the spirit and the mind.

The very fact that we were tempted to use the word 'neglect' in this context reveals a weakness in the argument, for at the very close of the selfsame chapter that records the repudiation of the flesh, the apostle warns against the 'neglecting of the body' (Col. 2:23) as a mode or means of fuller consecration! Have the members of the body been yielded in the past as servants of uncleanness and iniquity? They can be yielded just as surely as servants of righteousness and holiness (Rom. 6:19). The body of itself is neutral, neither moral nor immoral, it is but an instrument, and all depends upon the power that is in charge of its activities. The same epistle that reveals the depravity of human nature, says that it is 'reasonable service' on the part of the believer to 'present' his body as a living sacrifice, 'acceptable unto God' (Rom. 12:1). The mortal body can be 'quickened', the life lived 'in the flesh' can be sanctified. This new relationship, this exchange of masters, is very fully indicated in 1 Corinthians 6:19,20: 'ye are not your own, for ye are bought with a price: therefore glorify God in your body'. There is no authority for the added words 'and in your spirit which are God's'. It is not a change in the composition of the body that makes the difference, it is a change of masters. The following inscription of 200-199 B.C. will illuminate this passage :

'Date. Apollo the Pythian BOUGHT from Sosibus of Amphissa, for freedom, a female slave whose name is Nicaea, by race a Roman WITH A PRICE of minae and a half of silver ... '.

Here we have the words 'bought with a price', and not only so, but where the translator reads 'slave', the Greek has *soma* 'body'. The 'body' has changed masters by the process of emancipation by redemption, and in a society that was served by slaves, and where many a slave entertained the hope of one day purchasing his freedom, Paul's words would need no explanation. Whoever was thus 'bought with a price' could and should glorify the new master in his 'body'.

So, earlier in the chapter, the apostle said 'the body is ... for the Lord; and the Lord for the body' (1 Cor. 6:13).

In 1 Corinthians 9 the apostle brings the 'body' into the atmosphere of *race, prize* and *crown* (1 Cor. 9:24-27), and by the analogy of the contending athlete, who with the prize in view exercised self discipline, he said :

'I keep under my body, and bring it into subjection: lest that by any means, when I have preached to others, I myself should be a castaway' (1 Cor. 9:27).

The 'preaching' here is that of the 'herald' of the Greek contests; the becoming a 'castaway' is the condition of becoming 'disqualified' in respect of the crown.

The first epistle to the Corinthians gives the negative side, 'I keep under my body'; Philippians gives the positive, 'Christ shall be magnified in my body', and both epistles have a race-course and a prize in the background. It therefore needs both sides of the argument to state the truth. The body is made up of separate members.

'It is profitable for thee that one of thy members should perish, and not that thy whole body should be cast into hell' (Matt. 5:29).

'As we have many members in one body, and all members have not the same office; so ... ' (Rom. 12:4).

'The body is not one member, but many' (1 Cor. 12:14).

'The foot ... the hand ... the ear ... the eye ... the feeble ... the less honourable ... the comely' (1 Cor. 12:15-24).

'The tongue is a little member' (Jas. 3:5).

The apostle's members had, before his conversion, been employed in the upholding of Jewish tradition and of persecuting Christians, but after his conversion his 'hands' had ministered both to his own necessities and to those that were with him (Acts 20:34).

The apostle who wrote in the epistle to the Romans: 'their feet are swift to shed blood' and 'how beautiful are the feet of them that preach the gospel' (Rom. 3:15 and 10:15) knew by experience the truth of both statements.

At the stoning of Stephen the accusers laid their clothes at a young man's feet, who was called Saul (Acts 7:58); but a little later those self same feet were made fast in the stocks of a Roman prison (Acts 16:24). Paul could therefore truthfully say that these two members of his body, his hands and his feet, had magnified the Lord.

What was true of these two members of his body could be true of every member. His prayer was that his 'mouth' should be opened boldly as he made known the mystery of the gospel (Eph. 6:19). His ear, like the willing servant under the law had been 'digged'. He had said 'I love my master ... I will not go out free' (Exod. 21:5,6). Paul bore in his body the 'marks' (*stigmata* brand marks of a slave indicating the owner) of the Lord Jesus.

The body which he yielded to the service of the Lord, he calls in Philippians 3:21 a 'vile' body, according to the Authorized Version. This word 'vile' as used in modern English is scarcely correct; the Revised Version uses the word 'humiliation' instead. And such is the true rendering of the word *tapeinosis*, linked as it is with Philippians 2:8, which uses *tapeinoo* 'to be humble', the fuller consideration of which will come better in its place as we proceed.

The body in which Christ can be magnified is indeed 'this body of our humiliation', not only by its association with the Lord's rejection and humiliation, but by reason of the very constitution of human life, birth and maintenance.

The body, with all its wonder, is nevertheless a 'humiliation'. The whole process of life from birth to death has much in it that cannot be spoken about without reserve. Even the fact that at two or three intervals every day it is necessary to turn aside and partake of food in order to keep the body functioning is a humiliation, and belongs to the present disciplinary period. The fact that however much we desire otherwise, it is necessary to bring work to a stop, undress and spend a third of each day's twenty-four hours in sleep is another indication of present frailty. Yet in spite of these limitations, it is still gloriously possible for the believer to emulate the apostle and say 'these hands', 'my body', can now be the honoured instruments of grace. It is because this is a blessed fact, that we find the apostle saying 'let him that stole steal no more; but rather let him labour, working with his hands the thing which is good, that he may have to give to him that needeth' (Eph. 4:28).

Frances Ridley Havergal has crystallized the truth in the lovely words :

'Take my hands and let them move
At the impulse of thy love;
Take my feet and let them be
Swift and beautiful for Thee.

Take my voice and let me sing
Always, only, for my King,
Take my lips and let them be
Filled with messages from Thee'.

For me to live is Christ, and to die is gain

It will be remembered that we have seen the superb indifference which grace enabled the apostle to show in his service for the Lord, in spite of adverse circumstances. Provided Christ was preached, he rejoiced, even though some of this preaching added to his troubles. Provided Christ was magnified, Paul would be satisfied whether that magnifying demanded life or death for its exhibition. We now come to his concluding words :

'For to me to live is Christ, and to die is gain' (Phil. 1:21).

How are we to understand these words? On the surface the statement is divided into two parts. We can say: while he lived, his supreme object would be the magnifying of Christ, and if he died, then the prize of the high calling would be his. We are however somewhat sensitive to the apparent intrusion of personal gain here. It seems to fall short of the high ideal held before us by the apostle.

Other commentators have felt the difficulty too, as will be seen in the following. F. W. Grant, in his book 'Facts and theories as to a future state', quotes the book 'Bible *v.* Tradition' by Ellis and Read, as follows :

'Do you ask how then it would be gain to Paul to die? Paul does not say it would be gain to him. Fill up the ellipsis according to grammatical laws: For me to live will be gain to the cause of Christ, for Christ will at all events be magnified in my body, whether by my life or by my death. And for me to die is gain to the cause of Christ, for Christ will be magnified in my body, whether I die or live'.

The 'ellipsis' (or omission) and grammatical law may be illustrated by quoting from a letter which was received from the Rev. George Parker of Kingtse Kwan, China, in April 1915.

'Note the figure   Hendiadys of clauses.
Phil. 1:21.   Christ's gain distributed'.

In another letter the same writer speaks of the Hendiadys of Phrases which is illustrated by the passage :

'My soul doth magnify the Lord
My spirit hath rejoiced in God my Saviour'.

This is re-written :

'My soul and spirit, hath rejoiced in and doth magnify, Jehovah God my Saviour'.

This is followed by several passages by way of illustration. For example :

'Christ ... gain' means 'Christ's gain' (Phil. 1:21).

'In God ... in glory' means 'in God's glory' (Col. 3:3,4).

'Christ ... grace' means 'Christ's grace' (Gal. 5:4).

From this, Philippians 1:21 should read :

'For me to live is Christ's (gain), and to die is (Christ's) gain'.

'Not to Paul, but to Christ, as is clear from verse 20. To Paul, life and death were of no account, so long as the cause of Christ was advanced. His bonds had furthered the gospel, what might not his death do?' (*Companion Bible*).

To us with our modern depreciation of the doctrine of reward, such explanations are commendable. Paul is seen striking the high note of heroism to the last. And yet, when we read his own words as written, the explanations offered above seem very involved and somewhat strained. Moreover if we rule out personal gain from Philippians 1:21, we must face it in chapter 3:8 where the verbal form of the word translated 'gain' is there used in the phrase 'that I might win Christ', a passage in close logical connection with the 'prize' of the high calling (Phil. 3:14)!

The parallel epistle, 'Hebrews', certainly does not exhibit any sensitiveness in speaking of 'reward'. The believer is exhorted to endurance because of the 'recompense of reward' (Heb. 10:35) and the example of Moses is given in the list of those who obtained a good report, and he is said also to have had 'respect unto the recompense of the reward' (Heb. 11:26). Moreover, the writer of Hebrews actually incorporates this element of reward into both the nature of faith and the character of God, saying :

'He that cometh to God must believe that He is, and that He is the rewarder of them that diligently seek Him' (Heb. 11:6).

The primary meaning of *misthos* 'reward', is 'hire' paid for service. So *misthios* is a 'hired servant' (Luke 15:17); *misthoma* is a 'hired house' (Acts 28:30); *misthotos* is an 'hireling' (John 10:12), and Paul reasons on the word *misthos*, that to him that worketh is *the reward* not reckoned of grace but of debt (Rom. 4:4).

Kerdos, the word translated 'gain' in Philippians 1:21, is not so much 'hire' for service rendered but 'gain' acquired by trading. This can be seen in the use of the verb *kerdaino*, 'what is a man profited, if he shall gain the whole world, and lose his own soul?' (Matt. 16:26); and especially in the parable of the talents 'he also gained other two'; 'I have gained beside them five' (Matt. 25:17,20). So also in his epistle James speaks of those who 'buy and sell and get gain' (4:13). The word *kerdos* is translated 'lucre' in the phrase 'for filthy *lucre's* sake' (Tit. 1:11).

In Philippians Paul is a man entrusted with 'talents'. He is essentially 'a servant', and associates himself with 'bishops and deacons' (Phil. 1:1). He has a prize in view, and in chapter 3 he speaks of 'gain' and 'loss' (Phil. 3:7), and expresses the hope that he might 'win' Christ (Phil. 3:8).

Now it is beyond the power of any man to make the words 'that I may win Christ' mean that Christ may gain something by the apostle's effort. It is the same in Philippians 1:21. Paul is simple, he meant what the words imply 'to die is gain', for he would then have finished his course, and there would be laid up for him the reward of faithful service.

When the apostle denied himself and laid himself out to serve to the utmost in the gospel he did it that he might 'gain' the Jews, those under law, those without law, and those who were weak. This he conceived as a full compensation for anything he might be called upon to give up.

The actual words of Philippians 3:8 that are translated 'that I may win Christ' are *hina Christon kerdeso*, and the words of 1 Corinthians 9:20 'that I might gain the Jews' are in the original *hina Ioudaious kerdeso*. It will be observed that the language apart from the replacing of 'Christ' by 'Jews', is identical. Philippians 3:8 taken alone can only mean that Paul would find Christ to be his great reward even as he had found him to be his salvation, but Philippians 3:8 must be understood as we must understand 1 Corinthians 9:20. In what way did Paul expect 'to gain the Jews'?

We go back to the chapter and find that Paul had the right to 'eat and drink', to have a 'wife' as well as other apostles. The apostle reasons that if he had sown unto them spiritual things, it was no great thing that he should reap their carnal things. Yet he continues :

'Nevertheless we have not used this power; but suffer all things, lest we should hinder the gospel of Christ' (1 Cor. 9:12).

He continues his discourse, by bringing forward the analogy of the Jewish priesthood who were maintained out of the offerings, claiming the same support for the preacher of the gospel.

Paul however had something more in view than immediate gain or support. He said 'for if I am doing this preaching of mine own account, that is as a voluntary undertaking ("willingly" is misleading, Paul was perfectly "willing", but that is not his point), I have a reward, but if involuntarily (which was the case, Acts 9:15, etc.) with a stewardship have I been entrusted. What then is my reward that I while preaching, render the gospel without cost (i.e. what reward have I in prospect that induces me to preach gratuitously) in order not to use my power in the gospel?' He now proceeds to answer the question 'What prospect of reward could induce me to do this?' 'For being free from the power of all men, I am enslaved to all, that I might gain the largest number' (Alford).

From this the argument runs on to the 'race', the 'prize' and the 'crown'; the exercise of temperance, the preaching to others, the possibility of becoming disapproved (1 Cor. 9:24-27). It will be perceived that while the dispensation has changed and the high calling of Philippians 3, with its prize has come in, the atmosphere of both passages is the same.

The apostle had earlier still indicated the same attitude and expressed the same hope.

'We were allowed of God to be put in trust with the gospel ... nor of men sought we glory ... when we might have been burdensome, as the apostles of Christ. For what is our hope, or joy, or crown of rejoicing? Are not even ye in the presence of our Lord Jesus Christ at His coming? For ye are our glory and joy' (1 Thess. 2:4,6,19,20).

We can now return to Philippians 1:21 and in the light of Paul's own experience, we can read with understanding his words 'to die is gain'. Paul himself has told us in that parallel epistle, Hebrews, of others who deny themselves of immediate blessing because they had something 'better' in view. Abraham was willing to be a tent-dweller in the land of promise – because he had the heavenly Jerusalem in view; 'these all died in faith not having received the promises, but having seen them afar off, and were persuaded of them, and embraced them, and confessed that they were strangers, and pilgrims on the earth' (Heb.

11:13). 'Others were tortured not accepting deliverance, that they might obtain a better resurrection' (Heb. 11:35).

Paul also 'counted all things but loss' and preferred to count as his 'gain' the converts gathered to the name of Christ that would indeed be 'his crown of rejoicing' in that day. As Mrs. Cousins puts it in her poem on the life and death of Rutherford :

> 'If but one soul from Anworth
> Shall meet me on that strand,
> My heaven will be two heavens
> In Emmanuel's Land'.

It has been the blessed lot of those who serve with *The Berean Expositor* to receive little recognition for their services in this life but what reward can be compared with that which awaits them in that day when the Lord makes up His jewels, what crown so precious as that composed of fellow believers who have been brought into the light of grace? Philippians is practical. Philippians is addressed to 'servants' and it is fitting that these practical issues should be brought into the light. This is the Lord's encouragement, beside which all else can be counted 'loss'.

Yet what I shall choose I do not make known

We now come to one of the most controversial passages in the epistles of Paul, namely Philippians 1:22-26. It is appealed to by those who teach 'sudden death, sudden glory'. It is the passage brought forward to prove a conscious intermediate state, a state 'far better' than living here in the flesh. It is on the other hand referred to by those who believe that in death there is no remembrance, and the word translated 'depart' is rendered by them 'return', meaning by that the second coming of Christ, 'the return' of Christ being according to this teaching 'far better' than either living or dying.

We do not feel it necessary to make a digression here, and deal with the doctrine of the 'intermediate state'. We have on different occasions indicated the teaching of Scripture on this matter, believing the statements made therein, namely, that those that are dead are sleeping, that at the resurrection they awake, and that the interval between the two events (however long it may be by the time measurements of conscious beings using the light of day), is unknown and unobserved, that 'there is no work, nor device, nor knowledge, nor wisdom in the grave' (Heb. *sheol*, LXX, Gk. *hades*, Eccles. 9:10).

We are more concerned with the interpretation put upon this passage by those who are doctrinally sound regarding the state of death. These, in order, presumably, to rescue this passage from those who have used it to further their teaching of a conscious intermediate state before resurrection, have taught that Paul was pressed 'out of' the two, i.e. of either living or dying, by the overwhelming importance of the return of Christ, which is admittedly 'far better' than either. This interpretation, however, we are convinced errs as much on one side of the truth, as the interpretation which it opposes errs on the other. It has no specific bearing upon the immediate context or the general scope of the epistle, and has no light to throw upon the 'out resurrection' which awaits us in Philippians 3:11.

Consequently there is nothing for it, but to recognize both the gravity of the task before us, the eminence of those teachers from whom we differ, yet to recognize also the far greater importance of arriving at the meaning of the apostle, and through him the meaning of the Spirit who inspired the passage.

We have already discovered the 'scope' of the passage by discovering its 'structure', and we shall now seek by careful comparison and interpretation to present the meaning of the words employed.

First of all, we consider the scope of the passage. The structure of Philippians 1:21-26 has already been presented but we feel it would be useful to repeat it here.

Philippians 1:21-26

A 21.   TO ME (*emoi*) to live.   Christ.

   B 22,23.   **a** Live in flesh. Fruit.
      THE   **b** Paul's choice.   Not made known.
      STRAIT.   **c** Paul's desire. With Christ.

   B 24,25.   *a* Abide in flesh. Needful.
      THE   *b* Paul's confidence. I know.
      CONFIDENCE.   *c* Paul's continuance. With you all.

A 26.   BY ME (*emoi*) my presence.   Glorying in Christ.

A great deal of the controversy that has arisen over this passage finds its origin in the fact that we all have a tendency to pick on a few sentences, especially if they appear to contain some elements of controversial doctrine, and then employ all our powers in the defence of the doctrine we hold to be true, and in the defeat of the doctrine we hold to be false.

Many who clearly saw the teaching of Scripture as to the state of the dead, and the essential place of the resurrection, accepted with relief and without critical examination, an alternative explanation which by focusing attention on the 'return' of the Lord, removed this passage from the armoury of those who still believe and teach a conscious intermediate state. But in what are we profited if it should so turn out that in escaping from one error we have but perpetuated another, and what is more, have, in the process, suppressed a definite truth for which the epistle really stands and which it is essential that we should know?

The first thing that we must recognize is that Paul did not write 'verses 21-26'; he wrote 'an epistle', of which this section is an integral part. He was saying something in the early part of the epistle, of which these verses constitute both a sequel and a link. We have already discovered that the section Philippians 1:3-26 is divided into three parts by the recurrence of the word *pepoitha* 'confidence', and that confidence is not assurance of salvation, but assurance of continuance 'will perform' (v. 6); continuance 'bold to speak' (v. 14); continuance 'I shall continue with you' (v. 25). This continuance is concerned with one thing 'the gospel'. In the first place 'your fellowship in the gospel from the first day until now' (v. 5); in the second place 'the furtherance of the gospel' (v. 12); and in the third place 'the furtherance and joy of faith' (v. 25).

Any system of interpretation that ignores the 'scope' of a passage must sooner or later mislead, and to mislead in interpretation is to substitute chaff for wheat, human ideas for God's truth, and must be resisted.

A strong argument has been made of the fact that we read that the apostle in one breath tells us that *he did not know* what to choose between life and death, and *yet he had a strong desire* for something which was far better. If the apostle actually said this, it is reasonable to conclude that he was indeed 'pressed out of the two', i.e. of living or dying, by a third thing, namely 'the return' (*depart*) of the Lord, which admittedly would be far better than either living here in the flesh with all its attendant suffering, or of dying. However, there are two errors here. The first is a fallacy of *reasoning*, the second an error of *interpretation*.

First, the fallacy of reasoning. It is assumed that whatever Paul *desired* personally, that self same thing he would *choose*. But who that knows Paul, that has any acquaintance with his unselfish attitude, or that even reads on to chapter 2 and ponders the 'mind that is in Christ Jesus' can maintain such a teaching? The whole of the context reveals a man who rises above all selfish motives. He is in bonds, but his bonds have fallen out to the furtherance of the gospel, and so he rejoices. Some who preach the gospel do so with evil motives, 'supposing to add affliction' to his bonds. Still he rejoices that Christ is preached. No man who could say the 'what then?' of verse eighteen would necessarily *choose* what he most *desired*, we should rather expect him to set aside his own desires and to choose something quite the reverse, if the ministry of the gospel, the glory of Christ, or the blessing of His people should so demand. Such an attitude would stand self condemned as we read 'I have no man likeminded (one of equal soul with myself), ... for all seek their *own*' (Phil. 2:20,21). Any interpretation of Paul's dilemma that makes him seek 'his own' is therefore excluded.

Second, an error of interpretation. It is said that Paul *did not know* what to choose, but this is a manifest error, for the word *gnorizo* is never so used by Paul in any of his epistles! The Authorized Version uses an obsolete piece of English, 'I wot' connected with 'to wit', 'wist', as in Exodus 2:4, 'to wit what would be done', and Mark 9:6, 'he wist not what to say'. So we find 'to wot' translating the Hebrew *yada* 'to know' six times, and the Greek *oida* three times. In these instances the meaning is clear, it simply means 'to know' or 'to know not'. The word translated 'I wot' however in Philippians 1:22 is, as we have said, the Greek word *gnorizo* and is employed by Paul eleven times in the three great Prison Epistles. It should therefore be comparatively easy to arrive at the meaning of the word. Here are the occurrences :

'Having made known unto us the mystery of His will' (Eph. 1:9).

'By revelation He made known unto me the mystery' (Eph. 3:3).

'Which in other ages was not made known unto the sons of men' (Eph. 3:5).

'Unto the principalities ... might be known by the church' (Eph. 3:10).

'That I may open my mouth boldly to make known the mystery' (Eph. 6:19).

'Tychicus ... shall make known to you all things' (Eph. 6:21).

'Let your requests be made known unto God' "(Phil. 4:6).

'To whom God would make known what is the riches' (Col. 1:27).

'All my state shall Tychicus declare unto you' (Col. 4:7).

'They shall make known unto you all things' (Col. 4:9).

Any ambiguity in Ephesians 3:10 is removed by the Revised Version, which reads 'might be made known'.

The one other use of the word in Philippians itself shows that it means to make known. Elsewhere in the Authorized Version this word is rendered 'certify' once, 'declare' four times, 'do to wit' once, 'give to understand' once and 'wot' once.

It is evident therefore that Paul said in Philippians 1:22 'What I shall choose, I DO NOT MAKE KNOWN'.

These words in the mouth of any honest speaker mean that he *did* know himself but for certain reasons, stated or implied, he did not 'tell'. This rendering is the one found in Dr. Bullinger's *Critical Lexicon*, 'Wot ... *gnorizo*, to make known, declare, reveal'.

We have disposed of the fallacy of reasoning, and the false interpretations that have obscured the meaning of the passage, but we have more awaiting us. We have to examine the meaning of the words 'strait', 'betwixt' and 'depart', for each of these words has had meanings attached to them which they will not bear.

The meaning of the word translated 'depart'

Following on the assumption that Paul did not know what to choose is the suggestion that 'he was pressed out of the two, by reason of a third', and this 'third thing' was nothing less than the return of the Lord, which naturally would have been 'far better' than either living or dying.

Let us look at this word which some would translate 'I am pressed OUT'. We notice that Wordsworth in his commentary says 'yea, I am held together by the two – as in his body he was held at this time a prisoner between two soldiers, to whom he was bound by two chains'. Here, then, is an interpretation that is diametrically opposite to the preceding one. One authority says 'pressed out' the other says 'held together by'. It is evident that something has been misunderstood somewhere.

Alford suggests in his commentary that Paul's meaning can be expressed in the words, 'but I am perplexed by the two'. By 'the two' Alford means 'which have been mentioned, viz., *to zen* and *to apothanein* (to live and to die), not which follow'.

Here we find different authorities holding opposite opinions. One says the words *sunecho ek* means that Paul was 'pressed out', another says that he was 'held together'. One says Paul *referred back* to living or dying, another says he *looked forward* 'to the return of the Lord'. We must therefore either despair of arriving at the apostle's meaning, or make yet a further attempt by personal investigation to arrive at a just conclusion.

The Authorized Version translates *sunecho*: 'constrain, keep in, press, stop, throng, hold, be in a strait, be straitened, be taken with, be sick of'. The testimony of the Lexicons is equally direct.

Parkhurst's comment is 'to hold fast, to straiten, confine, constrain, bind'. Schrevelius is equally emphatic 'to hold or keep together, preserve, fasten, tie hard, curb, restrain'. Dr. Bullinger in his *Lexicon & Concordance* says the same, 'to constrain, to hold, to keep together'. The usage of the word in the New Testament fully confirms this meaning :

(1) To be taken by disease or fear (Matt. 4:24; Acts 28:8).
(2) To be thronged, as by a multitude (Luke 8:45).
(3) To be kept in, as by besieging army (Luke 19:43).
(4) To stop, as the ears (Acts 7:57).
(5) To be constrained or pressed (2 Cor. 5:14; Acts 18:5).
(6) To be held, as in an arrest (Luke 22:63).
(7) To be straitened (Luke 12:50; Phil. 1:23).

This list sets out the usage of *sunecho* as translated in the Authorized Version.

There is complete unanimity among translators and lexicographers therefore that when Paul used the word *sunecho* (and as the constraint here is not physical but mental) the rendering suggested by Weymouth, 'I am in a dilemma', is as near as one can hope to approach the apostle's meaning.

Following this word, the apostle uses the preposition *ek* which is translated by the Authorized Version 'betwixt'. Now in criticizing this rendering it may be a statement of fact that the word *ek* occurs 857 times in the Greek New Testament and that 165 of those occurrences are translated 'out of', but much relevant material has been left unexpressed. For example, on a number of occasions, the only way to render the meaning of *ek* is to translate it by the English 'with'.

'They bought *with* them the potter's field' (Matt. 27:7).

'Wearied *with* His journey' (John 4:6).

'Drunk *with* the wine ... *with* the blood of the saints' (Rev. 17:2,6).

Again, in some passages 'by' is the best rendering :

'The tree is known *by* his fruit' (Matt. 12:33).

'*By* thy words thou shalt be justified' (Matt. 12:37).

In Revelation 9:18 *ek* actually occurs twice, yet in spite of a desire for uniformity we are compelled to translate the word differently.

'*By* the fire ... which issued *out of* their mouths' (Rev. 9:18).

On other occasions 'by reason of' (Rev. 8:13), 'on' (Matt. 25:33), and 'through' (Gal. 3:8) are good renderings.

Exception has been taken to the translation 'betwixt', but no objection is lodged against John 3:25 'there arose a question *between* some of John's disciples and the Jews': it is evidently a good rendering, for there is no essential difference in 'betwixt' and 'between'.

To translate *ek* 'out of' in Philippians 1:23 is contrary to the meaning of *sunecho* which means to hold fast or bind.

Paul was held in suspense 'by reason of the two'. He was not 'pressed out of the two' into some hypothetical

'third'. What 'the two' are we are not left to conjecture.
Here they are :

> Having a desire to depart and be with Christ which is very far
> better.
>
> But, to remain in the flesh is more necessary for you.

Something *far better* for himself is weighed in the
scales over against something *more necessary* for the
saints – can we imagine the apostle making any other
choice, than that in spite of his own preference he would
continue in the witness a little longer?

We have not yet completed our examination of disputed
meanings in this passage. We must now deal with the
word translated 'depart'. This is the verb *analuo*. Dr.
Bullinger in his Lexicon says of this word 'to loosen again,
set free; *then*, to loosen, dissolve or resolve, as *matter* into
its elements (hence English analysis); then to unfasten as
the fastening of a ship, and thus prepare for departure (and
with the force of *ana* "back") to return (Luke 12:36)'.

The idea of 'departing' is expressed in the New
Testament by no less than twenty-three different Greek
words, which cover all phases of 'departing' as, going
from one place to another, travelling, withdrawing,
separating one's self, emigrating, and the like.

The Greek word *analuo* is not included in this set of
translations, it occurs but twice as follows :

'When he will *return* from the wedding' (Luke 12:36).

'Having a desire to *depart*' (Phil. 1:23).

Let us take the idea of 'return' as set forth in Luke 12.
Rotherham has the following rendering in his Emphasized
New Testament 'once he may break up out of the marriage
feast'. J. N. Darby is, as usual, cautious; he translates
'whenever He may leave the wedding'. It is evident
therefore that the idea of 'returning' is not necessarily
proved by Luke 12:36.

The root word of *analuo* 'to depart' is *luo* 'to loose' and in the use of the simple verb, or of its many combinations and derivatives, the primary idea of 'loosening' is never absent. This we can demonstrate from the use of the word in the New Testament.

Luo.   To unloose a shoe latchet, to loose a colt, to dissolve as the elements (Luke 3:16; 19:30; 2 Pet. 3:11).

Lutron   'a ransom'. Something that sets free (Matt. 20:28).

Lutroo   'redeem'. *Lutrosis* 'redemption' (Tit. 2:14; Heb. 9:12).

In combination we have *kataluo* 'to destroy', 'to dissolve' (Matt. 5:17; 2 Cor. 5:1).

Apoluo   'to release', 'to send away', 'to set at liberty' (Matt. 27:15; 14:23; Acts 26:32).

Analuo is no exception to the rule, and 'return' would be a good translation if there was no ambiguity about the word; but there are two ideas that are expressed in the word 'return' :

Of the *return* of the body to dust as it was,

AND

The *return* of a person from a distant place.

These are not synonymous.

It would be perfectly congruous to speak of the 'dissolution' of the body, but how can any one tolerate the idea of the 'dissolution' of the Lord in glory. The rendering of *analuo* 'to return' has only been possible because of its double meaning, and double meanings are the translator's pitfall. Now it is perfectly certain that when Paul used the word *analusis* in 2 Timothy 4:6 he meant his own 'departure', and in this passage *can refer to nothing else* than his own death. 'The time of *my departure* is at hand'. Even if we translated these words 'the time for my return', the meaning would still be unaltered. Dissolution, or analysis as the word becomes in English, is the only possible meaning of the apostle in 2 Timothy 4:6. In Philippians 1:23 Paul uses the verb *analuo*, in 2 Timothy 4:6 he uses the noun *analusis*. They are related together as any other verb and noun are, as 'sing' the verb is related to 'song' the noun. When Paul used the verb *athleo* in 2 Timothy 2:5 'to strive' and the noun *athlesis* in Hebrews 10:32 'a fight', there is no disharmony in the renderings and so it must be in every case. There is, however, a further reason to treat the two passages Philippians 1:23 and 2 Timothy 4:6 as common subjects, the two epistles are tied together by the repetition of another idea. In 2 Timothy 4:6, Paul also said 'I am now ready to be offered' *spendomai*, a word that is associated with the 'pouring out' of the drink offering (Exod. 30:9). This same word is employed in Philippians 2:17, 'If I be offered upon the sacrifice and service of your faith'. In Philippians the apostle 'desired' to depart, in 2 Timothy he said the time for his departure had come. In Philippians he had expressed his willingness to be poured out like a drink offering, in 2 Timothy he knew that the hour had come when he should be so poured out or 'offered'. In the presence of this witness it becomes impossible to translate *analuo* in Philippians 1:23 of the 'return' of the Lord, it can have but one meaning 'the return' if you will, but the return of the body to the dust; in fact, the ordinary or accepted meaning of the word *analusis*, 'analysis'.

To round the subject off and not leave any essential feature unexplained we turn once again to Luke 12:36. This verse actually speaks of the 'coming' of the Lord, as something *subsequent* to His 'departing'. The servants will *not* open the door when He *departs* from the wedding, but when He 'cometh and knocketh'. This passage is in no sense a contradiction of the Authorized Version translation of Philippians 1:23, rather it is a confirmation.

CHAPTER 4

Citizenship

Philippians 1:24-30

We have seen sufficient evidence to compel us to retain the word 'depart' in Philippians 1:23 and to reject the idea that Paul intended by the word *analuo* 'the return' of the Lord. There is another reason why the hope of the apostle could not be expressed in these terms which we must note before passing on.

During the Acts of the Apostles, the hope that was before the believer was 'the hope of Israel' (Acts 28:20), and the believers at Rome were instructed that their hope (A.V. trust) was embodied in the promise 'there shall be a root of Jesse, and He that shall rise to reign over the Gentiles; in Him shall the Gentiles trust' (or hope) (Rom. 15:12). This hope was to take place 'at the last trump' (1 Cor. 15:52) and the descent of the Lord was to be accompanied by the voice of the archangel, (1 Thess. 4:16), which links this aspect of the Lord's return with the prophecy and the people of Daniel (Dan. 10:21; 12:1). Had the unique character of the dispensation of the mystery, and the hope of its calling been perceived, no one could have put into the mind of the apostle, at the time when he wrote the epistle to the Philippians, the idea of the Lord's 'return'.

For the Lord to 'return' implies that He is coming back 'the second time' to the place and people of His rejection, which of course is blessedly true. The hope and constitution of the church of the mystery is however distinct from the promise made to Israel, from the setting up of a kingdom, the throne of David, the New Jerusalem, because it is blessed in a new sphere 'far above all', and the hope of this church is not so much to wait for the Lord 'to come' as to receive the call that shall make them 'manifest with Him in glory' (Col. 3:4). This will be the first movement of the second advent, but will in no sense be 'a return'. By the time Paul wrote the epistle to the Philippians the hope of the Lord's 'return' had been temporarily set aside, while the new dispensation of the mystery had its own special 'hope' of its calling.

Let us now re-read Philippians 1:21-26 in the light we have acquired :

'For to me living (is) Christ and dying (is) gain. But if living in the flesh (is Christ) this to me is the fruit of (my) work, and what I shall choose I do not make known. But (i.e. instead of making known) I am held in constraint (colloquially, 'I am in a fix') by reason of the two: (1) having an earnest desire to depart, and to be with Christ, for it were far better, but (2) the abiding in the flesh is more needful for you, and having this confidence, I perceive that I shall abide and continue beside you for your furtherance and joy of faith; that your rejoicing may be more abundant in Jesus Christ for me by my coming to you again' (Phil. 1:21-26).

'To depart and to be with Christ'. How are we to understand these words? Do they teach that there is an intermediate state? or do they teach that at death the believer goes straight to glory? We must remember that the apostle is not, in this passage setting out doctrine, he is expressing an ardent wish. He does not say 'to depart IS TO BE with Christ', he simply says he would choose if he had his own way 'to depart; and be with Christ', without dealing with the question of the passing of time or of a conscious or unconscious interval.

Let us illustrate this point. Years ago it was our privilege to travel to Canada, and there to testify to the wonders of the Dispensation of the Mystery. Every moment of the time was a joy, and the time spent away from home was ungrudgingly given. When however the last meeting was concluded we said to the gathering, 'Now that the witness is over, it would be natural to desire and *to depart, and to be* with dear ones at home', but no one misunderstood us. We, and they, knew that the train must be taken from Toronto to Quebec, the ship taken from Quebec to Southampton, and the journey completed to Hutton. In the same way Paul expressed himself in

2 Corinthians 5. He did not enunciate as a doctrine 'absent from the body IS TO BE THEN AND THERE present with the Lord'. He positively declared that he did NOT wish for the 'unclothed' condition, what he said was that he was 'willing rather to be absent from the body, and to be present with the Lord' (2 Cor. 5:1-8). So in Philippians, the apostle's desire overleaps all intervening time, even though, like the train and the ship, such time remains as a fact, though unrecorded.

The apostle's 'conversation' was 'in heaven'. For him, death had ceased to have any 'sting', it would be a falling asleep to awake satisfied in the image of his Lord. Any attempt to extract a conscious intermediate state from Paul's intense desire here expressed is manifestly unjustified. The alternative before the apostle, was to continue here in this life a little longer, and he was constrained to make this his choice for several reasons.

It was 'more needful' for the Philippians. Although the apostle had 'a strong desire' to depart – *epithumeia* being translated in Colossians 3:5 'concupiscence'; and in Ephesians 2:3 'lust' – yet the 'need' of the believer was stronger. There is a sense of 'constraint by force' in the word *anagkaios* 'needful', the word used by the apostle here and which is translated mostly 'necessary' and 'necessity' and occurs again in Philippians 2:25, providing another example of the unselfish service of the apostle. He put the 'more needful' over against the 'far better' and left us a blessed example of one who sought indeed the mind that was in Christ Jesus.

'And having this confidence'. How does this expression of confidence arise? In Philippians 2:24, Paul reverts to the subject of his continuance and ministry saying 'but I trust in the Lord that I also myself shall come shortly' where the same Greek word *pepoitha* 'trust' occurs, that is translated 'confidence' in Philippians 1:25. In Romans 14:14 the original reads *oida kai pepaismai ... hoti* 'I know and am persuaded ... that' which inclines

Lightfoot to translate Philippians 1:25, *touto pepoithos oida hoti* 'of this I am confidently persuaded, that, etc'. Being persuaded that his continued presence in the flesh would be advantageous to the Philippians, Paul knew that his life of ministry would be extended for a period.

'Abide and continue' *'Meno kai parameno'*. It will be seen that the word translated 'continue' is literally 'to abide beside', the double expression being similar to our 'bide and abide', to find a dwelling and also to continue for a period of time. Merely to 'bide' here in the flesh was no longer desirable to the apostle. *Meno* is absolute, *parameno* is relative, it has personal contact and fellowship in mind as well as mere continuance.

Length of life, says a poet, is not measured by the ticks of a clock, but by heart beats. Mere continuance of existence is no synonym in the estimate of Paul for 'life'. For me, said he, to live is Christ.

'Your furtherance and joy of faith'. Translators are divided in their endeavour to express the apostle's intention in these words. Bishop Middleton says, in his great work on the Greek article :

'Of these words there are various translations, which I forbear to enumerate. My objection to the greater part of them is, that they disjoin *prokopen* "furtherance" and *charan* "joy" as if *pisteos* "faith" did not depend on the former of these as well as on the latter. That this, however, is the construction, I infer from the omission of the article before *charan*. So in verse 7 of this chapter we have "the defence and confirmation of the gospel"'.

On the other hand Weymouth translates the passage 'to promote your progress and joy in the faith', while J. N. Darby has the note 'progress and joy go together, not progress – and joy in faith', and Rotherham reads 'for your advancement and the joy of your faith'. It is a nice point, and the grammarians will probably differ to the end of time. In actual practice there is little or no difference, however the passage is read. The 'furtherance' of the *believer*, and the furtherance of the *faith which he believes* go hand in hand; and again, the *furtherance* of the believer, will necessarily be accompanied by *joy* in the faith.

The apostle does not say in conclusion 'that your rejoicing may be more abundant by my coming to you again', which would most certainly have been true, what he does say is 'that your rejoicing may be more abundant IN CHRIST JESUS for me by my coming to you again'. Christ was the centre and the touchstone of Paul's life and ministry. In the original the two phrases come together *en Christo Iesou en emoi* 'in Christ Jesus in me' ('Christ Jesus' is the reading of the Revised text). Therefore while we, with Paul, give Christ the place of pre-eminence, and avow that his mere presence apart from Christ would have been no cause for abounding joy, yet on the other hand there is a very precious association between the Lord Who was all in all, and the earthen vessel that bore His name. Doubtless the Lord could sweep aside all human agents, and carry on His work without their feeble and often blundering aid, but He does not choose so to act, and it is the glory of grace that He links His own Name and Salvation with that of the servant He has chosen 'in Christ Jesus in me'. Let us bring our present meditation to a close with these gracious and inspiring words.

Conversation, life and citizenship

Just as we find the apostle returning in chapter 4:11-20 to the theme 'fellowship in the Gospel from the beginning' (Phil. 1:3-26), so we find 'conversation' (Phil. 1:27 to 2:5), has its sequel in chapter 3:20,21, and although we shall not leap from one section to its corresponding member, but take the epistle as it is written, we set out Philippians 1:27 to 2:5 together with 3:20 to 4:10, so that it may be in the back of our mind while we concentrate on the earlier portion. The structure of the epistle as a whole is given in the first chapter.

Conversation. Stand fast.

(Phil. 1:27 to 2:5, and 3:20 to 4:10) C and C page 8.

C | C 1:27.   Conversation,
                    worthy of the gospel (*politeuo*).*
    D 27.   Stand fast (*steko*).*
      E 27.   With one spirit and one soul.
        F 27.   Striving together (*sunathleo*).†
          G 28.   Not terrified by adversaries.
            H 29,30.   Conflict seen and heard to be in me
              I 2:1-3.   Esteem others better than self.
                J 4.   Look on things of others.

C 3:20,21. Conversation in heaven (*politeuma*).*
    D 4:1.   Stand fast (*steko*).*
      E 2.   Same mind.
        F 3.   Striving together (*sunathleo*).†
          G 4-7.   Not anxious. Garrisoned.
            I 8.   If any virtue, reckon these things.
          H 9.   Things learned, received,
                   heard and seen in me.
        J 10.   Your care of me.

The coming of the apostle to the Philippians would be for their furtherance and joy, but that coming, though hoped for with great longing, was nevertheless subject to delays, and so the apostle follows the record of his own willingness to spend himself on their behalf, with an exhortation to a worthy walk in the meantime.

Monon 'only'. The word isolates a thought and puts it into prominence 'this only would I learn of you' (Gal. 3:2); 'ye have been called unto liberty, only use not liberty for an occasion to the flesh' (Gal. 5:13). The 'furtherance' of the gospel and of faith is not a matter merely of soundness in doctrine, it is intimately associated with loyal and loving practice. By the word 'only' Paul focuses the attention on the words 'conversation' and 'becometh'.

---

* *Only occurrences in this epistle.*   † *Only occurrences in the N.T.*

Today, the first meaning that is attached to the word 'conversation' is 'familiar or intimate talk' and this later meaning of the word gives us the modern 'conversationalist'. The dictionary however reveals that the primary meaning of the word has to do with the manner of life rather than with speech.

The root of the verb 'to converse' is the Latin *versor* 'to dwell' or 'to be occupied', and the *Oxford Dictionary* gives as *the first* meaning of the word conversation, 'the action of living or having one's being in or among', and the second meaning is given as 'the act of consorting with others; living together; commerce, society, intimacy'. *Lloyd's Encyclopaedic Dictionary* gives as the first meaning 'the act or state of residing or sojourning in any place; residence, dwelling' and places 'intimate talk' *seventh* in the list of meanings! It is evident therefore, even from the Authorized Version, that the apostle was deeply concerned with the Philippians' 'manner of life'.

The word 'conversation' occurs seventeen times in the Authorized Version of the New Testament and although three Greek words are thus translated, in every case manner of life is in view. The Greek words are *anastrophe, tropos, politeuma* and these Greek words are in turn, derivatives of *strepho* 'to turn' and *polis* 'a city'. *Strepho* is a prolific root giving a variety of words of equally varied meanings, *anastrophe* being translated 'conversation' in each of its thirteen occurrences, and in every case 'manner of life' not 'intimate talk' is intended.

The word employed by Paul in Philippians 1:27 is *politeuo*. It is therefore evident that he intended something distinct from that which is implied by the derivatives of *strepho*.

Polis is the word translated 'city' throughout the New Testament (for example Matt. 2:23; Acts 16:12; 21:39; Heb. 11:10). It will be observed that Acts 16:12 refers to

Philippi, and says of it 'which is the chief city of that part of Macedonia and a colony'.

After discussing different interpretations which have been offered on the meaning of Acts 16:12, Christopher Wordsworth, D.D., says, 'the true solution is probably to be found in the Hellenistic sense of the word *meris*, viz. a *frontier*, or strip of *borderland*, that by which it is *divided (merizetai)* from some other adjacent territory. Philippi was colonized by the Romans as a *border city*, to defend the frontier against Thrace'. The Philippians would therefore appreciate the allusions in the epistle to 'defence' and 'striving together'. Moreover, Philippi was a colony, and this fact would enforce the apostle's appeal to the Church in that city. A colony in those days had many privileges, and one that is important to us consisted in the conception that Rome was transplanted, as it were, and reproduced as a *colonia*. When therefore the apostle says 'our conversation (*politeuma*) is in heaven' (Phil. 3:20), or 'only let your conversation (*politeuo*) be as becometh the gospel' (Phil. 1:27), he is saying, in effect, remember that as a 'colony' you represent Rome though actually severed from it by distance and difficulties, so remember that while here on earth, you show by your life that your true citizenship belongs to heaven.

Associated with this word 'conversation' are the other variants of *polis*, such as *politeia* 'freedom,' 'commonwealth' (Acts 22:28; Eph. 2:12), *polites* 'citizen' (Acts 21:39), and *politeuomai* 'to live' (Acts 23:1).

Where the Philippian citizen would be proud of the status of 'colony' enjoyed by his city, and would seek to so comport* himself that he did not lower the ruling city of Rome in the eyes of others, so the Philippians were exhorted to live as citizens of heaven, 'as becometh the gospel of Christ'.

---

* Comport = behave, conduct or bear one's self.

The spiritual blessings with which the believer is so freely endowed, are nowhere richer or higher than in the Prison Epistles, and it is here in the three great epistles of the Mystery, that the word *axios* is employed.

'Walk *worthy* of the vocation' (Eph. 4:1).
'Be as it *becometh* the gospel of Christ' (Phil. 1:27).
'That ye might walk *worthy* of the Lord' (Col. 1:10).

Axiology is a term used in the 'Philosophy of Values' or of 'worth', it is probably derived from *ago* as it refers to a pair of scales, in which, when the weights on each side are equal, 'they *agousi* bring or draw down the beam to a level or horizontal position' (Parkhurst). So *axios* is found in Romans 8:18, where the words 'to be compared' are added by the translators, with this thought of balance in mind.

The reader is probably acquainted with the diagram that has appeared in *The Berean Expositor* and *The Testimony of the Lord's Prisoner*, exhibiting the structure of the epistle to the Ephesians as a pair of balances, pivoted upon the word 'worthy' of Ephesians 4:1, and showing the two sets of teaching, namely, seven sections devoted to doctrine, being balanced by seven corresponding sections devoted to practice. It is not surprising therefore, in such a practical epistle as this to the Philippians, to find the apostle using the word 'worthy' in a similar way.

The Gospel must be preached, it must be believed, but it must also be defended, furthered, and confirmed by a worthy walk and manner of life if true balance is to be maintained.

In the passage before us, the worthy manner of life is expressed by the apostle in the following words :

'That whether I come and see you, or else be absent, I may hear of your affairs, that ye stand fast in one spirit, with one mind striving together for the faith of the gospel' (Phil. 1:27).

In addition he speaks of being 'nothing terrified' by their adversaries, and of being graciously given the privilege of not only believing but of suffering for Christ's sake, rounding the exhortation off with a reference to his own example.

The faith of the gospel

We have seen that 'conversation' refers to the manner of one's life and involves the idea of citizenship. The apostle was concerned about the 'affairs' of the Philippians, and desired that they should be of such a high standard that their worthiness should be maintained whether he himself were personally present or absent. The word translated 'absent' is *apeimi* and is found only in Paul's epistles always with reference to his presence or absence from a particular assembly, and occurs seven times.

There is a note of censure in the reference in 1 and 2 Corinthians :

'For I verily, as absent in body, but present in spirit, have judged already, as though I were present, concerning him that hath so done this deed' (1 Cor. 5:3).

'Now I Paul myself beseech you by the meekness and gentleness of Christ, who in presence am base among you, but being absent am bold toward you ... such as we are in word by letters when we are absent, such will we be also in deed when we are present' (2 Cor. 10:1,11).

'I told you before, and foretell you, as if I were present, the second time; and being absent now I write to them which heretofore have sinned, ... Therefore I write these things being absent, lest being present I should use sharpness' (2 Cor. 13:2,10).

Apart from the element of censure which we may not always merit, there is a lesson here for us all. We are still able to read Paul's epistles, though Paul himself is 'absent' and these epistles are tantamount to his personal presence with us in our gatherings, and should be treated accordingly.

Writing to the Colossians, Paul was able to adopt a different strain saying 'for though I be absent in the flesh, yet am I with you in the spirit, joying and beholding your order, and the stedfastness of your faith in Christ' (Col. 2:5). This is much nearer to the spirit manifested in Philippians 1:27. In Colossians he speaks of 'stedfastness' (*stereoma*), in Philippians 1:27 he exhorts the believer to 'stand fast' (*steko*), both of which words the Lexicons derive from *stao* 'to stand'. The apostle speaks of this attitude as the 'affairs' of the Philippians 'that I may hear of your affairs'.

'Affairs' with Paul may refer to the 'business' of life *pragmateia* (2 Tim. 2:4), a word derived from *pragmateuomai* 'occupy' (Luke 19:13), and is used in Ephesians 6:22 of Paul's affairs. In Ephesians 6:21, where the apostle says 'that ye may know my affairs and how I do', the word 'affairs' there translates the phrase *ta-kata* 'the things respecting' anyone, and in Philippians 1:27 'affairs' translates the phrase *ta peri* 'the things concerning' any one. This phrase *ta peri* is used by Paul four times in the epistle to the Philippians: 'your affairs'; 'your state'; 'how will it go with me' (Phil. 1:27; 2:19,20,23).

We can say that the apostle was 'concerned' about the things 'concerning' the believer and particularly their attitude in the face of opposition, employing the figure *Paronomasia*, often found in the writings of Paul.

'That ye stand fast in one spirit, with one mind striving together for the faith of the gospel' (Phil. 1:27).

Here we have the fourfold concern expressed by the apostle regarding the Philippians' 'affairs'. (1) That they stand fast. (2) That this standing fast shall be *in* one spirit and *with* one mind. (3) That they should 'strive' together. (4) That this united effort should be 'for the faith of the gospel'.

These items are further expanded as the epistle proceeds. The negative aspect is introduced in Philippians 2:3, 'let nothing be done through strife or vain glory'. The 'likemindedness' which the apostle looked for is illustrated by Timothy, 'I have no man like minded who will naturally care for your state' (Phil. 2:20), and what the apostle means by 'striving together' is illustrated by Philippians 4:3, where he speaks of those who 'laboured with' him, using the same words that are translated 'striving together'.

'*Stand fast*'. Paul uses this word seven times in his epistles, once (Rom. 14:4), it is employed of a servant who to his own master, stands or falls, but in other passages it is used in the sense of 'standing fast' to something.

Taking the passages in the order in which they were written (which assumes that Galatians was written first), we have the following sequence :

'Stand fast in the liberty wherewith Christ hath made us free' (Gal. 5:1).

'For now we live if ye stand fast in the Lord' (1 Thess. 3:8).

'Stand fast, and hold the traditions which ye have been taught, whether by word, or our epistle' (2 Thess. 2:15).

'Watch ye, stand fast in the faith, quit you like men, be strong' (1 Cor. 16:13).

'That ye stand fast in one spirit' (Phil. 1:27).

'Stand fast in the Lord, my dearly beloved' (Phil. 4:1).

It will be observed that while the exhortation to stand fast to something (liberty) comes once, and to stand fast in association with holding the teaching of the apostle comes once, in four passages the apostle urges the believer to stand fast IN, either in the Lord, in the faith, or in one spirit, suggesting that the manner and motive of the fight is as important in the sight of God, as the object for which we strive.

Any striving even though it be for liberty or for faith that is not at the same time 'in the Lord' is foredoomed. So also any striving *for* the faith if it be not also *in* the faith must fail. In the epistle to the Philippians the apostle stresses two spheres, (1) 'in the Lord', which must effectually rule out the incipient divisions suggested by the apostle in Philippians 4:1, and (2) 'in one spirit', which must be examined now more carefully.

'One spirit' is used by the apostle to emphasize 'unity' (1 Cor. 6:17; 12:13; Eph. 4:4), 'access' (Eph. 2:18), and a common purpose (Phil. 1:27). This expression is followed in Philippians 1:27 by the extension 'with one mind' *mia psuche*. Here it will be observed that the word usually translated 'soul' is rendered 'mind'. We may see some reason for the choice of this word *psuche*, if we read on in chapter 2. There we find 'one accord' translating *sumpsuchos* (Phil. 2:2), 'to be of good comfort' *eupsucheo* (Phil. 2:19), and 'likeminded' *isopsuchon* (Phil. 2:20). It will be observed that in this defence and confirmation of the gospel, the apostle brings together 'body', 'soul' and 'spirit' (Phil. 1:20,27,) and that both life and death, departing or abiding, are all subsidiary to the one great thing, the magnifying of Christ and the furtherance of the faith.

The strife is both whole-hearted and single eyed. Christ is first, fellow believers second, and self last. If these things are true of us, the victory is assured. The armour provided is the panoply of God and the sword of the Spirit cannot but prevail. The cause in which we fight is just, and it is of the very essence of truth that it must at length triumph. These features are in the background of the apostle's argument here. His one concern is the spirit in which the conflict is waged.

'Striving together'. *Sunathleo* means sharing the conflict together as in Philippians 4:3, where it is translated 'laboured with' the apostle in the gospel, even as *sunergos* means 'companion in labour' (Phil. 2:25); *sustratiotes* means 'fellow-soldier' (Phil. 2:25,) and *suzugos* means 'yokefellow' (Phil. 4:3). We in this day of declension, have to stand very much alone, and *strive alone*, even as the apostle has indicated in 2 Timothy 4. But the ideal, and that which should ever be the burden of our prayers and efforts, is that we 'strive together'. But this fellowship in the strife presupposes 'one spirit' and 'one soul', consequently all 'divisions' and 'strifes' and self seekings must be shunned as treachery and betrayal.

For what shall this striving be? 'For the faith of the gospel'. Among the last words penned by the apostle before he was 'offered' are these 'I have kept the faith' (2 Tim. 4:7). Writing to Timothy he said 'fight the good fight of faith' (1 Tim. 6:12). The faith which the apostle has in mind in Philippians is not so much the personal belief of the believer, but the purity of the message of salvation 'the faith of the gospel'. The Philippians were not only a company of saved people, they were also on a very high plane of spiritual growth and attainment. Yet the Philippian epistle contains more references to the 'gospel', in proportion to its length, than any book of the New Testament. For example, the gospel of Matthew contains but four references to the word *euaggelion*, even Romans has only nine references, whereas Philippians, though in comparison very much shorter, contains nine. This fact, while not detracting from the teaching of other Scriptures, does at least reveal the fact that high spirituality, running for the prize and seeking to attain to the out-resurrection, rather than reducing our interest in 'the faith of the gospel' quickens and expands it. The relations established in Philippians with the 'gospel' are suggestive. They are 'fellowship', 'confirmation of', 'furtherance of', 'defence of', 'conversation that shall be worthy of', 'striving together for the faith of' and 'service in' (Phil. 1:5,7,12,17,27; 2:22; 4:3,15.). Belief in the Gospel has already led to salvation, now fellowship with the Gospel leads on to triumph.

Striving supposes adversaries, and concerning these and for the encouragement of the Philippians in the presence of opposition, the apostle now continues his argument.

'And in nothing terrified by your adversaries' (Phil. 1:28).

The translation of *pturo* 'terrify', is a little too strong, the Revised Version modifies the rendering to 'affrighted'.

The Lexicons show that the word is especially applied to the shying or startling of a horse. This figure of a startled horse is very apt, for the opposition implied in the word adversary here suggests something partly concealed or hidden.

Antikeimai means 'one who lies over against' and is used by the apostle of the many adversaries which he associated with 'the open door' (1 Cor. 16:9), and the antipathy that exists between the flesh and the spirit which are 'contrary' the one to the other (Gal. 5:17). The apostle uses the simple word *keimai* in Philippians 1:17, when he said 'I am set' for the defence of the gospel, and he looked upon all who antagonized that gospel as 'set' on the other side and over against it. The stedfastness of the believer and the antagonism of the unbeliever provided both with a sign or token 'which is to them an evident token of perdition, but to you of salvation, and that of God' (Phil. 1:28).

The apostle's meaning here can be seen by comparing this passage with one written to the Church of the Thessalonians, a church belonging to the same district as that of the Philippians and reminded of the fact in 1 Thessalonians 2:2.

'We ourselves make honourable mention of you among the churches of God because of your patience and faith amid all your persecutions and amid the afflictions which you are enduring. For these are a plain token of God's righteous judgment, which has in view your being deemed worthy of the admission to God's kingdom, for the sake of which, indeed, you are sufferers. A plain token of God's righteous judgment, I say, since it is a righteous thing for Him to requite with affliction those who are now afflicting you; and to requite with rest you who are suffering affliction now' (2 Thess. 1:4-7; Weymouth).

'For unto you it is given in the behalf of Christ, not only to believe on Him, but also to suffer for His sake' (Phil. 1:29).

To this aspect of truth the apostle has already referred in verse seven, where he includes a share in his bonds as partaking of his 'grace' *'charitos'*. The word translated 'it is given' in verse twenty-nine is *charizomai*, 'graciously given'. To share the sufferings of Christ and the obloquy* of His Gospel, to stand alone if need be, to be misunderstood, misrepresented, and despised, instead of inducing a sense of injustice and leading to murmuring and to complaining, should be considered a privilege: for to stand where the truth is must ever be superior to anything that the antagonist can offer in exchange. The apostle rounds off this rather testing piece of teaching in his own familiar way, by enforcing his doctrine by his own inimitable practice.

> 'Having the same conflict which ye saw in me, and now hear to be in me' (Phil. 1:30).

He knew, and he shared. It was 'the same', and the 'conflict' was the gladiatorial *agona*; a crown was in view.

To this particular exhibition of the truth the apostle returned in chapter 4, when he said 'those things which ye have both learned, and received, and heard, and seen in me, do; and the God of peace shall be with you' (Phil. 4:9).

In the chapter which now follows, a greater and more wonderful example awaits us, an example so great that worship must ever be mingled with investigation, where grammar and grace walk together and prayer and praise must often interrupt examination.

---

* obloquy = abuse; being generally ill spoken of.

CHAPTER 5

The Mind which was in Christ Jesus

Philippians 2:1-11

The next great subdivision of this epistle commences at verse five of chapter 2 with the words 'let this mind be in you, which was also in Christ Jesus', but before this exhortation is uttered the apostle prepares the way in the four opening verses of the chapter which we have already found brings the structure of the passage to a close.

Commenting on Philippians 2:1-4, Lightfoot says :

'The apostle here appeals to the Philippians, by all their deepest experience as Christians and all their noblest impulses as men, to preserve peace and concord. Of the four grounds of appeal, the first and third ("consolation in Christ" and "fellowship of the spirit") are objective, the external principles of love and harmony; while the second and fourth ("comfort of love" and "bowels of mercies") are subjective, the inward feelings inspired thereby'.

Humility and unity appear to be of such importance here, that the apostle not only uses this fourfold argument in repeating its need from chapter 1:27, but follows it with the amazing example of Christ Himself (Phil. 2:6-11).

With such introduction and confirmation no reader who is a believer can treat such subjects as humility and unity but with the greatest reverence and concern. Perhaps it is not too much to say that more Christian service has been spoiled by the absence of these two graces, than by all else put together.

'If there be any consolation'. The word here translated 'consolation' is *paraklesis*, which the reader will recognize in the word *Paraklete* 'Comforter'. There is however good ground to believe that the modern idea of the word 'comfort' is absent both from *paraklesis* and from the English of the Authorized Version. The primary meaning of the English word 'comfort' is 'to make strong'.

'And the child waxed and was comforted' (Luke 1:80, Wycliffe).

This meaning is evident in the etymology of the word *com* 'with' *fortis* 'strong'. *Paraklesis* is composed neither of 'with' nor 'strong,' but of *para* 'beside' and *kaleo* 'to call'.

Paraklesis is translated 'exhortation' in Acts 13:15; Romans 12:8; 1 Corinthians 14:3; 2 Corinthians 8:17; 1 Thessalonians 2:3; 1 Timothy 4:13; and Hebrews 12:5 and Heb. 13:22. 'Comfort' in the sense of consolation is the rendering of *paramutheomai* (John 11:19,31; 1 Thess. 2:11; 5:14), and is used in Philippians 2:1 'comfort of love'.

The Greek word used by Paul therefore seems to occupy a place midway between 'to enstrengthen' and the old English word 'comfort' from the Latin, and 'to console'. It literally means 'to call to one's side' whether to aid, to console, or to beseech, as the case may be.

Moffatt's translation is suggestive in the light of what we have just seen. 'So by all the stimulus of Christ', and Rotherham also catches the spirit of the apostle when he renders the passage 'if there be therefore any encouragement in Christ'.

The Philippians by their very calling were 'in Christ'. 'For', 'through' and 'of' Christ meet us in Philippians itself more than 'in' Christ, for the words 'in Christ' refer rather to our blessed position by grace than to our outworking of the calling in suffering and endurance.

This POSITION 'in Christ' finds its EXPOSITION in the unfolding of grace in Ephesians. The apostle does not go over the ground again in Philippians, but says 'is there no encouragement in the fact that you are "in Christ"?' as though he would lead them to see that all he was asking of them was but 'their reasonable service'.

A.   The encouragement of being 'in Christ'.   *objective*
   B.   The comfort of love.   *subjective*
A.   The fellowship of the Spirit.   *objective*
   B.   Bowels and mercies.   *subjective*

Before the apostle proceeds to the second objective ground of appeal, 'the fellowship of the Spirit', he turns to the warmth and affectionate element of love, the encouragement of being 'in Christ' being associated with love, while the fellowship of the spirit is associated with mercies.

The word translated 'comfort' in the phrase 'comfort of love' is much nearer to the idea of consolation and soothing than the word has attached to it in English. *Paramutheomai* is related to *muthos* 'myth' and *musterion* 'mystery' by the common idea of keeping anything close, and it reappears in Philippians 4:12 in the word *mueo* 'instructed' or 'initiated' into a secret. *Paramutheomai* therefore has the idea of coming close to another, especially in a time of trouble, and so is appropriately found in the comforting of Martha and Mary (John 11:19), and when the apostle used the figure of a father comforting his children (1 Thess. 2:11). This comfort, said the apostle, is the comfort of love.

Love is used in Philippians in a way that marks off the epistle from Ephesians, as *fruit* is marked off from the *root*. We do not read of the love of Christ in Philippians, nor the love to all the saints, which are characteristics of the Ephesian epistle. The recurring phrase 'in love' which punctuates the epistle to the Ephesians and which is essential to its calling and walk is not found in Philippians. In Philippians which stresses the working out of truth, the running for the prize, the striving together for the faith, love is used four times and associated with knowledge and discernment, the preaching of the gospel, and the comfort and unity of believers (Phil. 1:9,17; 2:1,2).

He now turns and uses another pair as a ground of appeal, 'the fellowship of the Spirit' and 'bowels and mercies' which refer rather to contact with others, than what is internal and peculiarly our own as in the first pair. Again we may learn much by comparing Ephesians with Philippians. All the critical Greek texts justify the Revised

Version of Ephesians 3:9, where the true reading is 'the dispensation of the mystery' not 'the fellowship of the mystery'. By restoring this true reading we remove the only reference to 'fellowship' from the epistle to the Ephesians. The word moreover is not found in Colossians either. Philippians uses *koinonia* 'fellowship' three times and *koinoneo* 'to communicate' once.

'Your fellowship in the gospel'; 'If any fellowship of the spirit'; 'The fellowship of His sufferings'; 'No church communicated with me, as concerning giving and receiving, but ye only' (Phil. 1:5; 2:1; 3:10; 4:15).

It will be seen that in each case active participation is intended and a participation not of gifts and rewards, but of service and of suffering. In the three great Prison epistles the employment of 'fellowship' is peculiar to Philippians, so also the use of *pneuma* 'spirit' in that epistle, differs materially from its employment in Ephesians.

In Ephesians we read of the Holy Spirit of promise, the one spirit in which the believer has access, and which pervades the unity. In Philippians 1:19, the supply of the spirit of Jesus Christ, is seen implementing the answer to the believer's prayer for Paul. In one spirit, they are exhorted to stand fast (Phil. 1:27); the fellowship of the spirit is a ground of appeal to extend kindness and mercy to others (Phil. 2:1); and the essential nature of the worship of God (Phil. 3:3), rounds off the references to the spirit in Philippians. This fellowship of the spirit is accompanied by a deep love to fellow believers, 'bowels and mercies'.

In modern usage 'the heart' is generally referred to as the seat of the affections, and it is considered impolite today to refer to other parts of the viscera, such as 'bowels', 'liver' or 'kidneys' in this connection. In this, we have departed from the richer and more comprehensive language of Scripture and the ancients to our loss.

'In the Greek poets from Aeschylus down, the bowels were regarded as the seat of the more violent passions, such as anger and love; but by the Hebrews, as the seat of the tenderer affections, especially kindness, benevolence, compassion' (Thayer).

Splanchna 'bowels', gives us the verb *splanchnizomai* 'to be moved with compassion', a word used in the gospels twelve times and translated 'to be moved' or 'to have compassion'. Seven of these references speak of Christ's compassion, the others include the compassion of the Good Samaritan and the father of the prodigal son. Of the eleven occurrences of *splanchna* 'bowels' only one passage uses the word literally, namely Acts 1:18 where it speaks of Judas. The remaining ten passages, are translated 'tender mercies' 'inward affection' or where the literal word 'bowels' occurs, as in Philippians 1:8 and 2:1, the idea of mercy and compassion is intended without exception.

Instead of looking at this figurative use of the word bowels as of Hebrew origin and something far removed from Gentile thinking, we should remember that Luke alone of the four evangelists uses it (Luke 1:78); and apart from 1 John 3:17 every other reference is found in Paul's epistles. Then, when limiting our survey to Paul's epistles, we discover that two references only are found in the earlier epistles (2 Cor. 6:12; 7:15), the remainder being found in Philippians, Colossians and Philemon. Of all companies of believers therefore, the church of the mystery should be characterized by 'bowels of compassion'.

These four grounds of appeal, quoted from Lightfoot's commentary at the beginning of this chapter, are made by the apostle, that the Philippians should (1) complete the apostle's joy (see Phil. 2:2), (2) by being likeminded.

This general expression of accordance, says Lightfoot, is defined and enforced by the three following clauses: (*a*) a common love; (*b*) manifesting itself in complete harmony of the feelings and affections; and (c) producing an entire unison of thought and directs it to one end.

The redundancy of expression is a measure of the apostle's earnestness.

All this, the apostle will focus into one intense passage presently, when he says 'one thing I do' (Phil. 3:13), and his insistence upon unity of heart and mind and purpose is as surely necessary to the church, as is the basic unity of the Spirit revealed in Ephesians 4, or the newly created 'one new man' of Ephesians 2. Indeed, it reduces the unity of the Spirit, and the idea of the one body to a mockery when the members of such a unity fail to be of one mind and of one soul. Philippians is all the time presenting in its insistent appeal, the legitimate outworking of the truth revealed in Ephesians.

Pursuing this intense application of the truth, and realizing that the seeds of division were present (Phil. 4:2), the apostle now puts the case in the negative :

'Let nothing be done through strife or vainglory; but in lowliness of mind let each esteem other better than themselves' (Phil. 2:3).

Tapeinophrosune 'lowliness of mind' is a distinctly Christian grace. In classical Greek *tapeinos* had the sense of 'grovelling' and 'abject'. That it could have this conception still Paul makes evident by his use of it in Colossians 2:18, 'a voluntary humility' which is deprecated, but its use in the Christian sense in the same epistle 'humbleness of mind' (Col. 3:12), shows that it had a positive meaning when enjoined by the apostle. Lowliness should be the characteristic of all who have received such grace as is brought to them in the present high calling (Eph. 4:2).

The exhortation of the apostle in Philippians 2:3 gains meaning and point when we associate the word *tapeinophrosune* with *tapeinoo* 'to humble' and *tapeinosis* 'vile' which come in the same epistle.

The exhortation to exhibit 'lowliness of mind' is enforced by the example of Christ Himself, where the word *tapeinoo* occurs in Philippians 2:8 'He humbled Himself' and later in Philippians 4:12 where the apostle says of himself, 'I know both how to be abased', and in the reference to 'the vile body' or better 'the body of this humiliation' where *tapeinosis* is employed (Phil. 3:21).

The concluding exhortation if accepted as it stands in the Authorized Version 'let each esteem other better than themselves', is not always possible if one would be strictly and impartially true. It would not have been humility for Paul to have reckoned Demas 'better' than himself, or for Timothy to have considered Alexander the coppersmith as better than himself, for the example of Christ which immediately follows makes such a thought impossible. Weymouth seems to have sensed this and translates the passage :

'Do nothing in a spirit of factiousness or of vain glory, but, with true humility, let every one regard the rest as being of more account than himself; each fixing his attention, not simply on his own interests, but on those of others also'.

This naturally and easily leads us to the example of Christ, Who while He did not and could not esteem any other 'better' than Himself, did indeed think of others rather than think of Himself.

We are now ready to give undivided attention to this most blessed example of Christ, that occupies Philippians 2:6-11.

The three essentials in interpretation

We now approach a passage, which for the profundity of thought and majesty of doctrine, takes its place among the most wonderful pronouncements of Divine Revelation. The Person of the Saviour irradiates the passage with glory, the condescension of the Saviour like His love 'passeth knowledge'. The Reverend Professor A.B. Bruce, D.D, says of this passage, Philippians 2:6-11 :

'The diversity of opinion prevailing among interpreters in regard to the meaning of the principal passage bearing upon the subject of Christ's humiliation – that namely in the second chapter of St. Paul's Epistle to the Philippians – is enough to fill the student with despair, and to afflict him with intellectual paralysis'.

We do not intend discussing the various and conflicting interpretations that are here alluded to, but we do assure every reader, that we do not enter into this exposition without some due recognition of the nature of our task, fully conscious that without Divine aid our efforts will be in vain. In coming to any definite conclusion the reader may rest assured that we have patiently considered the arguments put forward by such standard exegetes as Alford, Bloomfield, Lightfoot, Ellicott, Meyer, Pearson, Bull, Wordsworth and many of the 'Fathers', in order that no contribution to the exposition of such a theme should be neglected or set aside without due consideration. We shall not, however, burden these pages with all the *pros* and *cons* thus examined, but will give scriptural and grammatical reasons for every step taken in the attempt to set before the reader the 'mind of the spirit', and would record our indebtedness to E. H. Gifford, D.D., whose articles in *The Expositor* of September and October 1896 blazed a trail that it has been a joy and a profit to follow.

There are three governing considerations which must be taken into account in the endeavour to arrive at a true understanding of this, or of any other passage in Scripture.

(1) The logical connection of the passage.

(2) The meaning of the words employed.

(3) The grammatical construction of the sentences.*

If we can come to a satisfactory conclusion on these three counts, we may reasonably expect, with the illumination granted by the Holy Spirit, to be enabled to perceive the truth of God as it is revealed in this passage.

---

*This grammatical construction necessarily interpenetrates the whole exposition and is not treated separately.

(1) The logical connection of the passage

Our first consideration therefore must be the logical place which Philippians 2:6-8 holds in the apostle's argument, and for this the context must be examined, and the literary structure discovered.

In the structure of the epistle as a whole, which the reader will find on page 8, the passage before us is found to be in correspondence with 3:4-19 as follows :

D   2:6-11. The Sevenfold Humiliation
                 of Christ.   *Example.*

D   3:4-19. The Sevenfold loss of Paul.   *Example.*

If this be a true summary of these two passages, the key thought is 'example'.   Now wherever we meet with example in the epistles we can be sure that we are not dealing with such basic doctrines as Redemption, Sin, Death, Forgiveness or Justification, for it is a perversion of the truth to teach that we are saved, forgiven or justified by the example of Christ.   Whenever His example is brought to bear upon the believer, discipleship, service and reward are in view.   These we have already realized are the distinctive features of Philippians.   While the passage under review leads us into the very heart of the mystery of godliness 'God manifest in the flesh', it was not written to teach doctrine, to explain the nature of Christ, or to defend the doctrine of His Deity; it was written to enforce by example the exhortation given in the words :

'Look not every man on his own things, but every man also on the things of others. Let this mind be in you, which was also in Christ Jesus' (Phil. 2:4,5).

The pronoun *eautou*, which is translated 'his own things', occurs in this section as follows :

'Esteem other better than *themselves*'.

'Look not every man on *his own things*'.

'He made *Himself* of no reputation'.

'He humbled *Himself* and became obedient unto death' (Phil. 2:3,4,7,8).

Here it will be seen that the two passages addressed to the Philippians themselves find an echo in the two passages that turn their attention to the act of Christ.

Whatever we may discover the terms — 'the form of God', 'equal with God', 'no reputation' and 'form of a servant' — to mean, one thing is necessitated by the logic of the context, namely, that whatever the Saviour gave up for us men and for our salvation, He gave up that which was 'HIS OWN'.

The apostle had no hesitation in using this supreme example of Christ, to encourage the believer in his practical outworking of the truth. In the second epistle to the Corinthians three chapters are devoted to the 'collection for the saints', yet the apostle does not hesitate to enforce his appeal by a reference to the supreme example of Christ :

> 'For ye know the grace of our Lord Jesus Christ, that though He WAS RICH, yet for your sakes He BECAME POOR, that ye through His poverty might be rich' (2 Cor. 8:9).

While this passage does not contain the doctrinal terms that so enrich Philippians 2:6-8, yet the argument is the same. What the Lord gave up was His own, He WAS RICH, He BECAME POOR, and this simple fact we must keep steadily before our minds as we ponder the wonder of His voluntary humiliation as revealed in chapter 2.

Continuing our examination of the context and the structure, we find that there is a sevenfold humiliation of Christ recorded in Philippians 2:7,8, which is balanced by a sevenfold exaltation, recorded in Philippians 2:9-11. This is not all, however, for in the corresponding member D 3:4-19 we find Paul setting forth a sevenfold ground of confidence, which he once had (3:5,6) and which he subsequently counted 'loss'; this is followed by a sevenfold ground of gain which Paul enumerates (3:8-11).

In order that the bearing of the context and the balance of truth, wherein the example of Christ is set over against the example of Paul, we conclude this opening study in Philippians 2:6-8, by giving the structure of these related sections :

Philippians 2:6-11 and 3:4-19

Examples of Christ and Paul.

```
D │ K₁ 2:6  EQUALITY WITH GOD. ORIGINALLY (huparchon).
  │    L₁ 2:7,8      r   7. He emptied Himself.
C │                  s   7. A bond servant.
H │    Sevenfold     t   7. Likeness as a man.
R │    Humiliation.  u   8. Fashioned as a man.
I │              r   8. He humbled Himself.
S │              s   8. Obedient unto death.
T │              t   8. The death of the cross.

  │ K₂ 2:9  EXALTATION. THE NAME (inherited, see Heb. 1:4).
  │    L₂ 2:9-11     v   9. The Name above every name.
C │                 w  10. Every knee shall bow.
H │    Sevenfold    x  10. Things in heaven.
R │    Exaltation.  y  10. Things in earth.
I │                 x  10. Things under the earth.
S │                 w  11. Every tongue confess.
T │              v  11. Jesus Christ is Lord.

D │ K₃ 3:4    CONFIDENCE IN FLESH. ONCE.
  │    L₃ 3:5,6      a   5. Circumcised the eighth day.
  │                  b   5. Stock of Israel.
  │    Sevenfold     a   5. Tribe of Benjamin.
  │    ground of     b   5. Hebrew of the Hebrews.
  │    confidence.   a   5. Touching the law a Pharisee.
P │                  b   6. Concerning zeal,
a │                            persecuting the Church.
u │                  a   6. Touching righteousness of law,
l │                            blameless.

  │ K₄ 3:7,8  ALL THINGS COUNTED LOSS FOR CHRIST.
  │    L₄ 3:8-11     d   8. Excellency of knowledge of
  │                            Christ.
  │    Sevenfold     e   9. Found in Him,
  │    ground of           not righteousness of Law.
  │    gain.         f  10. That I may know Him.
  │                  g  10. Power of His resurrection.
P │                  f  10. Fellowship of His sufferings.
a │                  e  10. Conformity unto His death.
u │              d  11. The out (ek) resurrection.
l │
  │ K₅ 3:12-19  PERFECTION OR PERDITION.
```

Having seen the logical place of Philippians 2:6-8 in the argument of the apostle, we can now proceed to an examination of the terms used, for, as Gifford says 'The apostle's purpose is happily too clear to be obscured by any diversity of interpretation ... the apostle proceeds to enforce, by setting forth our Blessed Lord Himself as the supreme example of humility, self sacrifice and love; and he is thus led on to speak of those deepest and holiest mysteries of the Christian faith, the incarnation of the Son of God, His voluntary self-abasement, His obedience even unto death, yea, the death of the cross'.

The important terms that now await our prayerful and wondering examination are the following :

(a) 'Being', *huparchon*. 'Being in the form of God'.

(b) 'In the Form of God', *en morphe Theou*.

(c) 'Robbery', *harpagmos*.

(d) 'To be equal with God', *to einai isa Theo*.

(e) 'He made Himself of no reputation', *heauton ekenosen*.

(f) 'And took upon Him the form of a servant', *morphen doulou labon*.

(g) 'Was made in the likeness of men', *en homoiomati anthropon genomenos*.

(h) 'Being found in fashion as a man', *schemati heuretheis hos anthropos*.

Here, without contradiction is a list of words, whose doctrinal import is so great as well nigh to overwhelm the student as he approaches the task of their analysis. Yet these mighty words were written with intention, they have a definite meaning and they must have been within the comprehension of the Philippians, for otherwise the example which they are designed to indicate would be valueless. They are therefore within the comprehension of the average believer who is under the guidance of the Spirit.

(2) The terms employed (a) *Huparchon* 'Who being'

We open our investigation with the word *huparchon*, translated 'being', and ask the reader's patience while we endeavour to place before him the import of this word. The margin of the Revised Version reads 'being originally'. The reader will perceive that 'being' in the Authorized Version of Philippians 2:6 is not a translation of *eimi* 'to be'. It is a translation of *huparcho*. The justification for the Revised Version margin 'being originally' is seen when we learn that the word *huparcho* is made up of *hupo* 'under', and *archo* 'to begin' or 'originate'. This word appears in three verbal forms in the New Testament. *Huparxis* twice, *huparchonta* fourteen times, and *huparcho* forty-eight times. *Huparxis* is translated in the Authorized Version 'goods' or 'substance'. *Huparchonta* 'goods', 'substance', 'that one hath', 'the things which one possesseth'. *Huparcho* 'be', 'live', and idiomatically 'after'.

It will be neither reasonable nor necessary to investigate the whole of these sixty-four occurrences, but we can establish the meaning of the apostle by a few sample passages.

Huparxis occurs but twice and these occurrences we give. They 'sold their possessions and *goods*' (Acts 2:45). These 'possessions and goods' Peter recognized were the personal and private property of the believer, saying 'whiles it remained, was it not thine own? and after it was sold, was it not in thine own power?' (Acts 5:4).

'For ye had compassion of me in my bonds, and took joyfully the spoiling of your goods (*huparchonton*) knowing in yourselves that ye have in heaven a better and an enduring substance' (*huparxin*) (Heb. 10:34).

Huparchonta (The participle used as a substantive).

'Sell *that* thou *hast*' (Matt. 19:21); 'ministered unto Him of their *substance*' (Luke 8:3); 'the things which he *possesseth*' (Luke 12:15) and so throughout the fourteen occurrences.

That *huparcho* means 'pre-existence' the following will prove. 'If thou, being a Jew' (Gal. 2:14). This is emphatic, as Lightfoot says, 'born and bred a Jew', and Howson, 'the Greek means more than "being" and denotes that he was a Jew by birth, a Jew *to begin with*'.

There is, however, a need when translating *huparcho* 'being originally' to avoid the error into which not a few great writers have fallen. For example, Bishop Lightfoot, whose examination of 'form' or 'fashion' we shall refer to with profit presently, has put the matter like this :

'Does the expression *en morphe theou huparchon* refer to the pre-incarnate or the incarnate Christ?'

and he uses the expression 'point of time' several times in his exposition, as *huparchon* must 'be referred to a *point of time* prior to the incarnation'.

The Bishop assumes that the phrase 'being in the form of God' must refer exclusively *either* to the pre-existence of Christ, *or* to His incarnate state, 'it thus', says Gifford, 'excludes the obvious and most important alternative, that it *may apply to both*'.

First, we observe that being an imperfect participle, *huparchon* points to an indefinite *continuance* of being. The imperfect expresses an action in the course of performance, *not yet ended*. For example, we have the imperfect *on* in combination with the aorist (as in Phil. 2:6) in John 11:49, 'And one of them, named Caiaphas, *being* the high priest that same year, *said*'. No one would suggest that immediately Caiaphas finished what he 'said', that he ceased 'to be' high priest. This, however, is not a perfect illustration as the word used is the participle of *eimi* 'to be'. Let us see the usage of *huparchon*.

'And, behold, there was (*huparchon*) a man named Joseph, a counsellor ... he ... went unto Pilate and begged the body of Jesus' (Luke 23:50-52).

It is impossible to suggest that Luke intended by the use of the word *huparchon* that Joseph ceased to be a counsellor as soon as he had begged the body of Jesus!

Or again, in Acts 2:30,31, we read of David that 'being a prophet ... spake of His resurrection'; there can be no thought that David ceased to be a prophet as soon as he spoke of the resurrection of Christ.

Paul's usage of *huparchon* with an aorist verb is found in 2 Corinthians 8:17 and in 12:16.

'But *being* more forward ... he went unto you'.

'*Being* crafty, I caught you with guile'.

'Did Titus cease to be zealous at the moment of starting to visit the Corinthians? Or does St. Paul mean, in his ironical statement, that in the opinion of the Corinthians, he ceased to be crafty as soon as he had once caught them with guile? It is impossible, I think, to find or imagine passages more exactly parallel in grammatical construction to Philippians 2:6 than these two examples of St. Paul's own use of *huparchon*' (Gifford).

The earliest direct quotation of Philippians 2:6 that is in our possession is found in the letters of the Churches of Lyons and Vienna to their brethren in Asia (Eusebius, Historia Ecclesiastica v. c.2). The letter speaks of those who had been tortured for their faith :

'They were so zealous in their imitation of Christ, Who being in the form of God counted it not a prize to be on an equality with God – that though they were (*huparchontes*) in such honour, and had borne witness not once nor twice, but many times ... they neither proclaimed themselves martyrs nor suffered us yet to address them by that name'.

Had these sufferers ceased to be held in honour as martyrs, there would have been no humility on their part in refusing the title, and they could not have been considered as imitators of Christ, if they refused a title which did not really belong to them.

It will be seen therefore that so far as the word *huparchon* is concerned, there is no need to limit our interpretation of Philippians 2:6 to *either* Christ's pre-existence *or* to His humanity. It has been wrongly assumed that the existence 'in the form of God' must have ceased at the moment indicated by the verb *ekenosen* 'He made Himself of no reputation'. This is not the case.

To maintain this position, however, necessitates an examination of the meaning of the expression 'the form of God', for if this means, as Whitby, Macknight, Calvin and others have maintained 'the visible glorious light in which the Deity is seen to dwell', 'the form of a king consists of the external marks which indicate a king, etc.'; then most certainly the Lord Jesus Christ in His humiliation had no such 'form', no such 'marks'. This, however, we hope to show is a misconception. It is confusing the 'form of God' with 'being on an equality with God' and we only make this observation here to prevent any reader misunderstanding our reference to Whitby, Calvin and others, for we believe they are wrong and have missed the meaning of the apostle.

This, however, cannot be urged until we have examined the phrase 'the Form of God' which we must now undertake.

(2) The terms employed   (b) *Morphe* 'Form'

We found that the word translated 'being' in Philippians 2:6 means something more than existence, it includes the thought of possession, of 'being originally', but does not necessitate the idea that when the Lord Jesus Christ took upon Him 'the form of a servant' He must necessarily have relinquished 'the form of God'. That can only be decided after the meaning of the 'form' of God has been ascertained.

There are a number of outstanding Commentators who teach that 'the form of God' means 'the divine appearance' of which Christ by His incarnation 'divested Himself'. Alford speaks of 'the act of laying aside the form of God'.

It is evident from these comments that in the mind of these writers 'the form of God' does not essentially differ from being 'equal with God'.

If by the word 'form' the apostle means 'external appearance' it would seem that the apostle has not expressed himself clearly, for :

(1) What is the external appearance of a 'slave' (servant)? Are there not tall slaves, dwarfed slaves, slaves of noble bearing, and slaves that cringe and fawn? Yet the same word 'form' is used.

(2) If 'form' refers to external appearance, then what is the added 'fashion' of a man? Was not that external? The same can be said of the two expressions 'the form of God' and 'the equality with God', which some confuse, but which we hope to show are not synonymous.

It is abundantly clear that by the 'form of a servant' the apostle means the 'status' of a servant. 'Form', says Lightfoot, means not 'external semblance but characteristic attributes'. It is conceded today, that the first meaning that attaches to the word 'form' does refer to outward appearance, but that is because it has come to be used of things, and it is the recognized tendency of words to degenerate with time. When it is used of God, it *cannot* possibly be used in this sense, for 'God is spirit', is omnipresent and can have no 'form' in the modern sense. We must enquire, therefore, into the way in which the word 'form' could be employed of God without reducing Him to 'shape and size'.

Bishop Lightfoot has an exhaustive treatise on the two words *morphe* 'form' and *schema* 'fashion' that cannot be reproduced here owing to the many references to the writings of the Greek Philosophers.

Aristotle criticized the saying of Democritus who had said 'anybody could see what was the form of a man' meaning that he might be known by his shape and colour.

Aristotle replied 'a corpse has the form (*morphe*) of the human shape (*schematos*), and yet nevertheless is not a man', meaning that while a corpse has the *morphe* of the human *schema*, it has not the *morphe* of a *man*. The form referred to something else.

The difference between 'form' and 'fashion' may be perceived in Romans 12:2, where the word *schematizomai* and *morphoomai* are used.

'Not to follow the fleeting *fashion* of this world (external), but to undergo a complete change, assume a new *form* (internal), in the renewal of the mind'.

Justin Martyr evidently used these two words with discrimination. He says: 'Christians do not believe the idols formed by men's hands to have the form (*morphe*) of God; they have only the names and the shapes (*schemata*) of demons; the form of God is not of this kind. His glory and form are ineffable. He thus appears to contrast the visible schemata of demons, with the invisible immaterial *morphe* of God' (see: Bishop J. B. Lightfoot *Saint Paul's Epistle to the Philippians* pp. 131,132).

Tyndale in A.D. 1534 translates the passage in Philippians 2:6 by 'the shape of God', and this again must not be read in the light of modern usage, but in the same way that Shakespeare uses the expression in *King Lear*. Lear had relinquished the throne, but owing to his daughters' great wickedness he says :

'Thou shalt find that I'll resume the *shape* which thou dost think I have cast off for ever'.

No reader of Shakespeare believes for an instant that King Lear referred to bodily appearance here. It was rather the relinquished 'status' of Royalty to which he referred.

On either side of the year in which the Authorized Version was produced, are two great writers, Hooker, A.D. 1594 and Bacon, A.D. 1620. Hooker says: '*Form* in other creatures is a thing proportional unto *soul* in living creatures' and therefore, to this writer, 'the form of God' would refer rather to 'the soul of God' if such a term could be permitted, than to an external shape. In Hooker's estimation 'form' meant not external appearance, but essence or attributes.

Bacon says: 'the form of a nature is such, that, *given the form, the nature infallibly follows* . Therefore it is always present when the nature is present, and universally implies it, and is constantly inherent in it. Again the form is such that, if it be taken away, the nature infallibly vanishes'. This cannot be true if 'form' refers merely to external shape, splendour, etc. Sugar is sweet whether it be in the 'form' of a cube, small grains, powder, or syrup. Bacon could not possibly have used the word 'form' in the sense of shape or appearance, or any thing accidental, for thus applied his words simply make nonsense.

As the glory of the Lord is at stake, let us spare no pains in arriving at just conclusions. We will therefore rewrite Bacon's lines in order that the error we are combating may be made evident :

'The external appearance of a nature is such, that given the external appearance, the nature infallibly follows. Therefore it (i.e. the external appearance) is always present when the nature is present, and universally implies it, and is constantly inherent in it. Again the external appearance is such, that if it (i.e. the external appearance) be taken away, the nature infallibly vanishes'.

Let us illustrate the 'essential' character of the word 'form' as distinct from 'accidental' characters.

Water is composed of two gases in chemical combination: hydrogen and oxygen. As one part of oxygen combines with two parts of hydrogen, the chemical formula for water is therefore H_2O, *and this formula (or form) never changes*. As Bacon observed, wherever we have the combination which is set forth by the symbols H_2O '*water*' 'infallibly follows', and as soon as that formula is altered water 'infallibly vanishes'.

Now, just as the apostle, when speaking of Christ, differentiates between 'form' and 'fashion', so we can go on to speak of the different 'states' in which the substance called 'water' may exist. Water may exist as a solid, a liquid or a gas. It may be ice, water or steam. Each of these states is associated with properties which are unknown and often contrary to the properties that mark the other states, yet however different a solid may be from a liquid, and both from a gas, the 'form' H_2O remains unchanged and unchangeable. The constant *morphe* of water is H_2O, its *schema* (fashion) may be either solid, liquid or gas. The 'form' of God *cannot alter*, though the 'fashion' which deals with appearance, may.

We do not think it profitable to devote time and space to extracts from the Greek Philosophers to prove that this meaning of 'form' was common among them. Those who could use the extracts to profit can find them in the treatise 'The Synonyms *morphe* and *schema*' in Bishop Lightfoot's 'Commentary on the Epistle to the Philippians', or in the book entitled 'The Incarnation' by Dr. E. H. Gifford.

'Thus it is clear', comments Gifford, 'that the philosophical sense of 'form' was as familiar to our translators as that of *morphe* to contemporaries of St. Paul'.

'For the interpretation of "the form of God" it is sufficient to say that (1) it includes the whole nature and essence of Deity, and is inseparable from them, since they could have no actual existence without it; and (2) that it does not include in itself anything "accidental" or separable, such as particular modes of manifestation, or conditions of glory and majesty; which may at one time be attached to the "form", at another separated from it. (3) The Son of God could not possibly divest Himself of the "form of God" at His incarnation without thereby ceasing to be God: so that in all interpretations which assume that "the form of God" was laid aside when "the form of a servant" was assumed, it is, in fact, however unintentionally and unconsciously, denied that Jesus Christ during His life on earth was really and truly God' (Gifford).

We must now pass to other equally important words and phrases in this most wonderful passage, and while carrying with us what we have already learned, we must reserve our judgment of the intention of the whole, until each clause has been examined.

No amount of weariness to the flesh, limitations of space, or flight of time can in any sense be weighed over against the seriousness of the passage we have before us; the fullest and most painstaking investigation is as nothing when compared with the awful and far reaching nature of the theme.

(2) The terms employed   (c) *Harpagmon* **'Robbery' or 'Prize'?**
                                          (d) *Isa Theo* **'Equality with God'**

We have seen that 'the form of God' must not be confounded with appearance, glory or any *accompaniments* of Deity, but that just as the 'form' of water H_2O remains constant, even though the 'fashion' changed, being sometimes ice, a solid, sometimes water, a liquid, and sometimes steam, gas, so Christ who originally subsisted in the form of God is here in Philippians 2:6-8, said to have exchanged the glory that He had before the world was, for the humiliation of manhood, servitude and ignominious death, without laying aside His essential nature, for to do so is an impossibility to either God or man.

In the clause that awaits us we have that act of laying aside indicated, He 'made Himself of no reputation'; the moral element involved 'He thought it not robbery to be equal with God', and an indication as to what He actually laid aside, namely the 'being on an equality with God' (R.V.). Taking the words as they come, we have to consider :

Ouch harpagmon hegesato to einai isa Theo. The adverb of negation 'not' is expressed in the Greek by the words *ou* and *me*. '*Ou* expresses full and direct negation independently and absolutely, whereas *me* expresses a dependent and conditional negation' (Dr. E.W. Bullinger's *Lexicon*).

Philippians 2:4 is an example of the use of *me*, Philippians 2:6, an example of the use of *ou*. The reader will realize that the form *ouch* is required because of the aspirate with which the next word *harpagmon* commences.

Harpagmon. This word occurs but once in the Greek New Testament in Philippians 2:6, where the Authorized Version translates it 'robbery'. It is derived from a root that means 'to seize, snatch, plunder, rob, pillage' (Schrevelius).

Harpazo, the verb, occurs thirteen times, 'the violent *take* it by *force*', 'the wicked. . . *catcheth* away', 'the wolf *catcheth* them', ' *pluck* ... out of my hand'.

Harpax occurs five times: '*ravening* wolves', '*extortioners*'.

Harpage occurs but three times: 'extortion', 'ravening' and 'spoiling'.

Diarpazo occurs four times, in each passage being translated 'spoil'.

Sunarpazo occurs four times, in each passage being translated 'caught'.

There is no ambiguity about the meaning of the word *harpagmon* therefore, the only question that arises is, does the word denote an *action* that is a 'robbery', as is indicated by the Authorized Version, or is it the *object* of an action that is 'a prize' as indicated by the Revised Version?

Gifford gives the following free paraphrase in order to place before the reader the two interpretations that are under consideration.

(1) With the active sense of 'robbery' or 'usurpation' we get the following meaning :

> 'Who *because* He was subsisting in the essential form of God, did not regard it as an usurpation that He was on an equality of glory and majesty with God, *but yet* emptied Himself of that co-equal glory, by taking the form of a created servant of God'.

(2) The passive sense gives a different meaning to the passage :

> 'Who *though* He was subsisting in the essential form of God, *yet* did not regard His being on an equality of glory and majesty with God a prize and treasure to be held fast, *but* emptied Himself thereof, etc.'.

What does the context demand?   In appealing to the example of Christ do we expect to read of a RIGHT which He CLAIMED? or to a GLORY which He RENOUNCED? Reader, think this over before proceeding.

Before we can fully express the intention of the apostle, however, we must consider the words translated 'to be equal with God'.

To einai isa Theo. – The Revised Version renders this passage 'counted it not a prize to be on equality with God'. To remove the possible ambiguity of the form 'to be', which might help the idea that 'To be on an equality with God' was something to be attained at some future time, we should render *einai* 'being', which for euphony we could render 'that He was' and so 'counted it not a prize *that He was* on an equality with God'.

The Authorized Version as we have seen reads 'equal with God' which the Revised Version corrects to 'on an equality with God'.   The Authorized Version looks to the being and essential nature of God, the Revised Version looks to the accompanying glory.

When the Jews charged the Saviour with making Himself 'equal with God' the singular *isos* is used (John 5:18), but in Philippians 2:6 the neuter plural *isa* is used, and this neuter plural cannot denote the *one* unchanging essence of Deity, but rather refers to the modes, states, manifestations and accompaniments of Deity.   The Saviour could once have been 'rich' and then for our sakes He could have become 'poor', but this would not have touched His essential nature. 'Rich' and 'poor' are modes of being, that can be taken up and laid aside. The LXX of the book of Job uses the plural form *isa* a number of times and mostly with the thought of 'like' rather than identity.

'A mortal born of woman *is like* an ass of the desert'.

'Let every unrighteous one be crushed *like* rotten wood'.

'Brass is hewn out *like* stone'.

'Thou hast counted me *as* clay' (Job 11:12; 24:20; 28:2; 30:19).

In none of these references equality of nature or essence is implied but likeness to some quality or attribute.

In the last reference the verb *hegeomai* 'to count' is used, just as it is employed in Philippians 2:6, 'He *thought* it not robbery' or 'He *counted* it not as a prize'. This word *hegeomai* plays an important part in Philippians, occurring altogether six times and translated in the Authorized Version 'esteem', 'thought', 'supposed' and 'count' (Phil. 2:3,6,25; 3:7,8 twice).

Taking *einai* in its usual sense, we find *hos* 'who' is its subject, and *isa Theo* as an adverbial predicate; thus not *the nature or essence* of God is intended, this has already been indicated by 'the form of God,' but *the mode, state, and accompaniments* of Deity. Lightfoot says, 'He divested Himself not of His divine nature, for this was impossible, but of the glories, the prerogatives of Deity; emptied, stripped Himself of the insignia of majesty ... rights which it was an act of condescension to waive'.

Looking at the passage as a whole, we see that 'in the form of God' finds its antithesis in 'the form of a servant' and the 'counting it not as a prize that He was on equality with God', finds its antithesis in the words 'but made Himself of no reputation'. Bishop Westcott, writing on John 1:14, 'The word was made flesh', says: 'St. Paul describes it as "an emptying of Himself" by the Son of God ... a laying aside of the *mode* of divine existence, and this declaration carries us as far as we can go in defining the mystery'.

(2) The terms employed (e) *Kenoo* 'He emptied Himself'

'*He made Himself of no reputation*'. – The Authorized Version has used the word 'reputation' twice in Philippians, the second occurrence being at 2:29 'hold such in reputation'. The Revised Version has wisely omitted the word 'reputation' in both passages, reading in 2:7 'but emptied Himself', and in 2:29 'hold such in honour', for two different Greek words are used.

The change, however, while it makes some aspects of the truth clearer, introduces other problems for, to a modern mind, there is something strange about the idea of anyone 'emptying himself'. In modern usage 'empty' places foremost in the mind the idea of 'a jug without water', 'a room without furniture' and 'empty vessels' (2 Kings 4:3), these come naturally to the mind. In order to avoid too crude an application of the figure of 'emptying a vessel' when speaking of the Saviour's humiliation, most of us slip into paraphrase and say 'He divested Himself' of His dignity and insignia of Deity, but this is confessedly an attempt to avoid a problem. The verb *kenoo* is cognate with *kenos* 'vain' and means 'empty'. That the word has a wider application than that of emptying a vessel, such expressions as 'seven empty ears' (Gen. 41:27), 'the sword of Saul returned not empty' (2 Sam. 1:22, see LXX) will show.

Where *kenos* is translated 'empty' in the Authorized Version of the New Testament it refers in the parable to the treatment of the servant by the wicked husbandmen, who 'sent him away empty' (Mark 12:3; Luke 20:10,11), and to 'the rich' who were 'sent empty away' (Luke 1:53); in most cases, however, *kenos* is translated 'vain', as for example, in Philippians itself 'run in vain' and 'labour in vain', where it is evident that 'empty' would have no meaning (Phil. 2:16).

The verb *kenoo* translated 'to make of no reputation', occurs five times in the Greek New Testament and the four occurrences other than that of Philippians 2:7, render the word 'make void', 'make of none effect', 'make ... void' and 'be in vain' (Rom. 4:14; 1 Cor. 1:17; 9:15; 2 Cor. 9:3). In Philippians 2:3 we find the word *kenodoxia* 'vain glory'. We remember with adoring wonder that in the Psalm of the Cross, we read 'I am poured out like water' (Psa. 22:14). He did indeed 'empty Himself'.

The reader will be conscious that we have considerable difficulty in arriving at the meaning in Philippians 2:7 in its use of the verb *kenoo*, and will appreciate the following account of our further search and of our ultimate satisfaction.

We observed, by a note in Thayer's Lexicon, that *kenoo* is used twice in the Septuagint and many a time when every other avenue of search has proved unfruitful, light has come by a reference to this Greek version of the Old Testament. There are but two passages and both are in Jeremiah and by this obscure and slender means we were led one step nearer to the truth.

'The gates thereof languish'; 'she that hath borne seven languisheth' (Jer. 14:2; 15:9). The word rendered 'languish' in the Authorized Version and *kenoo* in the LXX is the Hebrew *amal* 'to become weak'. So we find in 1 Samuel 2:5 words parallel with Jeremiah 15:9, 'she that hath many children is *waxed feeble*'.

In the garden of Gethsemane, when the physical body of the Saviour was almost at the end of its strength He said 'The flesh is weak' (Matt. 26:41). The apostle said of Christ 'He was crucified through weakness' (2 Cor. 13:4) and Matthew, referring to Isaiah 53, said of Christ, 'Himself took our infirmities, or weaknesses' (Matt. 8:17). And when speaking of the redeeming work of the Saviour, Paul could say 'the weakness of God is stronger than men'

(1 Cor. 1:25), and in this passage the 'cross' is prominent as it is in Philippians 2:8.

In the example of Epaphroditus given in Philippians 2, and as an extension of the example of Christ, the word translated 'weak' is there rendered 'sick', a sickness for the sake of others, a sickness that was nigh unto death, a 'weakness' endured in the spirit of Philippians 2:4,5, 'not regarding his life' (Phil. 2:25-30).

When the Lord 'emptied Himself' He at the same time 'humbled Himself', the word translated 'humble' being *tapeinoo*. This same word the apostle uses when he described his own condition, 'I know … how to be *abased*' (Phil. 4:12).

This same lowly estate is indicated in Matthew 11:29, when the Lord said 'I am meek and lowly (*tapeinos*) in heart', which same word is translated 'low degree' and 'low estate'. In Philippians 3:21 where the Authorized Version reads 'our vile body' the Revised Version reads 'body of our humiliation' *tapeinosis*, and the same word is used in Acts 8:33 where, speaking of Christ, it reads 'in His *humiliation* His judgment was taken away'.

The prophet Isaiah reveals that 'the child born' was at the same time 'the mighty God' (Isa. 9:6), and in the book of the Revelation the Saviour bears the name 'the Almighty', a name given elsewhere to 'the Father' (2 Cor. 6:18) and to the Creator (Rev. 4:8-11). This 'being on an equality with God' the Saviour renounced. From being 'Almighty' He stooped to the 'weakness' of Bethlehem's cradle, the 'weariness' of Sychar's well, the 'prostration' of Gethsemane, and the weakness, humiliation and shame of the cross.

The condescension is indeed His 'self emptying', but with these sidelights on the meaning of the term supplied by the two obscure references in Jeremiah we see something of its depth of meaning.

The Synod of Antioch (A.D. 269) records the testimony of Paul of Samorata :

'On which account the same God and man Jesus Christ in all the Church under heaven has been believed in as God having emptied Himself from being on an equality with God, and as man of the seed of David according to the flesh'.

The self emptying of the Son of God is directly linked with taking upon Himself the form of a servant. Bishop Mowle says :

'The Greek positively involves the conclusion that the "emptying" whatever it was, was coincident in time with taking the form of a servant. According to well recognized laws of Greek idiom the aorist verb ("He emptied") and aorist participle ("taking") in verse 7 give us one fact from two sides "He made Himself void" not anyhow, but *thus* "taking Bondservant's form". God has spoken His final message to us through a Son Who became also Bondservant. So, the *kenosis* itself (as Paul meant it) is nothing less than a guarantee of infallibility'.

'This', comments W. S. Hooton, M.A., D.D., 'is a startling turning of the tables'. But who shall venture to assert it is not true! It says neither yes nor no to the question, Was the Redeemer as Man, in the days of His flesh, Omniscient? It says a profound and decisive yes to the question is our Redeemer as Man, in the days of His flesh, to be absolutely trusted as the truth in every syllable of assertion which He was actually pleased to make. 'He Whom God hath sent speaketh the words of God'.

Quoting from the report of the Scripture Research Society for April 1917, on a paper entitled 'The Great Kenosis; and the mind of the saints', one speaker said :

'We are not bidden to think of our Lord contemplating equality with God as a thing which He possessed and would retain, but as a thing which He would lay hold of, so that He should possess it. Now with this explanation of the words let the negative be restored; Jesus Christ never so contemplated equality with God. He never was unpossessed of it. That was not what happened — on the contrary, He had got it, it was His own, and divesting Himself of it was not simply refraining from taking. That is the thought given by the word "robbery". He did not refrain from taking it, but *had* it and *gave* it up. He emptied Himself.

Now the horrible superstructure that has been placed upon that thought by some so-called interpreters of Scripture is that He made Himself fallible and made mistakes, and that we can criticise Him like any other human being. That thought has no place in Holy Scripture. Emptied Himself of what and how far? We do not know. We know that it includes some loss of glory, for He said "Glorify Thou Me with Thine Own self with the glory which I had with Thee before the world was". He emptied Himself of glory, He came down, and the glory which He had while on earth was not what He had been enjoying in heaven. He emptied Himself of riches − "Though He was rich yet for our sakes He became poor"; of knowledge, for "He grew in wisdom" as well as in stature; but of what else did He empty Himself, or how far He emptied Himself of these three, we have no dogmatic statement in Holy Scripture; and if we begin to make such statement, we are writing Scripture, not learning it'.

Another speaker said :

'There is a peculiar fallacy in the minds of many people. They think that limitation of knowledge is inaccurate knowledge. There are many children who have exact and retentive memories, and who remember exactly. They will answer correctly the question that is put to them. Those children to that extent may, humanly speaking, be called infallible, because they are correct up to the extent of their knowledge. If asked how much nine times nine is, they would say eighty-one. If asked how much nine hundred and ninety-nine times nine hundred and ninety-nine is, they might say that they could not tell, their knowledge did not extend so far. Limitation is not inaccuracy; and this seems to be the silly mistake made by a great school, that because our Lord had limited Himself therefore He would make mistakes. Infallibility and omniscience are totally different things'.

Finally, reverting to the problem raised by the words 'He emptied Himself', the opening speaker said of one who had taken part :

'I thank him for his remarks, but I think that his going back to the expression "divesting Himself" rather tends to weaken the teaching of the passage before us than to strengthen it. That divesting was self evident, but the Kenosis, that He *poured Himself out*, we do not get until we come to Calvary'.

We now return to Philippians to make one further comment. There, in chapter 2, awaits us in the example of the apostle, an illustration, so far as such is possible, of the 'self emptying' of the Son of God.

> 'Yea, and if I be offered upon the sacrifice and service of your faith I joy, and rejoice with you all' (Phil. 2:17).

The word *spendomai* refers to the 'drink offerings' that accompanied the Sacrifices under the Levitical law. We will give full proof of this when we reach the verse in the course of exposition, but will conclude this study with the paraphrase given by Bishop Lightfoot :

> 'I spoke of my severe labours for the Gospel, I am ready even to die in the same cause. If I am required to pour out my lifeblood as a libation over the sacrificial offering of your faith, I rejoice ... '.

We are irresistibly turned to Isaiah 53:12, where we read :

> 'He hath poured out His soul unto death',

and when we find that the word translated 'to pour out' *arah* is translated 'to empty' as pitcher, or a chest (Gen. 24:20; 2 Chron. 24:11) we feel that by strange and somewhat circuitous paths we have been led a few steps nearer to the meaning of the great passage which occupies the worshipping attention of our hearts and minds.

(2) The terms employed   **(f)** *morphe* **'The form of a servant'**
                                  (g) *homoioma* **'The likeness of men'**
                                  (h) *tapeinoo* **'He humbled Himself'**

Bishop Pearson, referring to the Authorized Version of Philippians 2:7, writes :

> 'Our translation of that verse is not only not exact, but very disadvantageous to the truth which is contained in it. For we read it thus: *He made Himself of no reputation and took upon Him the form of a servant, and was made in the likeness of men*, where we have two copulative conjunctions ("and" "and"), neither of which is in the original text, and three distinct propositions, without any dependence of one upon the other; whereas all the words together

are but an expression of Christ's exinanition*,? with an explication showing in what it consisteth: which will clearly appear by this literal translation, *But emptied Himself, taking the form of a servant, being made in the likeness of men.* Where if any man doubt how Christ emptied Himself, the text will satisfy him, *by taking the form of a servant*; if any still question how He took the form of a servant, he hath the apostle's resolution, by *being made in the likeness of men.* Indeed, after the expression of this exinanition, he goes on with a conjunction, to add another of Christ's humiliations. And being found in fashion as a man, He humbled Himself, etc., etc.'.

There is a definite descent indicated by the three verbs used by the apostle, *huparcho* 'subsisting', *einai* 'being' and *ginomai* 'becoming' or 'made'; the first refers to the eternal *subsistence* of 'the form of God', the second to the states and conditions that pertain to 'being on an equality with God', and the third to the entrance into a new sphere, '*made* in the likeness of men'.

Before the apostle tells us that in His great act of self abnegation the Saviour became man, he speaks of His taking 'the form of a servant'. This choice of words is evidently an intentional antithesis to the expression already studied, 'the form of God', and refers to an essential and characteristic attribute. As God He was *Despotes* 'Master', as man He was *doulos* 'a slave'. We must not limit this element of 'servitude' to the period when Christ was apprehended, bound, scourged and crucified, as some have done. 'Our Saviour in all the degrees of His humiliation never lived as a servant unto any master on earth' (Bishop Pearson).

'*The form of a servant* is here manifestly contrasted with *the form of God*. And in comparison with God EVERY CREATURE has the form of a servant and is bound to obedience towards God' (Bishop Ellicott).

'In the fulness of time Christ took our nature upon Him, He did wholly submit His reasonable will, all His

---

* 'He *exinanited* Himself' (*Phil. 2:7 Rhemish Translation*). The word is very rarely used today.

affections and desires, unto the will of His heavenly Father: and in this renouncing of the arbitrament* of His will, and in the entire submission of it unto the Will of His Father, did the *form of a servant*, whereof our apostle speaks, formally consist' (Dean Jackson).

So all embracive is the submission of the will of Christ to that of the Father, that in Matthew 26:39 the Evangelist uses the verb *thelo* 'not as I will', while in Luke 22:42 he uses *boulomai* as well as *thelo* 'if Thou be willing ... nevertheless not My will'. Of these two words, Dr. E.W. Bullinger says in his *Lexicon*, '*thelo* to will, to wish, to desire, implying the simple act of volition'; '*boulomai*, to wish, to desire, to have that desire from which *thelo* springs, to have a mind, intention, or purpose formed after mature deliberation'.

It is of the very essence of 'the form' of a servant, that will, desire, and purpose, should be entirely subservient to the One acknowledged as Master. When the mother of Zebedee's children made her request, she said 'grant that these my two sons may sit, the one on Thy right hand, and the other on Thy left, in Thy Kingdom'.

It is not within the province of 'the form' of a servant to 'grant' such a request, and so the perfect Servant said, 'to sit on My right hand, and on My left, is not mine to give'.

Not only in the course of His life and activities generally, but in those things that belong specifically to His ministry, the Saviour manifested at all times, the reality of His condescension.

'I can of Mine own Self do nothing: as I hear, I judge: and My judgment is just; because I seek not Mine own will, but the will of the Father which hath sent Me' (John 5:30).

Christ is pre-eminently set forth as 'The Sent One' in John's Gospel and it is written 'for He Whom God hath

---

* Arbitrament = power or liberty of deciding; choice, decision, determination.

sent speaketh the Words of God' (John 3:34). 'My doctrine is not Mine but His that sent Me' (John 7:16).

This is the first of seven such declarations found in this gospel (John 8:28,47; 12:49; 14:10,24, and 17:8). Not only did He, in perfect harmony with 'the form' of a servant, submit His will to and receive His message from the Father, but the mighty works that He wrought, are all attributed to the One that sent Him. The works that the Saviour did were 'given' Him to 'finish'.

> 'I have greater witness than that of John: for the works which the Father hath given Me to finish, the same works that I do, bear witness of Me, that the Father hath sent Me' (John 5:36).

The works that the Saviour did, were the works of Him that sent Him (John 9:4). 'If I do not the works of My Father', said Christ, 'believe Me not' (John 10:37).

So completely did Christ take upon Him 'the form' of a servant, that it could be written of Him 'even Christ pleased not Himself' (Rom. 15:3). This self-emptied servant therefore descended to depths which none of us could reach, and when the work of condescending grace was accomplished, He made it clear that He could use expressions which must for ever be beyond our right or power.

While all this is blessedly true, it would be an incomplete statement of truth to leave the matter there. This Servant was unlike any other. All others are servants by the very fact of their creation, He became a servant by an act of condescending love. Consequently when He knew that His hour had come, when He could say 'I have finished the work which Thou gavest Me to do' (John 17:4) a new note is struck. For the first and only time in Scripture the words 'I will' are uttered in any recorded prayer :

> 'Father, I WILL that they also, whom Thou hast given Me, be with Me where I am; that they may behold My glory, which Thou hast given Me: for Thou lovedst Me before the foundation of the world' (John 17:24).

This 'I will' is uttered in view of the day when 'the form of a servant' will have been put off, and glory again reassumed.

The expression 'in likeness of men becoming', neither necessarily implies nor excludes the reality of the nature which Christ assumed. That reality has already been affirmed by the words 'taking the form of a servant', even as reality is affirmed in the words 'the form of God'. The word translated 'likeness' is *homoioma* and is derived from the verb *homoioo* 'to make like', which verb is found in Acts 14:11, when the idolatrous people of Lystra said 'the gods are come down to us in the likeness of men'. What these pagans mistakenly applied to Barnabas and Paul, had been most blessedly realized when 'the Word was made (*became*) flesh and dwelt among us'. The Saviour, when He undertook the redemption of man, had a 'body' prepared for Him (Heb. 10:5) and because the men for whom He had undertaken were 'flesh and blood, He also Himself likewise took part of the same' (Heb. 2:14).

The apostle rightly says 'in the likeness of men' for, although the Saviour was most certainly man, and born of a woman, and living the normal life of man, yet He was most certainly not merely man, He was God manifest in the flesh, the God-Man, true God and perfect Man. Moreover the word *anthropon* 'men' is plural. He came in the nature common to all men — mankind, and so could be called 'The Son of Man'. The next words of the apostle, 'and being found in fashion as a man' (Phil. 2:8) take up the subject of the Saviour's *kenosis* or self-emptying, and focus our attention upon His culminating act of obedience, 'obedient unto death, even the death of the cross'. This culminating act of the One Who originally existed in the form of God and now is seen in the form of a slave, is further defined as an act of humiliation, 'He humbled Himself'.

The apostle looks backs to the great chapter of Messiah's sufferings (Isa. 53), where we read in the quotation made by Philip and recorded in Acts 8:33, 'in His *humiliation* His judgment was taken away'. 'This quotation is the LXX rendering of the Hebrew which Dr. Hudson translates "without restraint, and without a sentence He was taken away", i.e. He had no benefit of a formal trial, in which His innocence might have appeared. Pilate offered no restraint to the violent procedure of the Jews, nor did he pronounce legal sentence upon the Saviour' (Turpie.)

'He humbled Himself' and allowed Himself, the Lord of all, to be led as a sheep to the slaughter. In direct association with this humbling of the Lord is the humbling of His followers. First, Paul says 'I know both how to be abased, and I know how to abound' (Phil. 4:12), where the words 'to be abased' are a translation of the verb *tapeinoo* already used of the Lord in Philippians 2:8. Further, in the passage which speaks of 'our vile body' (Phil. 3:21) the word translated 'vile' is *tapeinosis*, which the Revised Version translates 'the body of our humiliation'. We shall discover that this passage has no reference to villainy or sin, for in the days when the Authorized Version was prepared the word 'vile' could be used of a raiment (Jas. 2:2), and a common phrase indicating the conditions of slavery is, as we all know, 'in durance vile'. The expression 'our vile body' refers to the voluntary conformity of the apostle and others to 'His death' (Phil. 3:10) which will come before us for fuller examination later. It is, however, essential to the argument of Philippians 2:6-8 that we should not forget that with all its solemnity and depth of doctrine, it is an example of the precept given in Philippians 2:4, the Saviour's 'humiliation' being the highest example and the conformity of the apostle one that most closely sought to carry that example into execution.

The word *heauton* 'Himself', in verses 7 and 8, are emphatic, 'Himself He emptied', 'Himself He humbled';

in both cases it was the voluntary act of Him Who subsisted in the form of God.

The lowest depths of the Saviour's humiliation and the extreme example of His willing obedience is seen in the death He died, 'even the death of the cross'.

In Paul's day crucifixion was the punishment meted out to a slave and a Roman citizen could not be subjected to such a degradation. Paul may suffer, Paul may suffer death at the hand of the Roman executioner, but he could not stoop so low as had His gracious Master (Cicero, Verr. i. 5; v. 64).

The Crucifixion has several aspects which vary according to the purpose of the writer in speaking of it. When Paul was dealing with the question of justification by faith apart from the deeds of the law, he stressed the fact that crucifixion fulfilled the statement of Moses (Deut. 21:23) and showed that Christ died under the curse of the broken law (Gal. 3:10-13). When Paul would level all boasting in human wisdom he preached Jesus Christ and Him crucified (1 Cor. 1 and 2). When he would exhort the Hebrews 'to run with patience the race set before' them, the apostle spoke of Christ Who 'endured the cross despising the shame' (Heb. 12:1,2). At the death of the cross the lowest rung in the ladder of the Saviour's humiliation is reached. The next movement is 'exaltation' and as we have followed step by step the seven-fold humiliation of our Saviour as recorded in verses 6-8, it will be our joy to follow the corresponding sevenfold exaltation that occupies verses 9-11.

The NAME which is above every name

Having referred to the seven-fold humiliation of the Lord and the subsequent seven-fold exaltation, it may be that some reader would appreciate the following set-out of this feature, which we give before proceeding.

Seven-fold Humiliation (Phil. 2:7,8).	*Seven-fold Exaltation* (Phil. 2:9-11).
(1) He emptied Himself.	(1) The Name above every other.
(2) A bond slave.	(2) Every knee shall bow.
(3) Likeness of a man.	(3) Things in heaven.
(4) Fashioned as a man.	(4) Things in earth.
(5) He humbled Himself.	(5) Things under earth.
(6) Obedient unto death.	(6) Every tongue confess.
(7) The death of the cross.	(7) Jesus Christ is Lord.

It is good to see something of what that joy was that was set before Him Who endured the shame of the cross and is now set down at the right hand of the throne of God (Heb. 12:1-3). The covering term for this complete and glorious reversal of His humiliation is expressed in Philippians 2:9 in the words 'God also hath highly exalted Him', and it is the delightful office of the seven-fold expansion of verses 9-11 to give some idea of what that high exaltation involved.

Before we can consider this high exaltation we must be clear concerning the humiliation of which it is both reward and consequence.

We read, 'Now He that ascended, what is it but that He also descended first into the lower parts of the earth?' (Eph. 4:9).

This 'descent' is two-fold. (1) Into the realm of creation at all; (2) And then, as a man, stooping to the death of the cross. The assumption of human nature was a condescension so great that the human mind cannot comprehend it, and had the Son of God assumed the form of the highest and most majestic of creatures, the stoop down would be something so tremendous as to be beyond our computation. This, however, was but the first stage of this gracious descent. The second stage is introduced by the words 'being found in fashion as a man' and these words are followed by a humiliation that went to the lowest depths of human degradation, 'the death of the cross'. All this moreover was an act of consummate 'obedience', the 'obedience of one' in fact upon which rests our eternal salvation (Rom. 5:19).

The exaltation of the Saviour was a direct consequence of His voluntary humiliation and in the nature of a public recognition. The words 'wherefore ... also' of Philippians 2:9, being in the original *dio kai*, suggesting the thought 'on this account'.

The exaltation of the Saviour, in one sense, was a return to the glory which He had before the world was (John 17:5), but in another sense it was a glory 'given' to Him consequent upon the finishing of His redeeming work and a glory therefore which the redeemed could share (John 17:4,5,22). This additional glory, consequent upon the completion of His great redemptive work, is set forth in great power in the first chapter of Hebrews. There the 'Son' is given wondrous titles.

As the Son, He had been constituted 'Heir of all things'. As the Son it could be written of Him 'Who being the brightness of His glory, and the express image of His Person, and upholding all things by the word of His power', how then was it necessary to say 'being made so much better than the angels, as He hath by inheritance obtained a more excellent name than they'?

Surely One Who was essentially the express image of the substance of God, could not but be infinitely above angels! The usage of the two words *hon* 'being' (verse 3) and *genomenos* 'having become' (verse 4) distinguishes between that which was *essential*, and that which was *awarded* and obtained by inheritance. In between the glories of His essential being and the reward of His exaltation, is interposed His redeeming work 'when He had by Himself purged our sins' and its glorious consequence 'sat down on the right hand of the Majesty on high' (Heb. 1:3,4).

'Wherefore God also hath highly exalted Him' (Phil. 2:9).

When Peter spoke of the exaltation of the Saviour he uses the verb *hupsoo* (Acts 2:33; 5:31), but when Paul speaks of the Saviour's exaltation in Philippians 2:9, he uses the verb *huperupsoo* 'to exalt highly'. This is the only occurrence of this superlative word in the New Testament and it occurs twice in reference to the Lord in the LXX. The first occurrence is in a Psalm of praise which opens with the words 'The Lord reigneth':

'For Thou Lord art high above all the earth: Thou art exalted far above all gods' (Psa. 97:9).

In the context will be seen the exhortation 'worship Him all ye gods', which is rendered in the LXX 'worship Him all ye His angels', and is quoted as of Christ in Hebrews 1:6 'When He bringeth in the Firstbegotten into the world, He saith, And let all the angels of God worship Him' (Heb. 1:6).

The second occurrence is found in the book of Daniel. Chapter 4 of that wonderful book is in itself a wonder, for it was not written by Daniel, it was not given to him by revelation, it is the actual transcript of the proclamation made by Nebuchadnezzar himself! After his proud boasting and humiliation Nebuchadnezzar was restored to his kingly estate and he 'extolled' and 'highly exalted' the King of heaven (Dan. 4:37).

Something of the character of Christ's exaltation is foreshadowed in these passages 'gods', 'angels' and 'pagan kings' using the word *huperupsoo* which is reserved in the New Testament to the exaltation of Christ alone. This super-exaltation will be travestied by the Beast, for 2 Thessalonians 2:4 says he 'opposeth and exalteth himself above all that is called God, or that is worshipped', where the word 'to exalt' here is *huperairomai*. *Huper* is associated with the Lord's ascension in Ephesians 1:21 and 4:10, where we read the

words 'far above all principality' and 'far above all
heavens'.

This high exaltation is expanded by the apostle when he
refers to the gracious bestowal upon the exalted Saviour of
'the name which is above every name' (Phil. 2:9).

The Revisers have rightly restored the article 'The
Name' and to a Hebrew 'The Name which is above every
name' can mean nothing less than the sacred name
Jehovah.

The ascension of Christ placed Him not only far above
all principality and power, might and dominion but far
above 'every name that is named, not only in this world,
but also in that which is to come: and hath put all things
under His feet' (Eph. 1:21,22). 'Every name that is
named' must include every Name of God, for we do not
need to be told that the exalted Christ is far above angels
or men.   Yet the stupendous consequences of such a
revelation leave us over-whelmed by their immensity.
What a sweep, from the infamy of the Cross to the name
above every name! The Psalm that supplies the prophetic
words 'all things under His feet' is the Psalm that begins
and ends with the words :

'O LORD our Lord, how excellent is Thy name in all the earth!'
(Psa. 8:1).

The LORD says in Isaiah 45 :

'… there is no God else beside Me; a just God and a Saviour; there
is none beside Me. Look unto Me, and be ye saved, all the ends of
the earth: for I am God, and there is none else. I have sworn by
Myself, the word is gone out of My mouth in righteousness, and
shall not return, *That unto Me* every knee shall bow, every tongue
shall swear' (Isa. 45:21-23).

The fact that this glorious Name was given to the Son
by the Father, shows that the 'Man' Christ Jesus is still
before us. Nothing could so emphasize the superlative
glory of 'Jesus', than that He should be graced with the
incommunicable name Jehovah, and nothing could so

emphasize the equally glorious fact that He Who was the Man 'Jesus' was nevertheless 'God manifest in the flesh'.

We meet His name in the opening of the New Testament 'Thou shalt call His name Jesus' with which the context links the name Emmanuel 'God with us' (Matt. 1:21,23). During the years of His humiliation that name 'Jesus' was associated with despised 'Nazareth' and it was this name and title that was displayed upon the cross, 'Jesus of Nazareth, the King of the Jews' (John 19:19).

Paul's first acquaintance with the Risen Christ was made on the road to Damascus. The terrifying vision caused him to cry 'Who art thou LORD?' for surely no One lower than God Himself could have so acted. To his intense surprise the 'Lord' replied ' I am Jesus' (Acts 9:5).

Paul's trembling and astonishment soon gave place to adoration and selfless devotion, and a steady course can be followed in his ministry that leads on from glory to glory, linking the 'Jesus' Whom he had persecuted to the 'Jesus' in Whose name every knee should bow.

Instead of reading 'At the name of Jesus' (Phil. 2:10) the Revised Version reads 'In the name of Jesus'. Whether we read 'At the name of Jesus' or 'In the name of Jesus', most assume that it is the name 'Jesus' that has been exalted to this high pinnacle of glory. The passage, however, does not say 'He exalted the name that had been borne by Him during His humiliation', but 'He gave to Him, Whose earthly name was Jesus, the name which is above every name, that is the name Jehovah, that in this name, Jehovah, the name given to Jesus, every knee should bow'. The universality of homage that the apostle visualized is expressed in extraordinary terms :

'Of things in heaven, and things in earth, and things under the earth' (Phil. 2:10).

Some see in this threefold division a reference to angels, to mankind and to the dead, but give no satisfactory reason for suggesting that the dead before the resurrection can be spoken of as bowing the knee and confessing that Jesus Christ is Lord.

Webster and Wilkinson say that this threefold division answers to that which the Pagan world made of their deities, and predicts universal submission to the true God, and they refer to the Iliad (3. 276-9) in proof.

Lightfoot, however, takes this threefold division to indicate 'the whole universe, whether animate or inanimate' and cites Revelation 5:13, Ephesians 1:20-23 and Romans 8:22 in passing.

'It would seem therefore that the adjectives here are neuter; and any limitation to intelligent beings, while it detracts from the universality of the homage, is not required by the expressions'.

Something of the intention of the apostle can be seen in the ascription of praise which constitutes Psalm 148, where not only angels, kings and all peoples are called upon to praise the Lord, but sun, moon and stars, dragons and all deeps together with 'Fire, and hail; snow, and vapour; stormy wind fulfilling His word'.

It is fitting that this should be, for 'the earnest expectation of the creature (creation) waiteth for the manifestation of the sons of God' (Rom. 8:19.) This universal acknowledgment is directed to one glorious goal 'that Jesus Christ is Lord, to the glory of God the Father' (Phil. 2:11). The fact that this is 'to the glory of God the Father' shows that Christ as the Mediator is still in view (1 Cor. 15:24-28), He is exalted in His Divine Manhood, as the second Man and the last Adam.

The title 'Lord' being as it is the LXX and the New Testament equivalent of the great name Jehovah (Rom. 4:8; Matt. 3:3), shows that this is 'the name which is above every name' given to Him, and confessed by all.

The goal of the ages will be reached when this universal acknowledgment here prophesied becomes an historic fact. It is the privilege of the church of the mystery to anticipate that day by its acknowledgment of Christ as 'Head over all things to the church' now.

This brings us back to Philippians 2:4,5, and the exhortation of verse 12, 'wherefore, my beloved'. Before we pick up the thread of the apostle's argument and pursue it through the record of the subjoined examples, of himself (Phil. 2:17), of Timothy (Phil. 2:20) and of Epaphroditus (Phil. 2:25), a brief summary of what we have learned concerning the voluntary self-emptying of the Saviour may prove of service.

Philippians 2:6-11

(1) 'Who being'. We have seen that *huparchon* denotes both the *pre*-existence and the *continued* existence of Christ in the form of God.

(2) 'Form' indicates essential nature; 'fashion' the perceptible mode of His existence, His state and relationships as a human being.

(3) 'To be on an equality with God' relates to the *mode* of existence, not to the essential nature of the One Unchanging Deity. This mode could be exchanged for another.

(4) The two expressions 'Thought it not a thing to be grasped at' and 'He emptied Himself' clearly indicate that at the incarnation Christ laid aside the glory that pertained to His essential nature and which will be resumed at the close of His great Mediatorial work (John 17:5). The 'emptying' finds an echo and explanation in the figure of the 'poured out drink offering' of Philippians 2:17.

(5) Christ becoming in the likeness of men and in the form of a servant links Him with the true nature of man which was made in the image and likeness of God.

(6) In this nature and by the body thus prepared for Him He humbled Himself until He could descend no lower, even to the death of the cross.

(7) Paul has thus shown us in brief outline the essential features of the Incarnation, the perfect Godhead and perfect Manhood united in One Divine Person Who is the subject of the whole passage.

'As to the manner in which those two natures are united in One Person, as to the degree in which the Deity was limited, or the Humanity exalted by their union, *during Christ's life on earth*, the apostle has said nothing whatever in this passage. ... The continuance of *the form of God* assures us that at least the moral attributes of the Godhead are faithfully represented in the one perfect image of the Father, His incarnate Word. And thus His every act of tender compassion, of patient endurance, and of loving self-sacrifice shines out in its perfect beauty as a revelation of God's own nature, and of His gracious disposition towards us' (Gifford).

'He clothes "eternal love with breathing life"' (Hutton).

CHAPTER 6

Working out the Truth

Philippians 2:12-30

The mighty revelation of Philippians 2:6-11, was not introduced by the apostle in order to treat of or to prove the deity of Christ, that doctrine is assumed throughout the passage, but that he might enforce by the greatest example known to man, the spirit inculcated in the words 'look not every man on his own things, but every man also on the things of others' (Phil. 2:4).

He now returns to the Philippians and urges them to another exhibition of Christian grace, enforcing it this time with the lower example of his own attitude. This exhortation and example occupy verses 12-18. This new section is linked with the preceding example of Christ by the word 'wherefore'. In one sense it could be said that the two passages, namely, Philippians 2:9 and 12 are linked together by the recurring word 'wherefore'

'Wherefore God also hath highly exalted HIM'.

'Wherefore my beloved ... work out YOUR OWN SALVATION';

and this would be true. The word 'wherefore' however is a translation of *dio* 'through which' in chapter 2:9, whereas it is a translation of *hoste* 'as besides' or 'so then' in chapter 2:12, a logical consequence.

In the case of Christ, the exaltation was 'in consequence of' the voluntary humiliation of the Son of God. In the case of the Philippians, the exhortation addressed to them, was 'as a consequence' of the pattern and example given them. The exhortation itself reads :

'Wherefore, my beloved, as ye have always obeyed, not as in my presence only, but now much more in my absence, work out your own salvation with fear and trembling. For it is God which worketh in you both to will and to do His good pleasure' (Phil. 2:12,13).

The apostle introduces his exhortation by the words 'My beloved'. Sometimes this title is employed as a simple statement of a very gracious fact 'to all that be in Rome, beloved of God, called saints' (Rom. 1:7). Sometimes it is introduced to temper a warning that might sound somewhat harsh 'as my beloved sons I warn you' (1 Cor. 4:14), or to add weight to an entreaty 'wherefore, my dearly beloved, flee from idolatry' (1 Cor. 10:14). Here in Philippians 2:12, the apostle gathers up the references to 'love' in 2:1 and 2, 'if any comfort of love', 'having the same love' and addresses his hearers as 'beloved'.

Even so, he still does not come at once to his theme. He does not say 'wherefore, work out', neither does he say 'wherefore, my beloved, work out', but he interposes yet a further clause to soften any feeling of doubt or censure that the ultimate appeal may appear to imply.

'As ye have always obeyed'. This is a gracious recognition of the longstanding character of these believers. 'Not as in my presence only' which might be construed in a derogatory sense apart from the words that follow, 'but much more in my absence' and so the apostle comes to his point.

'Work out' *katergazomai*. Out of the twenty-four occurrences of this word in the New Testament Paul is responsible for twenty-one. Of the twenty-one occurrences in Paul's epistles, two only are found in the Prison epistles, namely in Ephesians 6:13 and Philippians 2:12.

In Ephesians 6:13 the word is translated 'having done', with the marginal alternative 'having overcome'. The intention of the apostle is discovered by the place this word occupies in the structure of the epistle, Ephesians 1:19 to 2:7 'the mighty power inworked (*energeo*), balancing Ephesians 6:10-13 'the mighty power worked out (*katergazomai*), revealing that what is inwrought by grace (doctrine) should be worked out in life (practice).

Incidentally, this emphasizes the value of the structure in translating the Scriptures. The two words *energeo* and *katergazomai* come together in Philippians 2:12,13 and not being separated, as they are in Ephesians by several chapters, the translators have rendered them 'work out' and 'work in'. The apostle, therefore, in Philippians 2:12,13 is not enunciating anything new, he is but repeating in more concentrated form the teaching already given in Ephesians.

This word *katergazomai* is employed by the LXX to describe the work done by Bezaleel in the cutting of stones and in the carving of wood, where the Hebrew equivalent is *charosheth* 'to carve' (Exod. 35:33).

The Philippians were encouraged to be confident 'of this very thing' namely, that 'He which hath begun a good work in you will perform it until the day of Jesus Christ' (Phil. 1:6). This may include more than Philippians 3:21 expresses, but it cannot include less.

'Who shall change this body of our humiliation, that it may be fashioned like unto His body of glory, according to the working (*energeia*) whereby He is able to subdue all things unto Himself'.

It is not within the power of any mortal man, even though he be redeemed and a member of the body of Christ, either 'to will or to do' anything to contribute to this glorious goal. But there is an aspect of truth that links the 'working' of God with the co-operative 'outworking' of the believer, and that is before us in the exhortation :

'Work out your own salvation ... for it is God which worketh in you' (Phil. 2:12,13).

That intelligent personal co-operation is intended, the words 'with fear and trembling' make evident. Where it is the work of God alone, there is 'confidence' (Phil. 1:6), but where the voluntary act of the believer is involved, no such confidence can be expressed. 'Not as though I had already attained' and 'if by any means' must be the language employed when dealing with this aspect of the truth, even by the apostle himself.

Salvation from sin, the immediate result of believing the gospel of grace, is not the theme of the epistle to the Philippians. These were believers of long standing and of tried faith, having manifested active and self-denying fellowship in the ministry of the word.

The exhortation to work out his own 'salvation' therefore challenges the reader. Christ is called 'the Saviour' in Philippians 3:20, but it is a Saviour for Whom the believer 'looks', and His work is rather 'the redemption of the body' than redemption from sin. So is it with the other references to salvation in this epistle :

'This shall turn to my salvation' (Phil. 1:19).

'But to you of salvation, and that of God' (Phil. 1:28).

Paul was a 'saved' man, and those who were exhorted to withstand the onslaught of their adversaries were 'saved' men. We can sometimes help ourselves toward a conclusion by observing the opposite or the alternative to any word under discussion. In Philippians 1:28 the alternative to 'salvation' is 'perdition' and this word is the same that is translated 'destruction' in Philippians 3:19 and 'perdition' in Hebrews 10:39. Now in Hebrews the two key passages are :

'On unto PERFECTION' (Heb. 6:1) or 'back unto PERDITION' (Heb. 10:39),

even as the two key words of Philippians 3 are 'perfect' and 'perdition' (Phil. 3:12 and 19). It seems obvious therefore that by 'salvation' in Philippians, Paul is thinking of the full and complete attainment of the changed body, the out-resurrection and the prize of the high calling. It is 'the salvation (or that salvation *soterias ... tes*), which is in Christ Jesus with age-abiding glory ... if we endure, we shall also reign with Him' (2 Tim. 2:10,12).

Salvation is by grace, and not of works (Eph. 2:8,9), here the words used indicate origin. Salvation does not arise OUT OF works of any kind. Salvation however should lead to works, good works (Eph. 2:10), and whether we look back to the origin of our salvation or on to the goal we find that 'we are His workmanship' and that He has prepared beforehand these good works, in order that we should walk in them. Here we see the perfect blending of Divine grace and human response. So in Philippians, where another aspect of salvation is before the mind, the same gracious co-operation is manifest. There, not only 'the working' but 'the willing' are provided for.

Some have taught from this passage that inasmuch as 'the willing' as well as 'the working' is all of God (Phil. 2:13), that predestination in its most rigid sense must be believed, that the believer has no freedom either of will or of choice, that all is of God to the exclusion either of human responsibility or desire. Bloomfield writes 'It is worthy of observation that even Calvin in his annotation on this present portion, admits that *this* is no place in which to seek the doctrine of *gratia proeveniens*, nor, on the other hand, is it any suitable instrument by which to "beat down the doctrine of free will"'.

We may gain some light upon this passage by observing the usage of *energeo* in Ephesians 2:2; where the subject is the influence exerted on the minds of unregenerate men by the prince of the power of the air. Those who are thus energized are called 'children of disobedience', but this implies some measure of responsibility, any person or anything that has no option regarding its actions, can neither be rewarded nor punished, yet these 'children of disobedience' are also called 'children of wrath' (Eph. 2:2,3). Yet further, when the apostle enlarges upon this Satanic inworking, he links it up with 'the course of this world', and instead of saying that those thus energized were being forced by a mighty spirit to do things contrary to their own desires he actually says that they were 'fulfilling the desires of the flesh and of the mind', so that instead of the teaching of Ephesians 2:2,3 being that Satan forced men to sin against their will, he is seen using and co-operating with their own desires. Indeed, the word translated 'desires' here is *thelemata* 'wills', which brings this passage into line with Philippians 2:13, where the word 'to will' is *thelein*.

If the truth of Philippians 2:13 be that God irresistibly inworks in the believer both to will and to do, how is it that the apostle prefaces this statement with an exhortation 'work out'? These words are as unnecessary as they are illogical if the believer has no share in this outworking.

The outworking is an answer to the inworking of God, and this inworking is related to such gracious inducements and helps as the enlightenment of the eyes of the understanding, the verdict by the conscience, the attraction of the grace and beauty of truth and of salvation and the exposure of the hideousness of sin. All these the Lord uses to influence the believer 'to will and to work of His good pleasure'.

What does the apostle mean by the words 'of His good pleasure'? *Huper* is found seven times in Philippians (1:4,7,29; 2:9,13, and 4:10) and is translated 'for', 'of', 'in the behalf of', 'for ... make' and with the accusative case 'above'. Something of the apostle's meaning in the words 'of His good pleasure' can be seen in the words *'for* the truth of God' (Rom. 15:8) and *'for* the glory of God' (John 11:4), where something is worked out. 'Good pleasure' *eudokia*, is found in Philippians 1:15 where it refers to 'the good will' of those who preached Christ. In Ephesians the word is more definitely related to the great purpose of grace where, in chapter 1:5 and 9, we read of 'the good pleasure of His will' in relation to the predestination of the believer to adoption, and to inheritance (both high and wondrous favours), and so in Philippians 2, God is seen encouraging and helping the believer to the practical realization of His gracious calling.

On many occasions when one is meditating upon the meaning and intention of any particular passage of Scripture, the immediate context often supplies a key which all the probing into meanings of mere words fails to discover.

Some commentators have actually taught that with the opening of verse 14, Paul goes on to a fresh subject. Yet there are awaiting us in verses 14-16 suggestions that enable us to see that the salvation which the Philippians were exhorted to work out, is indeed, as we have already indicated, the full perfection of their calling.

'Murmurings'. The Greek word so translated is *gongusmos*, and is probably of *onomatopoeic* origin, that is a word formed in imitation of a sound, such as a buzz, whizz, hiss, cuckoo and peewit.

Gongusmos is probably derived from the murmuring sound of air in a shell, even as the English word mur-mur is a reduplication of a sound. This is the only occurrence of the word in Paul's epistles. The verbal form *gonguzo* is used by Paul but twice, and that in 1 Corinthians 10:10 where he speaks of Israel in the wilderness in elaborating his exhortation to 'so run that ye may obtain' (1 Cor. 9:24-27). Here we have a race, a running and a crown, with accompanying self discipline, followed by the example to be avoided of those who, though redeemed from Egypt, were overthrown in the wilderness. We have already established the fact that Philippians and Hebrews are parallel, and here we perceive that Hebrews 3, 4, expands at length what is condemned by the apostle in Philippians 2:14.

'Disputings'. The Greek word so translated is *dialogismos*. This word can mean 'reasoning', that is the exercise of the highest faculty of the human mind, and in its plural form it can mean 'reasonings' which take on an evil sense and, like 'disputatious', generally indicates an attitude of mind inimical to faith.

Consequently, such is the heart of man, although the word occurs eight times in the Gospels, it is never used in a good sense, and of the six occurrences in the epistles, not one is translated reasoning, in a good sense, but 'imaginations' which are vain; 'doubtful' and 'doubting', 'thoughts' that are either vain or evil, and 'disputings'. Israel after they began to murmur, soon began to rebel and dispute the wisdom and love of God and the authority of Moses their leader. They even went so far as to say 'let us make a captain, and let us return into Egypt' (Num. 14:4). It was as a counter to this danger, that the apostle spoke of 'forgetting those things which are behind' as 'he pressed toward the goal'. This murmuring and disputatious spirit must be shunned by all who seek to serve the Lord acceptably :

'That ye may be blameless and harmless, the sons of God, without rebuke' (Phil. 2:15).

Not that you may be 'sons of God', for no abstention of any kind can make a person a son of God, so the emphasis must be placed on the kind of son of God intended, i.e. the sons of God WITHOUT REBUKE. A similar process of argument is found in Matthew 5:44,45, 'Love your enemies ... that ye may be the children of your Father which is in heaven'; not that loving one's enemies can ever make a person a child of God, but love does make such a relationship manifest. In this same chapter of Matthew we have the exhortation 'Let your light so shine before men, that they may see your good works, and glorify your Father which is in heaven' (Matt. 5:16).

In like manner, the Philippians were told that they were placed in the midst of a crooked and perverse generation, (not 'nation' as in the A.V.), among whom they appeared (not 'ye shine', but *phainesthe* 'appear' as it is translated in Matthew 2:7) as lights in the world. The word translated 'lights' may refer to the heavenly bodies (Gen. 1:14), but the context so emphasizes that they shine or appear in the midst of a crooked and perverse generation as to favour the figure borrowed both from Scripture and profane usage, namely that of carrying torches to guide passengers along the 'dark and narrow streets of ancient cities' (see *Aristoph*).

Bishop Wordsworth comments upon this passage saying:

'The Christians little thought, when they read these words of the apostle, that some of their number would soon be literally made to be *phosteres*, or lights in the streets, by the Emperor, in that city. One form of their martyrdom was to be covered with pitch and tar, and then lighted as torches' (*Tacitus*).

This is the first development of the great example of Christ, further and fuller expansion is to follow, but with this exhortation before us, how wonderful the service of the Lord becomes.

Poured out as a drink offering

(With a special note an Proverbs 8:23)

We now pass from the supreme example of Christ's utter humiliation on our behalf to that of the example of, possibly, the closest follower that the Lord ever had, namely, the apostle Paul. Not one of the other apostles had so many advantages in this life as he had, not one went so far in renouncing all that life held dear for the sake of Christ and His truth.

To this the apostle returns in chapter 3 and sets out at length how indeed he had counted all things but loss for the excellency of the knowledge of Christ Jesus the Lord, but before he gives his renunciation in detail he follows the example of Christ's humiliation, with his own.

Lifted from its context such a recital in such proximity might have the appearance of boasting or of some form of competition. Taken with its context, it will reveal the apostle's intense concern, lest he should appear to be lecturing others and exhorting others to self denial, while failing to act upon his own principles and advice. This personal note has already been struck at the close of chapter 1, it is sounded again in chapter 3:1-14, and is restated with emphasis in chapter 4:9. Returning to chapter 2, we read:

'Yea, and if I be offered upon the sacrifice and service of your faith, I joy, and rejoice with you all' (verse 17).

The words translated 'and if' are *ei kai* (literally) 'if even', the stress being placed on the word 'if', the word 'even' belongs to that which is assumed. Appendix 118, 2a of the *Companion Bible* reads :

'*ei* = if. Putting the conditions simply :

(*a*) Followed by the *Indicative* Mood, the hypothesis is assumed as an actual fact, the condition being unfulfilled, but no doubt being thrown upon the supposition (1 Cor. 15:16)'.

Where the stress is laid upon *kai* 'even if', the strangeness belongs not to the thing assumed but to the making of the assumption.

The word 'offered' used by Paul here occurs but twice in the New Testament; here in Philippians 2:17 where the apostle expresses his willingness to be offered, and in 2 Timothy 4:6 where he announces that he was about to be offered.

Service and ministry under the law were essentially associated with 'sacrifice and offering', and the complete fulfilment of the Levitical law by the one offering of Christ, has so filled the vision of the believer under the dispensation of grace, that one blessed and holy feature that pertains to all Christian ministry has been either misunderstood or neglected.

The opening words of the practical section of Romans, introduces this sacrificial element into Christian service.

'I beseech you therefore, brethren, by the mercies of God, that ye present your bodies a living sacrifice, holy, acceptable unto God, which is your reasonable service' (Rom. 12:1).

When the apostle would expand his exhortation to walk worthy, in the Ephesian epistle, he says :

'Walk in love, as Christ also hath loved us, and hath given Himself for us an offering and a sacrifice to God for a sweetsmelling savour' (Eph. 5:2).

Writing to the Colossians the apostle speaks of this sacrificial character of his ministry saying :

'Who now rejoice in my sufferings for you, and fill up that which is behind of the afflictions of Christ in my flesh for His body's sake, which is the church' (Col. 1:24).

In Philippians itself there is a very lovely illustration of sacrificial service :

'But I have all, and abound: I am full, having received of Epaphroditus the things which were sent from you, an odour of a sweet smell, a sacrifice acceptable, wellpleasing to God' (Phil. 4:18).

Here the great-hearted apostle would, as it were, say, do not think merely of the spectacular 'offering' that I may be called upon to make – the lowly service of those who ministered of their substance can be also graced with this most precious title 'a sacrifice acceptable'.

There are, however, sacrifices that set forth in type the offering of Christ, an offering offered once, which can neither be repeated nor shared by others.

The offering therefore of Philippians 2:17; 4:18 and of Colossians 1:24, must fulfil some other type, if they fulfil a type at all. We therefore turn to the passage before us and observe that the word translated 'offer' is *spendomai*. The word sounds so much like the English 'spend', and the meaning of the word 'spend' is so illustrative of the apostle's meaning, that we may feel reluctant to acknowledge that the likeness is superficial only. Even though the apostle does not use the word *spendomai* in 2 Corinthians 12:15, when he says 'I will very gladly spend and be spent for you', the spirit is the same.

Between the writing of the preceding pages and the writing of the present, we have listened to the Archbishop of Canterbury preaching in Westminster Abbey, at the dedication of the memorial to the airmen who fell in 'The Battle of Britain'. He opened his address by giving a paraphrase of Matthew 10:39 :

'He that HOARDS his life shall lose it: and he that SPENDS his life for My sake shall find it'.

These words well illustrated the spirit that prompted the writing of Philippians 2:17.

Spendomai has a well defined meaning, 'to pour (i.e. offer) a drink offering', and this offering is not confined to the Levitical law. It was practised by the idolatrous nations outside Israel. It gives the word *sponde* 'a drink offering' and in the plural from *spondai*, it came to mean 'solemn treaty or covenant' secured and set forth by the pouring out of a libation. This in its turn gives the word *aspondos* 'implacable' (Rom. 1:31), 'truce breakers' (2 Tim. 3:3), the two translations revealing the origin and intent of the word.

The word *spendo* occurs about twenty times in the LXX, in most cases the reference is to the literal 'pouring out' of a drink offering.

(1) Jacob's offering at Bethel is the only reference to this custom before the law (Gen. 35:14). It was unaccompanied by any other sacrifice, but the intention of the patriarch is obvious.

(2) The references in the A.V. to the 'pouring out' of the drink offering in the tabernacle service (where the LXX uses the word *spendo*), are Exodus 25:29; 30:9; 37:16; Numbers 4:7 and 28:7. Exodus 25:29 calls for a word of explanation. There we read of 'bowls ... to cover withal', and in Exodus 37:16 and Numbers 4:7 of 'covers to cover withal', but in each case the margin reads 'pour out' which reading has been adopted as the true one in the Revised Version. Exodus 30:9 gives

a solemn warning against the pouring out of drink offerings and the altar of incense, showing that in some aspects of the work of Christ, fellowship is impossible and an intrusion, for verse 10 which immediately follows says: 'And Aaron shall make an atonement upon the horns of it once in a year' and in Leviticus 16:17 it is written 'And there shall be no man in the tabernacle of the congregation when he goeth in to make an atonement in the holy place'.

Neither the apostle's 'offering' of Philippians 2:17, nor the 'tribulations' which he endured (Col. 1:24) could ever be looked upon as in any sense supplementing the once offered and perfect sacrifice of the Son of God.

Something of the sacredness of the drink offering and the sense of complete surrender to God, may be seen in David's act after the three mighty men had, at the risk of their lives, brought to David water from the well of Bethlehem. He realized that such a 'drink offering' could not be made to mortal man, and so he poured it out before the Lord, saying 'Be it far from me, O LORD, that I should do this: is not this the blood of the men that went in jeopardy of their lives? therefore he would not drink it' (2 Sam. 23:16,17). There is no equivalent word in the LXX for 'jeopardy', because the Hebrew simply says *halak be nephesh* 'to go on with the soul' as the *Companion Bible* comments 'with their lives (in their hands)', or, as the Archbishop paraphrased the passage in Matthew, they did not 'hoard' their souls, they 'spent' them.

The apostle then, used a very intense and expressive figure when he spoke of himself being 'poured out as a drink offering upon the sacrifice and service of your faith'.

The reader will remember that of the Lord it is written, 'He emptied Himself' *ekenose*, a translation that is often set aside in favour of 'He divested Himself', but without warrant. The great self emptying of the Son of God is echoed at an infinite distance by this pouring out of his faithful follower. The offering of Christ was in itself perfect and needed no accompaniment to render it sanctified or acceptable. The 'offering' of Paul, by itself is valueless, it is only possible or acceptable when like 'the drink offerings' of the tabernacle it follows and accompanies the great sacrifice of Christ Himself.

The self emptying of the Saviour commences (Phil. 2) with taking upon Him 'the form of a servant', even as His further humiliation is associated with His subsequent obedience to the death of the cross. He indeed descended into 'the lower parts', that is 'the earth', and we look up from the foot of the cross to that glory which He had as being on equality with God and our senses reel at the tremendous descent.

We believe there are veiled hints in Scripture that there was an even more fundamental *kenosis* or self-emptying, which while we cannot pretend to comprehend we can at least indicate.

In order to enable the reader to see as far as the writer has attained in this most solemn yet enthralling subject, we must become acquainted with the meaning and translation of one or two key words.

We have seen that the 'self-emptying' of the Lord (Phil. 2:7) finds an echo in the 'offering' of Paul (Phil. 2:17). We have seen that the word *spendomai* 'offer' refers to the pouring out of a libation, or drink offering. We must now take the subject a stage further.

Spendomai is found in the LXX version eighteen times. This Greek word translates the Hebrew *nasak* fifteen times, the Chaldee *nesak* once. Two references, namely Exodus 25;29 and 37:16, are listed by Tromm under the Hebrew word *sakak*, with the note in brackets (*hic leg. nasak*).

Young's *Analytical Concordance* lists these two passages under the passive form of *nasak*. This means that *spendomai* finds its complete equivalent in the Hebrew word *nasak*. We must now consider the Hebrew word *nasak* itself.

We find that this word occurs in the Old Testament Scriptures twenty-six times, which leaves eight occurrences to be accounted for, eighteen, as we have seen, being translated by the Greek *spendomai*. In two passages the word is used of 'melting' or of a 'molten' image (Isa. 40:19 and 44:10). There is no essential difference here except that metal is in view instead of wine. The idea of 'pouring' is unchanged. The transition from 'pouring' to 'spreading' (Isa. 25:7) is reasonable, and it is an easy transition from 'spreading' as a vail, to 'covering' (Isa. 30:1; Exod. 25:29 and 37:16).

This leaves but two occurrences unaccounted for. They are Psalm 2:6 and Proverbs 8:23.

'Yet have I *set* my King upon My holy hill of Zion'.

'I was *set* up from everlasting'.

Here it will be observed the Authorized Version translates *nasak* 'set' and 'set up'. The Authorized Version margin of Psalm 2:6 tells the reader that the Hebrew word means 'anointed', and with this agrees Gesenius, who reads 'to anoint a king'. This moreover is the rendering found in Young's Literal translation; the reader will therefore see that we are not offering a 'private interpretation' of Psalm 2:6.

This leaves us one passage more (Prov. 8:23). Young's Literal translates this passage 'from the age I was anointed'. This great passage in Proverbs 8, takes the reader back to 'the beginning', 'before His works of old', 'or ever the earth was', 'while as yet He had not made the earth', 'when He prepared the heavens'. 'The Lord possessed Me in the beginning of His way' (Prov. 8:22). The verb 'to possess' occurs for the first time in

Genesis 4:1, where Eve said 'I have gotten a man — Jehovah' (see *Companion Bible*). The verb is *qanah* and gives us the name 'Cain', which in the Hebrew is spelt with a Q. Eve at a cost (Gen. 3:16) had acquired Cain, the one she fondly imagined was the promised seed who should bruise the serpent's head. In this she was mistaken but the element of suffering in the acquiring is nevertheless a fact to be remembered. *Qanah* is used mostly in connection with the 'buying' or 'purchasing' of land, and especially in connection with the office of the Kinsman-Redeemer. The idea of acquisition at some cost is present in every occurrence of the word and this brings us back to Proverbs 8. At the 'beginning of His way' before creation itself came into being a redemptive note is sounded. It was a condescension for God Who is Absolute to stoop to make contact with the limitations of the conditioned.

However wonderful the titles of the Lord may seem to us, it was a self-emptying of Himself for Him to assume the condition indicated by the title 'The image of the invisible God'; 'The brightness of His glory'; 'The express image of His person'; 'The Word'. This condescension anticipated creation, even as the *kenosis* subsequently preceded redemption. This leads us to Proverbs 8:23 'I was *poured out as a drink offering* from the age, from the beginning or ever the earth was'.

We do not intend to suggest that we comprehend all that we have brought forward, we felt that at least we should put the reader in possession of the facts; but for ourselves, our attitude in view of what little we have glimpsed, is to put our grammars and lexicons aside, take off our shoes from off our feet, and recognize that the place upon which we stand is holy ground.

The superb 'hazard' of Epaphroditus

By his references to Timothy and Epaphroditus (Phil. 2:19-30) the apostle rounds off his illustrations of 'the mind which was in Christ Jesus'.

'But I trust in the Lord Jesus to send Timotheus shortly unto you'.

'Him therefore I hope to send presently, so soon as I shall see how it will go with me'.

'I trust in the Lord that I also myself shall come shortly'.

'Yet I supposed it necessary to send to you Epaphroditus'.

The movement of the apostle's mind is made clear by these passages. He was confident that he would be spared to serve a little longer (Phil. 1:24,25), but until his release was officially announced he must remain a prisoner. In order that the Philippians may know the affairs of the apostle and that he also might likewise hear of theirs and be comforted, he planned to send Timothy. However, even though he planned to send Timothy 'shortly' it was useless sending him until Paul could definitely see 'how it will go with' him. Consequently he fell back upon the good offices of yet another messenger in Epaphroditus whose longing to return to the Philippians is explained. Intertwined with this very human account of plans projected and postponed, we learn something of the character of these two men, and the characters that are revealed provide further illustrations of that spirit of selflessness which the apostle had inculcated in Philippians 2:4, and shown in the great example of the Lord Himself, and had supplemented by his own attitude to the service of the faith.

The apostle possibly looks back to what he had said in verse 12, when he urged the Philippians to some measure of independence during his absence. He assures them now, that he did not intend leaving them without some spiritual assistance, hence the plan to send Timothy. Timothy is seen as an example to the Philippians in the words employed by the apostle in commending him :

'I have no man likeminded who will naturally care for your state'.

Isopsuchon, 'equal soul' or 'like-minded', was a word with which Timothy would have been familiar by the reading of the LXX. It occurs in Psalm 55:13 'a man ... mine acquaintance' (Margin Heb., a man according to my rank), the Hebrew word meaning 'estimation' in the sense of a money equivalent, and so translated twenty-one times in one chapter of the law, i.e. Leviticus 27.

This would lend a certain weight to the thought that Paul was comparing Timothy with himself. On the other hand, Lightfoot says *'likeminded*, not with St. Paul himself, as it is generally taken, but with Timotheus', and gives his reasons by supplying the words that Paul would have to have used to give the word *isopsuchon* this meaning. It is possibly a moot point, but the fact remains whether the comparison be between Paul and Timothy, or between Timothy and others, that he was exceptional. There were no others then present wrote the apostle 'who will naturally care for your state'.

'For all seek their own, not the things which are Jesus Christ's' (Phil. 2:21).

'Their own'. The apostle uses the same word that we find in Philippians 2:4. The 'all' cannot include such faithful fellow workers as Epaphroditus or Luke the Beloved Physician, it is rather a generalizing upon the nature of humanity, 'all' naturally 'seek their own'. Timothy was an exception: he 'naturally' cared for the state of others.

The apostle advances a further proof of the character of Timothy.

'But ye know the proof of him, that, as a son with the father, he hath served with me in the gospel' (Phil. 2:22).

A man may honourably serve as a servant does a Master (Col. 3:22-24) and in that capacity he can 'serve the Lord Christ', but the highest form of service is that which is seen in the ministry of the Lord. While indeed He took on

Him the form of a servant there was nothing servile about His obedience. He indeed 'served as a Son with the Father' and no higher conception of service is to be found either in the pages of Scripture or in the testimony of experience. This digression on the quality of Timothy's service is in keeping with the theme of the epistle. As we have seen, Philippians is the epistle of service (Phil. 1:1).

The word *dokime* 'proof' (Phil. 2:22) finds its correspondence in 2 Timothy 2:15, *dokimos* 'approved', where Timothy is addressed as 'a workman', service still being uppermost.

The date of Timothy's journey to Philippi being somewhat dependent upon the apostle's knowledge of his affairs, and seeing that another faithful messenger was already eager to return to that city, the apostle speaks of the bearer of the epistle, Epaphroditus.

Bloomfield expands the apostle's thought thus :

'But (since these things, though probable are uncertain, that you might not be any longer ignorant of the state of my affairs), I judge it necessary to send Epaphroditus, though he be not quite restored to health; yet lest you should hear any false tidings of my fate, or his, I thought better to send him now, without waiting for another opportunity'.

It is a well established fact that Epaphras is an accepted contraction of Epaphroditus, even as Silas is of Sylvanus, or Apollos of Apollodorus.

It has been a matter of speculation as to whether Epaphras (Col. 1:7) and Epaphroditus (Phil. 2:25) are not one and the same person. Epaphras was a native of Colosse, 'one of you' (Col. 4:12), but Epaphroditus is not so called when writing to the Philippians. Both Epaphras and Epaphroditus are described by the apostle in similar terms. Epaphras is described as 'our dear fellowservant who is for you a faithful minister of Christ', while Epaphroditus is described 'my brother and companion in labour, and fellowsoldier, but your messenger, and he that ministered to my wants'.

But these things prove nothing. Epaphras may have been another fellow servant, quite distinct from Epaphroditus. Both names were very common. We will therefore confine ourselves to the record in Philippians. Epaphroditus 'had hazarded his life', or had 'not regarded his life', that he might supply the service which the Philippians were prevented from rendering to the apostle.

The Received Text of Philippians 2:30 reads *parabouleusamenos* 'regarding', but the critical texts read *paraboleusamenos* 'hazarding' and this has been accepted without comment in the Revised Version.

As a law term *parabolos* was the deposit made in an appeal case as a security, and so a 'stake'. There is, however, the possibility that the apostle when speaking of 'the hazard' run by Epaphroditus was indulging in a gracious piece of word-play. Before the reader can expect to follow this possible play on words, a little digression will be necessary.

First, the reader will perceive that the name Epaphroditus contains the name of the goddess Aphrodite, the Roman Venus. Secondly, we must remember that the apostle was well acquainted with the game of dice, for he uses it in Ephesians 4:14, where the word 'sleight' is the translation of the Greek *kubeia* 'dice', from which comes the English word 'cube'; the word dice is the plural of the word 'die', the 'die' giving us the figure 'the die is cast'.

Dice, similar to those in present use were found at Herculaneum, where the gamesters were overwhelmed at the time of the destruction of Pompeii.

The game of dice was so popular that the Emperor Augustus wrote a treatise on it. We learn that the highest throw, three sixes was called *Aphrodite* or *Venus* (cf. the 'love' terms in tennis), the three aces being the lowest possible throw and called 'the dog'.

Augustus wrote 'whoever threw a dog or a six paid a denarius to the bank for every die, and whoever threw a Venus won everything'. Mark Antony wasted his time at Alexandria, playing dice, and the Emperor Claudius wrote a book on the game.

Now in Philippians we have the terms 'win' (3:8), 'loss' (3:8), 'hazard' (2:30), 'one thing' (3:13), 'prize' (3:14), 'Venus' (*Epaphroditus* 2:25) and 'dogs' (3:2).

We can of course not prove from these allusive notes that Paul did actually use the hazard of the game of dice to comment upon, and to commend the greater hazard run by Epaphroditus. We do know that he had no scruples in using the game of dice to illustrate his point (Eph. 4:14), any more than he had any reservation in using most fully the language of the Greek sports, including terms associated with the boxing ring (1 Cor. 9:24-27) and the theatre (1 Cor. 4:9, 'spectacle' being in the Greek *theatron*) and that it could be in entire accord with his custom, thus to seize upon the associations of the name Epaphroditus and the 'hazard' he had run to encourage both this servant of the Lord and all who learned of his example, thus to 'win Christ'.

The fact that no miracle of healing was wrought upon Epaphroditus in spite of the intense anxiety his illness caused the apostle, demands some very definite explanation.

We believe that we have no call to labour this point. Granting the Dispensational boundary of Acts 28, and taking this fact to its logical conclusion, we already know that any attempt to put into operation Pentecostal conditions in the absence and dismissal of the Pentecostal People (Israel) is entirely unscriptural because undispensational.

CHAPTER 7

All Things Loss

Philippians 3:1-10

Chapter 3 opens with the word 'finally'. The word is repeated in chapter 4:8, and as the matter stands in the Authorized Version it looks as though the apostle was bringing his epistle to a conclusion, when further teaching demanded an extension. That Paul occasionally does make an extension with what looks like an after thought, the parenthesis of Ephesians 3:2-13 illustrates.

Many commentators and translators, however, feel that 'finally' is not a suitable translation for the words *to loipon*. Moffatt's translation reads 'well then', and Dr. Macknight's is 'now my brethren', with the comment, '*to loipon* is put for *kata to loipon* "as for what remains"'. 'Now then, besides, moreover, it remaineth, and henceforth' are employed in the Authorized Version as well as 'finally' to interpret these words, and they adhere more closely to the basic meaning of *loipos*, which means something 'left' from *leipo* 'to leave' or 'to lack' (Luke 18:22). Where *loipos* occurs elsewhere in Philippians it is translated 'other' (1:13; 4:3).

It is therefore unnecessary to create a difficulty by translating the words *to loipon* here 'finally', when a translation that adheres more closely to the basic meaning makes far better sense. We accordingly translate Philippians 3:1

'As to what remains, brethren, rejoice in the Lord',

the ground of that rejoicing being the theme, discussed both negatively and positively throughout the remainder of chapter 3.

Two Greek words are employed by the apostle in this exhortation to rejoice, *chairo* and *kauchaomai*. The first word *chairo* is a word of sheer joy. The second word *kauchaomai* belongs to a different family; it means 'to boast, vaunt, brag'. *Chairo* occurs in Philippians 1:18; 2:17,18,28; 3:1; 4:4,10. In the form *sugchairo* 'to rejoice together' it is found twice, Philippians 2:17,18. *Chara*, joy itself, occurs in Philippians 1:4,25; Phil. 2:2,29 and 4:1. *Eucharisteo* reveals its association with thanksgiving, Philippians 1:3; 4:6. *Charis* 'grace' Philippians 1:2,7; 4:23 shows how essentially the rejoicing inculcated by the apostle is separated from any confidence in the flesh. Finally *charizomai* 'to graciously give' (Phil. 1:29; 2:9) completes the references to this root in Philippians.

The second word *kauchaomai* is not so prolific. As a verb it occurs in Philippians 3:3; as a noun in Philippians 1:26 and 2:16.

'To write the same things to you, to me indeed is not grievous, but for you it is safe' (Phil. 3:1).

'I am repeating this word "rejoice" in my letter, but that does not tire me and it is a safe course for you' (Moffatt's Translation).

It will be seen from this extract from Moffatt that he has decided that the words 'the same things' refer to the exhortation to rejoice. Some commentators think that the apostle refers to what he is about to say, namely 'Beware'. Alford says on this matter :

'*Charein* is in fact the ground tone of the whole Epistle, see 1:18; 2:17; 4:4, where *palin ego* "again I say", seems to refer back again to this saying. So that there is no difficulty in imagining that the apostle may mean *chairete* "rejoice", by the *ta auta* "these things"'.

It seems therefore that the apostle refers to his repeated exhortations to rejoice in the Lord, which he now expands and explains.

First he says that to himself, such a repetition was not 'grievous'. Secondly, he says that for the Philippians, such a repetition was 'safe'.

Okneros 'grievous'. Of persons it means slothful; of things, tedious (Matt. 25:26; Rom. 12:11). The grammarians derive the word from *ou kinein* 'not moving' (from which comes the modern 'cinema') and suggests

delay, tediousness, hindrance, rather than grief. In effect
Paul assures the Philippians that repetition need not hinder
progress in truth, it may even help, for, said he, it was
'safe' *asphales*, which is a compound of *a*, a negative, and
sphalo 'to supplant, to trip up the heels'.

The words *asphalos* and *asphaloo* are found in the LXX
version of Genesis 6:14 where we read that Noah was
instructed 'to pitch' the ark within and without 'with
pitch'. The word has come into our own language as
'asphalt', a bituminous substance used for the surface of
roads.

The positive form of the word *asphales* does not occur
in the New Testament. The LXX employs *sphaleros*
'slippery' in Proverbs 5:6, where the Authorized Version
reads 'her ways are moveable'.

It will be seen that the apostle chose an apt word when
he wrote to the Philippians. He was about to speak of a
race and a prize, and prefaces his exhortation not only by
his own example, but by the choice of a word that was
used of a 'slippery path' and of being 'tripped up by the
heels'. Moffatt's translation, 'a safe course', therefore will
be the more fully appreciated by the reader who knows the
associations of the word translated 'safe' with a pathway.

The apostle now gives a threefold warning 'beware'.
'Beware' stands for three phases of awareness in the New
Testament. It translates *phulasso* 'to be on guard', it
translates *prosecho* 'to take heed', and it translates *blepo*
'to behold, or to see'. 'See', as in the exhortation to walk
circumspectly in Ephesians 5:15, 'look to yourselves', as
in 2 John 8. It is this word that is used by the apostle in the
third chapter of Philippians.

The word of warning is directed to three potential
dangers, or perhaps a threefold potential danger.

'Beware of dogs, beware of evil workers, beware of the concision'.

The Rabbinical writings reveal that the Jews referred to the Gentiles as 'dogs'. Midrash Tillin says 'the nations of the world are likened to dogs'. However, even the Talmudists said that the last days would be characteristic of corruption and apostasy, for the Babylonian Talmud says of Israel in the days when the Messiah comes 'the faces of that generation shall be as dogs'.

'This ignominious name, like a stone cast at the heathen, at length fell upon their own heads' (Lightfoot).

The dispensational place of Israel at the time when Philippians was written was *lo-ammi* 'not My people', but the apostle's words here show that Israel were not merely marking time, they were fast degenerating, the title once used to speak of the outside Gentile now being used of them, and used by one who by race and upbringing was an Israelite himself!

The Philippians are warned of 'evil workers'. The Lord tells us Himself that He will say to some who had eaten and drunk in His presence, 'depart from Me, all ye workers of iniquity' (Luke 13:27).

The stress seems not so much on evil doers, but of those 'who actually wrought, professedly for the Gospel' (Alford) and throws into prominence 'the workman' commended in 2 Timothy 2:15. The apostle uses the word translated 'workers' of his fellow labourers who were in many cases 'fellow teachers' (Rom. 16:3; Phil. 2:25; 4:3). In the third case these evil workers are called 'the concision'. *Katatome* is an intended disparagement, 'circumcision' being *peritome* and 'rightly dividing' being *orthotomeo*, each word being a variant of *temno* 'to cut'.

Circumcision, instead of being an honourable sign, a sign of covenant relationship with God, and a sign of self denial in the flesh, had degenerated to a mere ostentatious barbarity, and so far had Israel fallen, that the apostle uses of them the identical word found in the LXX for the

forbidden 'cutting in the flesh' (Lev. 21:5), practised by
the priests of Baal (1 Kings 18:28) and the heathen.

The true meaning of circumcision as over against this
degeneration had already been made known when writing
to the Romans.

> 'For he is not a Jew, which is one outwardly; neither is that
> circumcision, which is outward in the flesh, but he is a Jew, which
> is one inwardly; and circumcision is that of the heart, in the spirit,
> and not in the letter; whose praise is not of men, but of God' (Rom.
> 2:28,29).

In Colossians the apostle advances a further statement
concerning the true intent of circumcision :

> 'In Whom also ye are circumcised with the circumcision made
> without hands, in putting off the body of the sins of the flesh by the
> circumcision of Christ' (Col. 2:11).

But in Philippians he brings the spiritual teaching of
true circumcision to its climax, and just as he uses the
word 'beware' three times, associating the warning with
'dogs', 'evil workers' and 'the concision', so now he
expands the character of true circumcision in a threefold
description:

> 'For we are the circumcision, which worship God in the spirit, and
> rejoice in Christ Jesus, and have no confidence in the flesh' (Phil.
> 3:3).

The idea of worship should be confined to the word
proskuneo, which is so translated in the Authorized
Version of the New Testament sixty times. In Philippians
3 the apostle uses the word *latreuo* which, while it is
translated in the New Testament 'worship' four times, is
rendered 'serve' sixteen times and 'do service' once.*

The word has been variously derived. One
Lexicographer says that it comes from the word *tromou*
meaning 'to tremble', as of servants (Eph. 6:5). Another
says that it is derived from *latris*, 'to serve for hire'. In

---

* See articles entitled 'Worship' in *The Berean Expositor*, Vols. 33-35.

classical Greek the primary meaning of *latreuo* is 'to work for hire', and the secondary meaning 'to serve the gods'. The reader will see that *latreuo* enters into the composition of the word 'idolatry', the 'service' of that which is 'seen'.

Philippians as we have seen is the epistle of service. It is addressed by Paul and Timothy in the capacity of 'servants', not only to the believers at the Church at Philippi, but to 'the Bishops and Deacons'. Worship (*proskuneo*) is in spirit (John 4:23) and service (*latreuo*) is in spirit also (Phil. 3:3). We serve (*douleuo*) in newness of spirit (Rom. 7:6). Our Christian life began in the spirit (Gal. 3:3), and we are exhorted to walk in the spirit (Gal. 5:16).

In the realm of the spirit there can be no boasting in the flesh. This is the first mark of true circumcision, consequently the apostle continues :

'and rejoice in Christ Jesus' (Phil. 3:3).

As we have already observed the true Greek word meaning 'rejoice' is found in Philippians 3:1, but the word so translated in chapter 3:3 means rather 'to boast'. In every day use, *kauchaomai* means 'to brag'. Some Lexicons deduce the word from *auchen* 'the neck, which', says Parkhurst, 'proud, vain-glorious persons are apt to carry and toss in a remarkable manner'. So the Psalmist (Psa. 75:5), 'speak not with a stiff (retorted) neck' (compare Isa. 3:16).

If this derivation be true then Paul has used words twice which employ the use of the neck figuratively. In chapter 1:20, the word 'earnest expectation', *apokaradokia*, means 'to look forward expectantly, as with the neck stretched out, and the head thrust forward'. In one case it is the figure of the athlete, in the other the figure of a braggart that is evoked by the word used. The one commended, the other condemned.

We can understand the choice of this word *kauchaomoi* in Galatians 6:14, 'God forbid that I should glory (boast), save in the cross of our Lord Jesus Christ'. This is the second mark of true circumcision. The third mark is the negative statement 'and have no confidence in the flesh' (Phil. 3:3). Paul had already shown that his confidence was in the Lord (Phil. 1:6,25; 2:24), here he is but restating the fact in negative terms.

The mention, however, of any confidence in the flesh makes the apostle think of his past days as a Pharisee and leads him to give the great 'profit and loss' account which occupies verses 4-9. This passage is both structurally and doctrinally in correspondence with the passage of Philippians 2:6-11, and must be given separate and careful attention.

Boasting in the flesh 'I more'

In the opening of this section, which commences with verse one of chapter 3, the apostle has declared positively that the true believer 'boasts' in Christ Jesus and then puts the matter negatively saying that such has 'no confidence in the flesh'. From one point of view, this is true of all men. No man really has any ground of confidence in himself, but, alas, countless millions have never learned this most fundamental of lessons. Moreover, in Philippians the apostle is not dealing so much with foundation truth as with the believer's subsequent outworking of the grace already bestowed upon him. Consequently we have in Philippians, the 'prize' rather than the 'hope', and the figure of the athlete and the race course is employed to enforce the great example of Christ which has already been given in chapter 2. While it may be universally true that no man has any ground of confidence in the flesh, the special purpose of Philippians demands that this shall not be accepted merely as a truism, but as a truth associated with intelligent and experimental co-operation. From this angle if the words are to ring true, the apostle feels that something personal is called for so that the condition 'no confidence in the flesh' shall be the better appreciated. It could be recorded to the credit of

Moses, that he 'refused to be called the son of Pharaoh's daughter' *because the offer had been made to him.* No such credit could be given to his brother Aaron, for no such opportunity had opened to him. The apostle evidently felt that it was necessary that he should show that this repudiation of any boasting in the flesh was something more than the proverbial attitude to 'sour grapes' and so he proceeds to show that if any other man thought that he had a ground of confidence in the flesh, then, he, the apostle, could beat him in his boasting, he could say 'I more'. *Mallon* is the comparative of *mala* 'much', the superlative being *malista*, which comes in Philippians 4:22 and is translated 'chiefly'. The English 'more' is used to translate a variety of Greek words, *eti* is related to time or endurance, *pleion* with bulk, *perissos* with abundance and *meizon* with magnitude, but *mallon* is expressed best by the adverb 'rather', as will be found in such passages as Ephesians 4:28; 5:4,11 and also in Philippians 1:12. The adjective 'rathe' has dropped out of common use, but most readers will call to mind Milton's phrase 'the rathe primrose' which means 'early, premature, coming before others, or before the usual time'. Now in an epistle which uses the figure of a race course, the use of *mallon* 'rather' is pointed, far more so than words that mean bulk or abundance, and while the idiom of our language will not permit the translation 'I rather', it should be retained in the back of the mind, and Moffatt's translation 'I can outdo him', though far from being literal, retains the sense in a way that no literal rendering can do.

Writing to the Galatians, with another purpose in view, the apostle had said that he 'profited in the Jew's religion above many my equals in mine own nation' (Gal. 1:14), or as Moffatt renders the passage, 'how I outstripped many of mine own age and race', where again the word *prokopto* translated 'profited' or 'outstripped' is a word of progress.

The apostle substantiates this claim, by advancing evidence under three heads :

(1) *He was a pure Israelite*, circumcised the eighth day, of the stock of Israel of the tribe of Benjamin, a Hebrew of the Hebrews.

(2) *He was by conviction* a Pharisee and a persecutor of the church.

(3) *He was in person* 'blameless' so far as the righteousness of the law was concerned.

In some contexts such a catalogue would be no commendation. The Roman would say with Pilate 'Am I a Jew?' or with Gallio, that he 'cared for none of these things'. The Greek would consider that his philosophers ranked much higher than the Jewish prophets and would reckon the claims of Paul to be 'foolishness'. Writing to believers, however, the apostle's claims would be forceful.

The apostle was not only circumcised, but had been circumcised the eighth day, the emphasis being upon 'the eighth day'. In this respect Paul had the advantage of a proselyte who would naturally not be circumcised until later in life, and by this rite he was in covenant with the God of Abraham. Further, he was of 'the stock' of Israel (*genos*). He was of this genus, race, family, lineage. He could not only say 'I was born free', he could say 'I am by birth an Israelite', he was one of the true and favoured seed. Abraham had other descendants such as those of Ishmael and those of Esau, but none of these could lay claim to the peculiar and privileged name of Israelite.

The Roman Governor gave the title to the crucified Saviour, 'King of the Jews', but the Lord's own countrymen use the more exclusive title 'King of Israel' (Matt. 27:29,37,42). In these things the apostle could boast that he was ahead of his contemporaries. There were, moreover, differences of degree within the favoured ranks of Israel, for some of the tribes went early into idolatry and captivity, leaving Judah and Benjamin to hold the fort at Jerusalem. Paul moreover claimed that he was an 'Hebrew of the Hebrews'. The title Hebrew in the Old Testament is used by Gentiles to indicate the people of

Israel and is never used by Israel without some sense of national antagonism. In the New Testament the word changed its meaning a little, and is placed in contrast with *Hellenistes*, 'Grecians', Greek speaking Jews (Acts 6:1). Paul not only claims that both of his parents were of pure stock, but that although he was born at Tarsus in Cilicia, and not in Palestine, he was nevertheless not to be reckoned as an *Hellenist*, being a Jew through and through. In addition to all this, Paul had been a Pharisee. In Acts 26:5 he said of himself 'that after the most straitest (strictest) sect of our religion I lived a Pharisee'. On another occasion he said 'I am a Pharisee, the son of a Pharisee'. At this distance and with the conception usually entertained by believers today, there was little ground for boasting in Paul's claim to be a Pharisee, for the word has passed into common speech to indicate 'conceit', 'self-righteousness', 'hypocrisy' and 'formalism'. Now no one in his senses would include in a list of excellencies, the claim that he was a 'conceited, self-righteous, hypocritical formalist' — the title Pharisee therefore must have had other connotations in Paul's day. Josephus in the introduction to his works, says of the Pharisees 'I ... began to conduct myself according to the rules of the sect of the Pharisees, which is kin to the sect of the Stoics as the Greeks call them'.

The boast of Paul and the context of the above quotation from Josephus shows that there was another side to Pharisaism than that which is popularly supposed. The Talmud enumerates seven different kinds mostly hypocritical and mean. The 'Shechemite' Pharisee obeyed the law merely out of self interest; the *Nitki* 'trembling' Pharisee outdid 'Uriah Heep' in false humility; the *Kinai* or 'bleeding' Pharisee, hurt himself continually by walking into walls and posts, because, forsooth, he was so modest that lest he should see a woman, he walked with eyes fixed upon the ground! But there was another class of Pharisee who were 'Pharisees from love', actuated by a feverish anxiety to fulfil the law, the title given them in the Talmud being expressed by Dean Farrar in the words 'Tell-me-anything-more-to-do-and-I-will-do-it-Pharisee'.

The name Pharisee is derived from the Hebrew *parash* 'to separate', and Paul seems to allude to this meaning when in Romans 1:1 he says of himself, 'separated' unto the gospel of God, the Greek *aphorismenos* resembling the *sound* of the word Pharisee as well as sharing its meaning. The Pharisees overloaded the law with minute scruples, they strained at gnats yet swallowed camels, they set themselves an impossible task, and then set about devising ways in which their self imposed task could be avoided.

'Under the dignified exterior of the Pharisee lay a wildly beating heart; an anxious brain throbbed with terrible questionings under the broad phylactery ... in all the struggle to achieve his own righteousness – this struggle so minutely tormenting, so revoltingly burdensome – there seemed no hope, no help, no enlightenment, no satisfaction' (Dean Farrar).

Such a moral conflict forces the sufferer to extreme attempts at self-justification, and this is often expressed by extra zeal in persecuting those who differ.

Paul had consented to the death of Stephen, yet could he ever forget that forgiving spirit, that face like an angel, that masterly and convincing résumé of Israel's history? Yet, to allow such thought a moment's space was suicidal, he must crush out this disturbing questioning by greater zeal, hence his request for permission to extend his inquisition even to Damascus.

'Concerning zeal persecuting the church' (Phil. 3:6).

The word translated 'persecute' is the Greek *dioko*. The word means 'to pursue' and is used in Philippians 3:12, 'follow after' and 3:14 'press toward' in its primitive meaning. At first sight this fact gives colour to the suggestion that in Philippians 3:6 Paul is not speaking of *persecuting* the church, but of his zeal in *pursuing* it with the intent that he may become a member. Philippians, however, is not the only epistle that employs *dioko* in two meanings. This double usage is found in 1 Corinthians.

'*Follow* after charity' (1 Cor. 14:1), 'being *persecuted*, we suffer it' (1 Cor. 4:12) and 'I am ... not meet to be called an apostle because I *persecuted* the church of God' (1 Cor. 15:9).

In Galatians we have a parallel with the apostle's ground of boasting 'in the Jew's religion' which we have been studying in Philippians 3, and here we are left in no doubt as to his meaning, he says 'I persecuted the church of God and WASTED IT' (Gal. 1:13). The five occurrences of *dioko* in Galatians are all translated 'persecute' (Gal. 1:13,23;   4:29;   5:11;   6:12), concerning which no alternative is possible.

The substantive *diogmos* is translated 'persecution' in its nine occurrences, as *dioktes* is translated 'persecutor' in its one occurrence (1 Tim. 1:13), even though in 1 Timothy 6:11 *dioko* is once again rendered 'follow' in a good sense.

The primitive meaning 'pursue' is colourless. What one pursues, and why, is left to the context to decide. A man may pursue a method, a plan, a course of studies or he may pursue a fugitive, or a legal action, and in English, as in the Greek, pursue and persecute are both derived from the same root word, and the same fallacious argument which mistranslates Philippians 3 might just as well be used when explaining these two allied English words.

It is clear that both in Galatians 1 and in Philippians 3 the apostle introduces the persecution of the church as one of a series of proofs of his intense Pharisaic zeal, a zeal which culminates in Philippians 3 with the claim 'touching the righteousness which is in the law, blameless' (Phil. 3:6).

Paul does not assert here that which he so continually disproves, that either he or anyone could attain unto righteousness by the works of the law, he says that so far as a zealous conformity to all that the law demanded, as viewed from the standpoint of a Hebrew and a Pharisee, his manner of life was beyond reproach. Here he reaches the summit of his excellencies. Concerning his race he was an Israelite, concerning his tribe the honoured tribe of Benjamin, concerning the law a Pharisee, concerning zeal a persecutor, concerning that righteousness which was in the law blameless. Here, said Paul, is a catalogue of excellencies, a ground of boasting in the flesh which defies competition. As in the Epistle to the Corinthians the apostle confessed that he had become a fool in his boasting, so here, he no sooner completes the enumeration of his excellencies while a Pharisee, than he reveals their utter worthlessness when seen in the light of Christ and His great salvation. All that we have seen is the justification of the apostle's 'I more', but we now are to learn his true estimate of these fleshly attainments.

All things counted loss

The Saviour, in condescending mercy, laid aside unspeakable glory when He took upon Himself the form of a servant and the fashion of a man; Paul's repudiation of those things that were gain for Christ is indeed put in structural correspondence with the great example of chapter 2:6-8, but, oh! the poverty of the comparison. Paul exchanged empty shadows for Divine substance, formalism for grace, vanity and vexation for glory beyond dreams, yet this example must suffice – so infinite is the distance between the Lord and the greatest of His followers. While circumcision, and the purity of his stock is enumerated, the whole seeming advantage of his earlier position is focused on the idea of that righteousness which is in the law. So, when he now repudiates all his so-called gains, he specifies none except that righteousness of God which is by faith, summing up all his gains in that one blessed fact.

In one sense Paul and his Master have something in common. Christ gave up His own things (Phil. 2:4-8) and Paul gave up his own righteousness which is of the law, but there the parallel ends, for such a righteousness is described in the Scriptures that Saul the Pharisee believed, to be but 'filthy rags' (Isa. 64:6).

'But what things were gain to me, those I counted loss for Christ' (Phil. 3:7).

With these words Paul turns from any ground of confidence in the flesh that at any time he may have held, gladly to relinquish every real and imagined advantage for the excellency of the knowledge of Christ Jesus his Lord.

The depth of the apostle's feeling is revealed in little grammatical points and items of emphasis. For instance 'gain' is really plural, whereas loss instead of being in the plural, and so rendering the passage ordinary, is in the singular. Then the apostle does not say that these things 'are' but 'were' gain – it is all a matter of the past. The word 'loss' is put by the apostle at the very end of the sentence for the sake of emphasis. Paul is here making out, perhaps, the most wonderful balance sheet ever prepared by man. Here is his 'profit and loss' account. Here is Paul's estimate. Six times does the apostle use the verb *hegeomai*, and these occurrences are important enough to justify their inclusion here.

'Let each *esteem* other better than themselves' (2:3).

'Who ... *thought* it not robbery to be equal with God' (2:6).

'Yet I *supposed* it necessary to send ... Epaphroditus' (2:25).

'Those I *counted* loss for Christ' (3:7).

'Yea, doubtless, and I *count* all things but loss' (3:8).

'And do *count* them but dung' (3:8).

It will be seen that these references fall into two groups. The exercise of this discrimination on the behalf of others, and the exercise of this discrimination both by Christ Himself and by the apostle.

A (2:3). The esteeming of the things of others as of prior importance.

B (2:6). Christ's attitude to being on equality with God.

A (2:25). The esteeming of the needs of the Philippians.

B (3:7,8). Paul's attitude to whatever he once prized under the law.

We have already seen the parallel that exists between Philippians and Hebrews, we shall not therefore be surprised – but recognize with joy the consistency of Truth – to find that Hebrews contains the words translated 'esteem' six times also, other epistles of Paul containing but one occurrence each. In Hebrews 11:24-26 we have the example :

> 'By faith Moses, when he was come to years, refused to be called the son of Pharaoh's daughter; choosing rather to suffer affliction with the people of God, than to enjoy the pleasures of sin for a season; *esteeming* the reproach of Christ greater riches than the treasures of Egypt; for he had respect unto the recompence of the reward'.

'When he was come to years'. In every other occurrence of *megas* in the epistles of Paul, as in the rest of Hebrews, the word is translated 'great'. The word seems to have been chosen in order that a two-fold truth might be stated.

Moses had become great, so great that he could have become heir to the throne of Egypt had he so chosen. Yet he voluntarily exchanged such dazzling greatness for a long life of labour and reproach. This use of the word *megas* is justified by a reference to the LXX of Genesis 26:13. There is, however, warrant for the Authorized Version, the Revised Version endorsing it by the translation 'when he had grown up'. An instance from classical Greek is found in Homer's Odysseus 2 verse 314, where Telemachus, the son of Odysseus, who was an infant when his father left for Troy, after twenty years, says :

'I was an infant but now I am grown up' *(nun epee de megas eimi)*.

This is the only possible rendering of *genital megas* in the LXX of Genesis 38:11, 'be grown'. Moses' act is set over against that of his parents when he was a babe. Hebrews places the position of a babe over against that of the 'perfect', or arriving at adulthood, and so by these interrelated references we see that Moses had reached 'perfection', as the term is used both in Hebrews and in Philippians.

In Hebrews 11:24 the apostle is actually quoting from the LXX of Exodus 2:11, where the Hebrew original uses the same words that are found in Genesis 38:11. Moses' action is described as a 'refusal' and a 'choosing' because of an 'esteeming' and a 'respecting'.

The refusal employs the word *random*, generally translated 'deny'. In Matthew 10:33 and in 2 Timothy 2:12, the 'refusing' or 'denying' is the denying of the Lord by the believer with consequent loss of reward or crown. In Acts 7:35 Stephen employs the self same word when he said that Israel 'refused' Moses at the first time. It would therefore appear by comparing the records of Acts 7, Exodus 2, and Hebrews 11, that the refusal or denial was mutual. Moses was denied or refused by Israel. He would not deny nor refuse his Lord, but denied or refused the offer of Egyptian greatness. Moses did not merely act negatively, he 'chose'. It is very probable that the apostle employs the figure known as *paronomasia* or rhyming words, *random* being the Greek word translated 'refuse' and *airwoman* the Greek word translated 'choose'.

Here, once again is a definite link with Philippians, the word being employed but once by the apostle elsewhere, and that in Philippians 1:22, 'what I shall choose I wot not', where the apostle's choice is most obviously parallel to that made by Moses. We have already shown that the words 'I more' of Philippians 3:4 translate the adverb *mallon* 'rather', and are not surprised to find the same word in Hebrews 11:25 'choosing *rather*'.

Moses 'chose rather' to suffer affliction with the people of God, esteeming the reproach for Christ greater riches than the treasures of Egypt. In this he acted as Paul did. In the sequel, we find the apostle placing over against all the 'gains' which he had as an Israelite and a Pharisee, the desire that he might know the fellowship of the sufferings of Christ, and be made conformable unto His death. In both cases there is nothing morbid about such a choice, for Hebrews 11 frankly tells us that Moses had respect unto the recompence of the reward, even though he chose to suffer, and Philippians 3 tells us that Paul had the 'out-resurrection' and 'the prize' in view.

We return to the epistle to the Philippians with our understanding enlightened by this inspired commentary.

'Yea doubtless, and I count all things but loss for the excellency of the knowledge of Christ Jesus my Lord; for Whom I have suffered the loss of all things, and do count them but dung, that I may win Christ' (Phil. 3:8).

In moments of ecstasy and excitement, high claims may be put forward which in calmer moments may call for great modification. The apostle knew this, and in Galatians, after saying 'But though we, or an angel from heaven, preach any other gospel unto you than that which we have preached unto you, let him be accursed', repeated the statement 'as we said before, so say I now again' (Gal. 1:8,9).

So here in Philippians 3. What he had once said he now repeats. He changes the verb from the perfect to the present, 'I do count' and expands 'what things ... those' into 'all things'. The word 'loss' *semi*, occurs in but two other passages in the New Testament namely, Acts 27:10 and 21, 'damage', 'loss', where the reference is to the wreck of the ship by which Paul was brought on his journey to Rome. The experiences of that journey left a deep impression upon the apostle's mind and provided him with imagery in preaching the truth which we are to discover again when considering the eleventh verse. When he says 'if by any means I might attain unto' (Phil. 3:11) he uses the words with a true feeling of the hazard that must be run, for these very words occur in Acts 27 (verse 12), and the consequent shipwreck was still vivid in the apostle's mind. The verb *semi* is found in a context parallel in theme with that of Philippians, namely in Matthew 16:26 and in 1 Corinthians 3:15. Far better, said the apostle, to suffer loss now, than to suffer loss when standing before the judgment seat of Christ. The word *semi* is used by Artaxerxes as recorded in the Septuagint, where we read :

> 'And whosoever shall not do the law of thy God, and the law of the king, let judgment be executed speedily upon him, whether it be unto death, or to banishment, or to *confiscation* of goods, or to imprisonment' (Ezra 7:26).

When writing to the Hebrews, the apostle included among the things which they had suffered for Christ's sake 'the spoiling' of their goods. This is but a variant of the 'confiscation' of goods and provides yet one further link with Philippians 2 and 3, for the verb 'to spoil' used in Hebrews 10:34, *wharfage* and the word 'robbery' *wharfages* of Philippians 2:6, are both derived from the same word and establish another correspondence between the great examples of Christ (Phil. 2) and that of the apostle (Phil. 3); the 'robbery' of the first passage being intentionally reflected in the 'loss' of the second.

While Josephus makes it clear that the Greek word *subalpine* can be translated 'dung' as is found in the Authorized Version, the Revisers have put in their margin 'refuse' which is adopted by most modern translators. Ecclesiasticus uses the word in connection with 'sifting with a sieve'. Dr. Bullinger says that the word is probably derived from *cushy balloon* 'to cast to dogs' and so 'refuse'. It would not be beyond the apostle to look back to his reference to 'dogs' in Philippians 3:2 and to think, that once, as a bigoted Pharisee he had called the Gentiles dogs, who were permitted but the 'crumbs' that fell from Israel's table, so now to confess a complete revulsion of feeling and liken all that the Jew valued most as so much refuse, fit only to be thrown to dogs. The apostle had a goal in view 'to die is gain', 'I press toward the mark for the prize', so here he expresses it 'that I may win Christ'.

We have discussed at some length these words 'that I may win Christ' on pages 52-57, where the parallel passage 'to die is gain' is examined. We will not repeat ourselves here, but would refer the reader back to the argument there set out to show in what way the apostle hoped to 'win' Christ. It is a truth that belongs to our present calling and is of vital importance to all who would run the race and finish the course.

Justification by faith, a fundamental doctrine

The apostle has given a detailed list of his 'gains' as pertaining to the flesh, and has announced that he counted all such gain as so much 'refuse' that he might win Christ. This new and blessed estimate he now proceeds to expand and he does so under a series of aspects of Divine truth :

(1) His position in Christ, and his perfect justification by faith (3:9).
(2) His desire to attain unto the resurrection of the dead (3:11).
(3) His reaching forth for the prize of the high calling (3:14).
(4) His heavenly citizenship (3:20).
(5) The future transfiguration of this 'vile' body (3:21).

'And be found in Him, not having mine own righteousness, which is of the law, but that which is through the faith of Christ, the righteousness which is of God by faith' (3:9).

It is evident by this passage that the apostle saw that all his early 'gains' as a Jew and a Pharisee could be summed up under the heading 'the righteousness which is in the law'.

In Philippians 3:9 we have the apostle's own summary of his great doctrine 'Justification by faith without works of law'* as set out in the epistles – Galatians and Romans. This summary falls into two parts :

(1) Found in Him.
(2) Righteousness by faith. This second item is further subdivided.
  (*a*) Neg. Not mine own righteousness, which is of the law.
  (*b*) Poss. But that which is through the faith of Christ.

In its turn (*b*) is further distributed, thus :
  (*c*) This is a righteousness of God.
  (*d*) It is by faith.

'And be found in Him'. The word 'find' has several shades of meaning in the New Testament. It may be the finding that comes of seeking (Luke 15:4); or it may be a finding, without seeking, and by accident (Matt. 13:44). The word is used also of 'obtaining', 'computing', and 'knowing how'. There is, however, a further use, and one which bears upon Philippians 3:9, that is 'to find by a judicial enquiry'. So in Luke 23:2, 'we found this fellow'; Luke 23:4, 'I find no fault in this man'. The apostle uses the word in this sense in Galatians 2:17, 'we ourselves also are found sinners'. In view of the day of judgment and the need for a perfectly righteous standing before God, Paul had learned that even though he piled the scale high with his fancied gains, he would still, like Belshazzar, be 'found wanting'. When that day comes, he said, to be found in Him, will more than counterbalance all that the world could give, or the flesh could possibly gain.

As a sinner saved by grace Paul's one ground of hope was to be 'found' in Christ. As a servant entrusted with a stewardship, he realized that first and foremost it is required in stewards that they be 'found' faithful.

---

* For a full exposition of the doctrine of Justification, the reader is directed to the book by the author entitled *Just and the Justifier*.

The apostle summed up the blessedness of his new ground of acceptance under grace by the words 'in Him'. There are seven forms in which this position is expressed in the epistles of Paul.

(1) In Christ Jesus our Lord.   Rom. 8:39.
(2) In Christ Jesus.   Rom. 3:24; Gal. 3:14 (R.V.).
(3) In the Lord Jesus.   Eph. 1:15.
(4) In Jesus.   Eph. 4:21.
(5) In the Lord.   Eph. 4:1 (margin), Phil. 4:1.
(6) In Christ.   Eph. 1:3; Phil. 2:1.
(7) In Whom, in Him.   2 Cor. 5:21; Eph. 1:4,7.*

These references are but a selection of the many found in Paul's epistles under these headings and they are according to the Revised Text, which differs in many places from the Authorized Version.

It would take us too far afield to examine the distribution of these titles, but it does fall within our legitimate enquiry to observe how they are used in Philippians.

We observe that 'in the Lord' occurs eight times; 'in Christ Jesus', seven times; 'in Christ', four times; 'in Him', twice and 'in the Lord Jesus', once.

'In Christ Jesus' refers particularly to doctrinal truth and position by grace, whereas 'in the Lord' has reference rather to service. We are not surprised therefore to find that in Philippians, an epistle of service, the phrase 'in the Lord' is used far more frequently than those which refer to doctrine and position.

---

* The reader who wishes to continue and complete the comparisons between the epistle to the Ephesians and that to the Hebrews, should note that in addition to those already set out in the articles entitled 'Comparing Spiritual Things with Spiritual' in Vol. 24 of *The Berean Expositor*, should be recorded that not one of these seven forms is found in Hebrews.

The doctrinal idea contained in the phrase 'found in Him' is one aspect of a great truth variously expressed by the terms 'in Adam', 'in the flesh', 'in the world', 'in the law', 'in the spirit', 'in newness of life', 'in Isaac', 'in sin', 'in heavenly places' and the many other phrases that stress the question of position and sphere that is such a marked feature in the doctrine of the apostle.

When the apostle expressed his great desire 'to be found in Him', he was establishing yet another corresponding feature with the great example of Christ recorded in the second chapter. There it is written 'and being *found* in fashion as a man', which follows the great step down already indicated by the words 'was made in the likeness of men' (Phil. 2:7), as status follows nature. As we have already seen, 'found' often implies some sort of judicial finding and so the apostle institutes a most lovely contrast. When Christ was 'found' in fashion as a man, it led Him at length to the death of the Cross. When Paul is 'found' in Christ, it leads him to a perfectly righteous standing in His Lord. The rich fulness of this expression 'found in Him' is now expanded. The index of this position in Christ is Righteousness, but as the apostle had but recently spoken of his own righteousness which is in the law, his first motion is to repudiate it entirely, saying 'not having mine own righteousness, which is of the law', which he follows by the positive 'but that which is through the faith of Christ' (Phil. 3:9), which in its turn is explained to be (*a*) the righteousness of God, which is (*b*) by faith.

Let us not hastily pass over the words 'the faith of Christ'. The expression 'the faith of Jesus Christ' and its variants occur in Paul's epistles as follows :

'Even the righteousness of God which is by faith of Jesus Christ' (Rom. 3:22).

'By (Through) the faith of Jesus Christ ... justified by the faith of Christ' (Gal. 2:16).

'The promise by faith of Jesus Christ might be given to them that believe' (Gal. 3:22).

'Boldness and access with confidence by the faith of Him' (Eph. 3:12),

and the passage under review in Philippians 3:9.

The inter-relationship of these passages can be exhibited as follows, placing the epistles quoted in their chronological order, concerning which there is complete unanimity among authorities.

A_1	Gal. 2:16.	Justification by faith.	*Personal testimony.*
B_1	Gal. 3:22,23.	The Promise, to those 'shut up'.	
A_2	Rom. 3:22.	Justification by faith.	*Doctrinal statement.*
B_3	Eph. 3:12.	Access, to those 'far off'.	
A_3	Phil. 3:9.	Justification by faith.	*Personal testimony.*

It will be seen that not only are Galatians 2:16 and Philippians 3:9 in the nature of a personal testimony, but they both follow references to Paul's 'profit' (Gal. 1:14) or 'gain' (Phil. 3:7) in the Jew's religion. In Galatians 3:22, we are taken back in the context to a promise made four hundred and thirty years before the giving of the law, and in Ephesians 3, to a period called 'the beginning of the world'. The inter-relation of these passages is much more complex and illuminating than this cursory examination reveals, but while we cannot pursue the theme further here we commend the comparison to the earnest student.

We have omitted the reference to Romans 3:26, 'him which believeth in Jesus'. In the first place the Authorized Version does not give a satisfactory rendering of the original. Conybeare and Howson render the passage 'that He might be just and (yet) might justify the children of faith', saying in a footnote '*ton ek pistols* is not fully represented by the Authorized Version. It means "him whose essential characteristic is faith", "the child of faith"' (compare Gal. 3:7,9). The word *Yeses* is omitted by some of the best MSS. and is introduced in others with variations which look as if it had been originally an interpolation. It is omitted by Tischendorf.

The usual interpretation of the words 'the faith of Jesus Christ' makes them refer to the believer's faith in Christ. This, applied to Romans 3:22 would make it read :

'The righteousness of God has been manifested through the believer's faith in Jesus Christ'

which is not a true statement of doctrine.

In Romans 4:12 we have the expression 'that faith of our father Abraham', which cannot mean the believer's faith in Abraham, but Abraham's own faith.

In the LXX the Greek word *pistis* often means faithfulness and often translates the Hebrew words *emplane* and *Amman*. 'The faith of God' (Rom. 3:3) is practically synonymous with 'the truth of God' (Rom. 3:7); where *ek* is used in these references in the phrase *ek pistols* 'out of faith', it is set over against *ek gnome* 'out of law'. The righteousness which is reckoned to the believer, arises out of the utter faithfulness of Christ his Redeemer. The adjective *pistols* occurs some sixty-six times in the New Testament and over fifty of these occurrences are translated 'faithful'. While some passages use *ek*, Philippians 3:9 uses *dia*. The teaching of the apostle may be seen if set out as follows :

A   Not mine own righteousness which is *ek gnome*, 'out of law'.
  B   But that which is *dia pistols Christly*,
       'through faith of Christ'.
A   That righteousness which is *ek Theou*, 'out of God'.
  B   On the condition of faith, *epi Te pieties*.

Here are the two possible sources of righteousness, 'law' and 'God'. Here are the two channels of righteousness, through faith of Christ, and on condition of faith in Him.

Law as a source of righteousness is entirely repudiated by the apostle, leaving him the righteousness which is of God in which to glory. As the apostle has used both *ek* and *dia* in relation to 'the faith of Christ' it will be as well if we note the passages which contain the one or the other of these prepositions.

Dia   'through' is used in Galatians 2:16 (1st);
        Romans 3:22; Ephesians 3:12; Philippians 3:9.

Ek   'out of' is used in Galatians 2:16 (2nd) and
        Galatians 3:22.

Philippians 3:9 is of extreme importance for another reason. We do not find in Ephesians, Philippians or Colossians an exposition of the great doctrine 'justification by faith', for the apostle is there dealing, not with the foundations but with the superstructure.

It would be a false and dangerous inference, however, to deduce from the absence of the doctrine that the great foundation truth of the apostle's Gospel no longer obtained. The Church of the One Body needs a righteous standing and a salvation by grace, as surely as the believers of any other calling. Philippians 3:9 is the apostle's own résumé of this great truth, and its introduction into Philippians assures every believer that the basic teaching of Romans 1 to 5 is as fundamental to the revelation of the mystery as it is for the salvation of Israel.

CHAPTER 8

The Prize of the High Calling

Philippians 3:11-21

Paul the master builder, not only laid a foundation, he built thereon. Here, in Philippians the building is not salvation but rather the things that accompany salvation, the working out of salvation, fruit that may by its abounding give evidence of the root hidden from view. Consequently, we have in Philippians 3:9 and 10 the following sequence :

'And be found in Him ... That I may know Him'.

The first of these aspirations is doctrinal, the second is experimental. The first is concerned with righteousness, the second with resurrection, but a resurrection that is peculiar and unique.

Paul did not need any proof of the fact of the Lord's resurrection, his conversion revolves around the overwhelming fact, that it was 'Jesus' Whom he was persecuting that spoke to him from heaven. What Paul desired to know was the '*power*' of that resurrection. It is not possible to think of resurrection, without thinking also of mighty power. When Paul spoke of Christ in resurrection he said 'and declared to be the Son of God with power ... by the resurrection from the dead' (Rom. 1:4). Though He was crucified through weakness 'yet He liveth by the power of God' (2 Cor. 13:4), and the prayer for the Ephesians reaches its culminating point in the first chapter, with a desire that they should know 'what is the exceeding greatness of His power to us-ward who believe, according to the working of His mighty power, which He wrought in Christ, when He raised Him from the dead'. This 'power that worketh in us' (Eph. 3:20) meets us in Philippians. It is available to enable the believer to work out his own salvation as God works in (Phil. 2:13), and more pointedly, at the end of chapter 3, when speaking of the glorious transfiguration of the believer in resurrection, we read 'who shall change our vile body, that it may be fashioned like unto His glorious body, according to the *working* whereby He *is able* (*Tunisia*, power is *dunamis*) even to subdue all things unto Himself' (Phil. 3:21).

When the apostle cried 'that I may know Him and the power of His resurrection', it is this aspect of resurrection that the apostle has before him. He knew the historic fact; he knew its fundamental character for all doctrine; he knew all preaching and all faith were vain without it, but he also realized that there was a personal and experimental side to the fact of resurrection that had a peculiar bearing upon the great theme of the Philippian epistle. Let us follow the apostle in his quest:

(1) That I may know Him and the power of His resurrection.
(2) The fellowship of His sufferings.
(3) Being made conformable unto His death.
(4) If by any means I might attain unto the resurrection of the dead.

It will be seen that this four-fold sub-division falls into an introversion:

A   That I may know. Power. Resurrection. Something to attain.

B   Fellowship of His sufferings. ⎱ Something
                                   ⎰ to endure
B   Conformity to His death.   in the process.

A   If by any means I might attain. Resurrection. The consequence.

It is evident that the prayer, 'that I may *know* Him', speaks of a knowledge beyond that which is historical or even doctrinal. A person may be said 'to know' when a subject has simply come within the sphere of his perception, and where this aspect of knowledge is intended the Greek word *Ouija* is used, a word that is derived from *eider*, 'to see, or perceive by means of the senses'. This knowledge, however, is not deep, it lies near the surface of things. To know as represented by the word *ginosko*, implies insight, acquaintance and personal relationship. This knowledge influences the one who knows and is deeper. It is this word *ginosko* that the apostle uses in Philippians 3:10. Relation with the object is readily seen in such passages as 'Who knew no sin', 'I had not known sin'. The special use of the word 'know' in Matthew 1:25 and Luke 1:34, shows how intimate this knowledge is considered to be. In Philippians 3:10, the apostle was not seeking fuller information about the person and history of Christ, he was not concerned about the numbers of prophecies that were fulfilled by His advent, he desired a closer, more intimate acquaintance, a personal relationship that involved suffering and shame, a fellowship and a conformity. When the fuller meaning of knowledge is perceived, we can the better understand how it is that it stands at the very dividing of the ways in the third chapter of Genesis, and will be the great and glorious possession of the redeemed in the ages to come (Isa. 11:9).

This intimate, personal knowledge of Christ, if taken in its widest scope, is so vast, that like the Love of Christ 'it passeth knowledge'.

Here in Philippians 3:10, the apostle's desire is focused upon one aspect of His great work, 'the power of His resurrection'. Even so, we must remember that he has given evidence in other epistles that he was acquainted with this mighty power. He speaks of it in Ephesians 1:19, 3:7,20 and 6:10, in relation to believing, ministry, answer to prayer and Christian warfare, but here, in Philippians, he has something more in view. He desires to attain unto the resurrection of the dead (a term that awaits examination) and he perceives that this is only possible by a descent and ascent with Christ comparable in his limited degree, to the great humiliation and exaltation of Philippians 2:6-11.

The great sacrifice which the Saviour came to offer and which underlies the whole plan of salvation, was completely accomplished when He died 'the just for the unjust'. For this purpose He had been born and to make this offering 'a body had been prepared Him'. Moreover, in making this offering He laid down His life voluntarily, for He said 'no man taketh it from Me'. To this, however, man's wickedness and enmity added the cross, the shame and the sufferings, and *in these* aspects of His great sacrificial work, the believer may have some fellowship.

Christ is said to have suffered 'being tempted'; to have learned obedience by the things which He suffered; and being reproached, to have suffered 'without the gate' (Heb. 2:18; 5:8; 13:12).

Peter speaks of Christ suffering for us and thereby 'leaving us an example', associating this suffering with that endured by the believer who with a clear conscience takes unmerited evil patiently, and actually telling the believer that in these things he can 'follow His steps'. It will be found that this is the character that attaches to the sufferings of Christ in the New Testament. In *these* sufferings the believer can be a 'partaker' (2 Cor. 1:5-7; 1 Pet. 4:13). The reader will expect a reference to the apostle's statement that he filled up 'that which was behind of the afflictions of Christ in my flesh'; this we must include, but it should be noted that here the word is not *pathema* but *thlipsis*, often rendered 'tribulation' (Eph. 3:13; Rev. 7:14) and in many passages associated with future glory as a consequence.

The apostle desired to have 'fellowship' with the sufferings of Christ, and because of this, he also desired a deeper acquaintance with the power of His resurrection — without such power, such fellowship would have been suicidal. There are six references to 'fellowship' in Philippians, and they are all related to this self denying attitude.

These six references are so distributed through the epistle as to enforce upon us the peculiar aspect that the apostle had before him when he wrote Philippians 3:10.

'Fellowship' in Philippians

A   Phil. 1:5.   Your fellowship in the gospel
                      from the first day until now.

  B   Phil. 1:7.   Ye are all partakers of my grace.
                      Defence and confirmation of gospel.

    C   Phil. 2:1.   Fellowship of the Spirit. Leading
                      to the great descent and subsequent
                      exaltation of Christ (Phil. 2:6-11).

    C   Phil. 3:10.   Fellowship of His sufferings.
                      Leading to attainment of
                      resurrection and
                      prize of the high calling.

  B   Phil. 4:14.   Ye did communicate with
                      my afflictions.

A   Phil. 4:15.   Ye only communicated in
                      the beginning of the gospel.

The desire for the fellowship of Philippians 3:10 is therefore not only the logical sequence of the other usages of the word *koinonia* and its derivations, but is of the very essence of the epistle itself.

Just as there are two stages visible in the descent of Christ in Philippians 2:6-11 :

(1) He was made in the likeness of men.
(2) He humbled Himself to the death of the cross,

so in Paul's contemplated association with Christ's rejection, there are two stages :

(1) Fellowship with His sufferings.
(2) Conformity unto His death;

the one deeper and more terrible than the other.

It is possible to have fellowship with the sufferings of Christ, and still not be made conformable unto His death.

This conformity to His death leads on to the conformity of His resurrection, the apostle's goal, 'if by any means I might attain unto the resurrection of the dead'.

The doctrine of the identification of the believer, with the death and resurrection of the Saviour, is entirely a matter of grace, but there is an identification with His death and its shame and sufferings that is voluntary and experimental and is moreover the necessary prelude to attaining the resurrection of the dead. It is obvious therefore that not only must the conformity unto the death of Christ be something beyond the doctrinal identification of the believer with His death and resurrection, it is also equally obvious that the resurrection which was the object of the apostle's aim, a resurrection concerning which he entertained doubt, cannot possibly be the resurrection which is the blessed and certain hope of every believer.

The 'out-resurrection' and the word 'if'

Resurrection is not only a blessed hope, it is inescapable. The unjust, as well as the just, they that have done good, and they that have done evil, those who form the body of Christ, and those who stand before the great white throne, each and every son of Adam, Jew and Gentile, saved and lost, must be raised from the dead. The fact that the apostle could preface his reference to resurrection in Philippians 3:11 with an 'if', after having expressed his complete surrender to the grace of God in Christ, is of itself an indication that something exceptional is before us.

'If by any means I might attain unto'. No ambiguity attaches to the original here, the Revised Version makes but one alteration, the exchange of 'may' for 'might'. The simple way of 'putting the condition' is attained by using the particle *ei*, as in Philippians 1:22. In the passage before us, *ei* is combined with the adverb *pos* 'how', and so means 'if somehow'. The word *eipos* occurs but four times in the New Testament and in every case the contingency is very real and *the possibility of failure* is stressed. The passages are :

'If by any means they might attain to Phenice' (Acts 27:12).
'If by any means now at length, I might have a prosperous journey' (Rom. 1:10).
'If by any means I may provoke to emulation' (Rom. 11:14).
'If by any means I might attain unto the resurrection' (Phil. 3:11).

The grafting in of the Gentile, as a wild olive, failed to provoke Israel to emulation. The attempt to reach Phenice, ended in shipwreck. The original of Philippians 3:11 reads *eipos katanteso eis*, the original of Acts 27:12 reads *eipos dunainto katantesantes eis*. The differences are purely grammatical, *katanteso* being singular, and *katantesantes* being plural, and the added word *dunainto* being the addition of the word meaning 'be able'.

The experiences of the apostle recorded in Acts 27 must have left an indelible impression upon his mind, and as he pressed the words 'if by any means I might attain unto the resurrection' he knew, by actual experience, that there was the possibility of failing to arrive just as surely as the venture to attain unto Phenice met with disaster. Moreover, in the verse following he emphasizes the fact that he had not 'already attained', but that he 'followed after', still further adding 'brethren, I count not myself to have apprehended'. Contingency is the very atmosphere of the context. Now it is certain that Paul could have entertained no doubt concerning his standing in grace, or of his acceptance in the Beloved; his hope, like an anchor, was sure, and if he used words that expressed contingency and uncertainty, then it is morally certain that he was not speaking of the hope of the believer. In verse 14 he reveals that his uncertainty was related to a 'prize', and this attitude of mind he has already exhibited in relation to the same theme in 1 Corinthians 9:24 to 10:13.

The 'resurrection' therefore that was the object of the apostle's desires here in Philippians 3:11, for which he suffered and was willing to endure, must be something equivalent to 'the first resurrection' of Revelation 20:4-6, or the 'better resurrection' of Hebrews 11:35.

The words 'first' and 'better' stand visible for all to read in the passages cited, but neither the Authorized Version nor the Revised Version use any such qualifying prefix in Philippians 3:11. The Authorized Version reads :

'If by any means I might attain unto the resurrection of the dead',

and the Revised Version reads:

'if by any means I may attain unto the resurrection from the dead',

but that is all the difference there is between the two versions. The reader will by this time be desirous of consulting the original, and to this we accordingly turn.

The Received Text reads *ten exanastasin ton nekron* 'the out-resurrection of or from the dead'; The Critical Texts read *ten exanastasin ten ek nekron* 'the out-resurrection, that which is out from the dead ones'.

In order to appreciate the intention of the apostle here it will be necessary to review the teaching of the New Testament on this question of resurrection.

Two sects divided the religious beliefs of Israel into conflicting camps, the Sadducees and the Pharisees. Of the Sadducees it is written that they say 'there is no resurrection' (Matt. 22:23). When the Saviour challenged the faith of Martha concerning the resurrection of her brother Lazarus, she replied in the language of the common creed of the day 'I know that he shall rise again ... *at the last day*' (John 11:24). The simplest statement concerning the resurrection is that given by the apostle before the Sanhedrin, a belief which Israel and the believer could share 'and have hope toward God, which they themselves also allow, that there shall be a resurrection of the dead, both of the just and unjust' (Acts 24:15). Here in the words *anastasin nekron* we have the most elementary form in which the resurrection of the dead can be expressed, a form used by Pharisees, by Paul, by the sister of Lazarus and by the common people, for the Apocrypha, written long before Christ, contains the words *anastasin eis zoen* 'a resurrection unto life'.

It is therefore somewhat disconcerting to read in Mark 9:10 of the disciples that they questioned one with another 'what the rising from the dead should mean'. Are we to understand that the very disciples who had been selected to witness the transfiguration on the mountain, were not so mature in the faith as an unconverted Pharisee? Did Martha outstrip the apostles in this article of faith? Once again therefore we must turn to the actual words as recorded in the original before attempting a conclusion.

The words that troubled the disciples were those used by the Lord when He said : 'Till the Son of Man were risen from the dead' *ek nekron anaste* 'risen OUT FROM dead ones'. It is the presence of this word *ek* 'out' that caused the questioning. It was something additional to the common creed. It was this resurrection *ek nekron* that declared Christ 'to be the Son of God with power' (Rom. 1:4). The first to rise out from the dead was Christ, as Paul testifies in Acts 26:23 :

'That Christ should suffer, and that He should be the first that should rise *out* from dead ones'.

We now take one further step forward and discover a reference that is nearer to the form found in Philippians 3. *Tes anastaseos tes ek nekron*, in Luke 20:35.

'But they which shall be accounted worthy to obtain that world, and the resurrection, that which is out from the dead ones'.

Here it will be observed, we not only have words similar to those used in Philippians 3:11, 'accounted worthy to obtain', but a similar context. Believers can be accounted worthy to obtain that age at the out-resurrection, they may be accounted worthy to escape the dreadful things that are coming on the earth and to stand before the Son of Man, they were counted worthy to suffer shame for His name : and the persecutions which they endured were a manifest token of the righteous judgments of God, that they may be counted worthy of the Kingdom of God, for which they suffered (Luke 20:35; 21:36; Acts 5:41; 2 Thess. 1:5).

The word 'obtain' in Luke 20:35 is used by the apostle in 2 Timothy 2:10, 'that they may also obtain the salvation which is ... with eternal glory', where the context associates 'suffering' with 'reigning', and in Hebrews 11:35 'that they might obtain a better resurrection', which is an obvious parallel with the 'out-resurrection' of Philippians 3:11.

While Paul was sure of the 'Hope' of his calling, he could not be sure of attaining unto the 'Prize' of this same calling, and associated with that prize is the special resurrection, the out-resurrection and the desire for conformity unto the death of Christ which we have been considering. In the verse following the apostle makes it very clear that this uncertainty is legitimate, and one or two added words are employed in making this fact clear.

'Not as though I had already attained' ('Not that I have already obtained', R.V.), 'either were already perfect' ('or am already made perfect', R.V.), 'but I follow after' ('but I press on, R.V.), 'if that I may apprehend that for which also I am apprehended of Christ Jesus' ('if so be that I may apprehend that for which also I was apprehended by Christ Jesus', R.V.) (Phil. 3:12).

The Authorized Version, by repeating the word 'attain' in Philippians 3:12, gives a continuity to the apostle's argument, but as two very different words are employed, *katantao* in verse 11 and *lambano* in verse 12, the Revised Version is preferable. The change from 'attaining' to 'obtaining' moreover, reveals a change in the apostle's objective. He sought first to 'attain' to the out-resurrection and then subsequently to 'obtain' the prize. This comes out clearly when we remember that *lambano*, 'obtain', occurs in 1 Corinthians 9:24,25, 'one *receiveth* the prize', 'they do it to *obtain* a corruptible crown'.

It is moreover evident from the apostle's language, that one who 'obtained' the prize, could be considered as 'perfect'. Here the Greek reading *teteleiomai* 'I have been perfected' anticipates the triumphant *teteleka* 'I have finished' of 2 Timothy 4:7, where once again we have the race course, the conflict, and the crown.

The reader will recognize that in both of these Greek words, there is the common root *tel* which means that the 'end' has been reached, the race run. *Telos* 'end' (Phil. 3:19), gives us *teleo* 'to reach an end, or finish' (2 Tim. 4:7); and so *teleioo* 'to make perfect' (Phil. 3:12); and *teleios* 'perfect' (Phil. 3:15).

The apostle said 'I follow after', and what he sought for was that he might 'lay hold of' that for which he had been 'laid hold of' by Christ. The apostle's 'confidence' in chapter 1 and his 'diffidence' in chapter 3 show the two aspects of truth that present a perfect whole, two aspects which are expressed in Ephesians by the words 'the HOPE of His calling' and in Philippians by the words 'the PRIZE of the high calling'.

The prize of the high calling of God in Christ Jesus

The figure of a race, a conflict with a crown or prize at the end, is used by the apostle in more places than one. If this 'prize' is something for which we have been apprehended by Christ, then if for no other reason than to please Him, we should get to know what it is and how it may be obtained.

It is right for every believer to sing :

'Not for weight of glory, not for crown or palm,
Enter we the army, raise the warrior's psalm,
But for love that claimeth lives for Whom He died',

but it is also right for every believer to believe what God has said regarding 'the prize' that is attached to our 'high calling', as it is right that we should understand the high calling itself.

When one has perceived the riches of grace that characterize the calling of the Mystery, there is a temptation which is very strong, to put out the hand to save the ark of God, and to deny the possibility of 'reward' in the Prison Epistles, lest by so doing the character of grace should be impaired. While sympathising with this regard for grace, we must nevertheless resist it, for we must have a higher regard for 'truth' of which grace is a part, and truth demands that we shall allow a rightful place in the dispensation of the mystery to the undiluted meaning of 'race' with its 'crown', 'prize' and 'reward'.

Let us turn to the epistle to the Colossians, an epistle which stresses the fact of the believer's 'completeness' in Christ and let us observe what it says concerning this aspect of revealed truth.

In chapter 2 the apostle gives a warning against that attitude of mind that beguiles of the reward. The word that demands attention here is *katabrabeuo*. *Brabeuo* by itself means to be a judge or umpire, and so to assign the prize in a public game. But the addition of *kata* 'against' indicates an adverse judgment. *Brabeuo* occurs in Colossians 3:15 where the peace of God is said to 'rule (act the umpire) in your hearts' – a precious thought. *Brabeion* is a prize. It is found in 1 Corinthians 9:24 and Philippians 3:14, 'the prize of the high calling of God in Christ Jesus'. We are therefore not without guidance as to the subject of this second chapter of Colossians. It has to do with the prize. Now Colossians, whilst running very parallel with Ephesians, has much in its central section that bears upon Philippians, which is the epistle of the 'prize' and the 'perfecting', and if we look at the first chapter of Colossians we shall find in the idea of being 'presented', the two aspects of truth set forth by Ephesians and

Philippians. We shall distinguish between that which can never be lost, and that which may be lost, and return to Colossians 2 with clearer views :

The first presentation.

'In the body of His flesh through death, to present you holy and unblameable and unreproveable in His sight' (Col. 1:22).

The second presentation.

'Warning every man, and teaching every man in all wisdom; that we may present every man perfect in Christ Jesus' (Col. 1:28).

The first presentation rests solely upon the finished work of Christ; the second involves the idea which is found in the word 'perfect' – of pressing on to the end. In the first no effort of our own could ever present us 'holy'; in the second we stand in need of 'warning'.

Satan does not waste his energies in attempting to deprive us of our acceptance in the Beloved. 'Your life is hid with Christ in God'. Scripture nowhere says: 'Hold that fast which thou hast, that no man take thy *life*' but it does say: 'Hold that fast which thou hast, that no man take thy *crown*' (Rev. 3:11). Satan was permitted to touch everything belonging to Job except his *life*.

The same is true of all the redeemed. There is a prize to be won, a crown to be gained, but no man is crowned except he strive lawfully. If therefore Satan can turn the saint away from the fullness of Christ, and get him occupied with other means and ways – be they ordinances, days, feasts, meats, drinks, false humility, neglect of the body, unscriptural mediators, or any other thing save 'holding the Head' – then the prize is lost, the saint dishonoured, and above all the Saviour robbed, for what is a crown to us but an added crown to Him?

The apostle returns to the subject of 'reward' in his practical exhortations.

'*The reward of the inheritance*' (Col. 3:22-25). This phrase is the key to the apostle's object in writing the epistle. The Colossian believers, being members of the body of Christ, were already 'seated together in heavenly places in Christ'; already 'accepted in the Beloved'; already sure of their presentation 'holy and unblameable and unreproveable' in the sight of God. Already the apostle had said: 'giving thanks unto the Father, which hath made us meet to be partakers of the inheritance in light' (Col. 1:12). Words cannot make clearer the assured position of the believer nor the completeness of his acceptance. Nevertheless, before the chapter is finished we have found Paul 'warning' and 'teaching', that he may 'present every man perfect in Christ Jesus', and also at the close of the epistle we find Epaphras praying for the selfsame thing (Col. 4:12). The accompanying chart illustrates this point. As it is evident that neither Paul nor Epaphras has any doubt that what has already been written of the saints, as to standing, in Colossians 1:12,13 and 22 remains unalterably true, it becomes necessary to distinguish between the common 'inheritance of the saints in light' for which all believers have been made meet, and 'the reward' attaching to that inheritance, which was associated with individual faithfulness, in other words the prize attached to the high calling which, as in Philippians 3 is associated with 'perfecting' (Col. 1:28; 4:12).

We must distinguish between that 'holy, and unblameable, and unreproveable' position which is ours 'in the body of His flesh through death' and the possibility of being *blamed and reproved* for the things done in service. If we 'try the things that differ', we shall see that 'hope' is on a basis of pure, unalloyed grace, which excludes all possibility of either gain or loss, running or serving; and that the 'prize' is on a basis of reward, given only to those who strive lawfully. Knowing these distinctions we shall be saved a multitude of vexations, and moreover not be found false witnesses of God, for without doubt, He

teaches us that membership of the one body and participation in its one hope is entirely outside the range of attainment on our part. And with equal certainty He assures us that the *prize* of the high calling, the *reward* of the inheritance, and the *crown* of righteousness, fall within the category of attainment. True, nothing but grace will avail, but it is grace *used*. The reason for the apostle's assurance that our life is hid with Christ in God, is that we might know that life is not in question. He does not say in Colossians 2:18, let no man beguile you of your *life*, or *membership*, or *position* – these are never in question. But he does echo the words of another dispensation and say: 'take heed, that no man take your *crown*'.

In 1 Corinthians 9:24-27 the apostle enlarges upon this figure of the race and the crown, supplementing his own inspired figures of the 'ensamples' provided by Israel in the wilderness (1 Cor. 10:1-13).

Grace is emphasized in the epistles of Paul written before Acts 28 as an examination of Galatians and Romans will demonstrate.

No single chapter repudiates the flesh and its efforts more strongly than does the first chapter of 1 Corinthians, yet the apostle sees no incongruity in stressing with equal emphasis the running of a race, the fact that only one receives the prize, and the necessity for discipline and temperance on the part of all who enter the lists, with the final warning, that he himself could possibly become 'disqualified' (*adokimos* 1 Cor. 9:27, not 'castaway') even as with many of Israel, though redeemed out of Egypt, the Lord was not 'well pleased' *eudokeo* (1 Cor. 10:5).

In the last epistle Paul wrote, he speaks not only of the association of 'crown' and 'running the race' in connection with himself, he applies the same principles to 'all them also that love His appearing' (2 Tim. 4:7,8); but he distinguishes very clearly between the unalterable position of those who 'died with Christ' as compared with the condition attached to 'reigning with Him' (2 Tim. 2:11-13). Life with Christ is one thing, reigning with Him is another.

We trust the passages which have been brought before our notice make it clear that the doctrine of prize, crown and reward is by no means absent from the epistles of the Mystery. We can therefore return to the passage in the third chapter of Philippians, which speaks of the 'prize of the high calling of God in Christ Jesus', assured that we are examining a passage of Scripture that applies with undiminished force to ourselves.

'Brethren, I count not myself to have apprehended: but this one thing I do, forgetting those things which are behind, and reaching forth unto those things which are before, I press toward the mark for the prize of the high calling of God in Christ Jesus' (Phil. 3:13,14).

'Forgetting ... I press'. What things did the apostle wish to 'forget'? What things if remembered would hinder his running and spoil his chances for the Prize? It cannot refer to the fact that Paul was once a Pharisee and an enemy of the Gospel, for this is remembered with deep appreciation of grace in 1 Timothy 1:11-16, and urged upon the remembrance of Timothy himself in 2 Timothy 1:3; 3:10-14.

In the twelfth chapter of Hebrews, in connection with running 'the race that is set before us', the apostle urged his readers to 'lay aside every weight', which turns us back to the sixth chapter where he says, 'leaving the word of the beginning of Christ, let us go on unto perfection' (Heb. 6:1 margin). The Hebrews were hindering their ability to run the race that was set before them, and to go on unto perfection, by clinging to the doctrines and practices of a dispensation that had passed.

So, even though the Philippians were called to salvation by the preaching recorded in Acts 16, and referred to in Philippians 4:15, they must nevertheless beware of bringing over from the Pentecostal dispensation, which had now fallen in abeyance, doctrines and practices which were once right and proper, but now obsolete and hindrances. They must forget the things that are 'behind'. For the apostle himself, the things that were 'behind' would embrace all that he had counted loss for Christ's sake, and for each one of us, there will be a similar personal assessment that we alone can make.

From the prison on the Palatine Hill at Rome (Phil. 1:13) Paul would hear the shouting and cheering of the multitudes as they encouraged their favourite charioteers in the *Circus Maximus*. Paul, though a prisoner, was also a charioteer, he too had a 'mark', he too 'stretched himself forward' as the racer did in the lists.

Clement of Rome, who is probably the same person as is mentioned in Philippians 4:3, associates *brabeion* the 'prize', with Paul's apostolic career. 'St. Paul gained the *brabeion* of endurance, having worn chains seven times for Christ' (probably an allusion to the seven rounds of the race course before the final run up to the 'mark'). From this Greek word for 'prize' *brabeion*, some think the English 'bravo' is ultimately derived.

Coming to the prize itself. Are we to understand the apostle to teach –

(1)   The prize, that is to say, the high calling of God?
(2)   The prize, that is to say, the upward call of God?
(3)   The prize which is attached to the high calling of God?

If the apostle is allowed to speak for himself, then *brabeion* 'the prize' is equivalent to a crown, both words being used in 1 Corinthians 9:24-27 and both words being used in connection with a race and conflict. *Katabrabeuo* is 'to beguile of reward' (A.V.), 'rob you of your reward' (R.V.) (Col. 2:18), and *ho brabeus* was the judge who assigned the prizes at the games, an umpire or an arbitrator.

It is exceedingly difficult to find support from any passage of Paul's epistles, that the prize was itself the high calling. Just as 'the reward OF the inheritance' in Colossians 3:24 means the reward attached to an inheritance already assured by grace (Col. 1:12), so the prize OF the high calling of God, means the prize which is attached to the high calling already received and entered by grace. However there is an objection to be considered here which involves a point of grammar.

The word translated 'high' is *ano*, an adverb, and as adverbs in English usually qualify verbs, some have taught that this fact settles the meaning of 'calling' and teach that Philippians 3 speaks of some future personal summons on high. While it is true that *ano* is an adverb *it is not true* that adverbs qualify verbs only, as can be demonstrated by the use of this very word in Paul's writings. 'Jerusalem which is above' (Gal. 4:26) uses *ano* to qualify the noun Jerusalem; 'seek those things which are above' (Col. 3:1), uses the phrase *ta-ano* 'the above things', so Philippians 3:14 employs *ano* to qualify the noun 'calling'. *Klesis* is not a verb and cannot be translated other than 'a calling or vocation'. It is used eleven times in the New Testament and ten of the occurrences are found in Paul's epistles, Ephesians 1:18; 4:1,4 and 2 Timothy 1:9 will indicate the way the word is used by the apostle.

It was Sir Robert Anderson who said, that those who translate Philippians 3:14 'the upward call' meaning a future 'summons on high', rarely complete the quotation. Paul *does not say* 'the prize of the high calling of God', what he does say is 'the prize of the high calling of God which is IN CHRIST JESUS'.

The out-resurrection segregates the believer who has obtained the prize but this special resurrection is not itself the prize for which the apostle was running. When at the last Paul could say 'finished' he then speaks not in generic terms of a 'prize', but in specific terms of 'a crown', which he also associates with 'reigning together' in the second chapter of the same epistle (2 Tim. 2 and 4). This association of prize, running and crown is found together in 1 Corinthians 9:24-27. There may be varieties in the crown awarded, but all will be of the nature of 'prize' or 'reward'.

The perfect, and the enemies of the Cross of Christ

The majority of commentators see no difficulty in the accepted translation of Philippians 3:15, 'let us therefore, as many as be perfect', or if they have had any problem the difficulty is left unexpressed.

Most take the word 'perfect' here to mean 'mature' as contrasted with 'babes' or immature, and in other contexts this interpretation is quite true (Heb. 5:14). If, however, we look back to Philippians 3:12 where the apostle says of himself that he was not already 'perfect' or 'mature', we shall have a difficulty in accepting the usual rendering of the fifteenth verse.

If Paul was not then 'perfect', who among the Philippians or his readers down the ages could hope to be? Further, it reflects upon the intelligence of the apostle to make him say (verse 12) that he was not 'mature', yet at the fifteenth verse to continue his argument with the word 'therefore' and assume that nevertheless both he and others were at the same time 'mature' or 'perfect'. It is an axiom that requires no demonstration to prove that a thing cannot both be, or not be, at one and the same time.

Conybeare and Howson sense the difficulty saying 'the translation in the Authorized Version of *teteleiomai* (verse 12) and *teleioi* by the same word, makes Paul seem to contradict himself', and their way out of the difficulty is to translate verse fifteen by 'ripe in understanding'. This, however, only conceals the difficulty from the English reader. Macknight is the only commentator we have consulted who realizes the difficulty, and he translates Philippians 3:15 'as many, therefore, as WISH TO BE perfect'.

Hosoi oun teleioi contains no verb. The 'be' is supplied in the Authorized Version to make sense. If we must supply a verb, why not keep the unity of the apostle's argument? Why make him contradict himself within the space of three verses? Why accuse him of using a term in two different meanings without the slightest warning to the reader?

As many as would be, or who wish to be perfect, makes all clear and straightforward. All who would emulate the apostle's desire and eagerness must emulate his 'mind', they must be 'thus minded', and we have only to go back to the opening of the great argument in the second chapter to realize that the apostle is turning back to the 'mind that was in Christ Jesus'. The Received Text reads :

> 'Nevertheless, whereto we have already attained, let us walk by the same rule, let us mind the same thing' (16).

The use by the Authorized Version of the word 'attain' in Philippians 3:11,12 and 16, to represent three different Greek words, has robbed the English reader of the means to appreciate the transition of thought in the apostle's argument. We have already observed that in verse 12, the word should be 'obtain'; we now draw attention to the original of verse 16, where *phthano* is the word translated 'attain'. Dr. Bullinger's *Lexicon and Concordance* says '*phthano*, to come or do before another, to be beforehand with, to overtake, outstrip; to come first'. It is this word that is found in 1 Thessalonians 4:15 and is translated 'prevent', which English word is from the Latin *proevenio* 'to come before'.

The recognition of this Greek word *phthano*, 'to outstrip', while it brings us closer to the apostle's language makes the suggested translation offered by Lewin untenable :

> 'But whereunto we have outstript, walk in the same'.

While it is of the very nature of a race, that competitors should endeavour to outstrip others, the race set before the

believer would appear to the worldling as though the prize
was awarded to the last man in rather than the first.

The Great Example set in chapter 2 appeared at all
points to be giving away advantages, His humble follower
Paul pursued the prize while at the same time counting all
things loss. Whoever won a race and 'esteemed the affairs
of others of far more importance than his own'? In this
competition there is no thought of elbowing the weak
brother out of the way, but rather of losing place and pace
while we pause to help him on to his feet. The apostle
exhorted the runner to 'lay aside every weight', yet at the
same time revealed that the law of Christ called upon every
entrant 'to bear one another's burdens'. This somewhat
paradoxical state could obtain only in the realm of grace.

The hymn expresses something of this quality when it
says :

> 'Through weakness and defeat,
> He won the meed and crown;
> Trod all His foes beneath His feet
> By being trodden down'.

Some MSS. omit the words 'by the same rule, let us
mind the same thing', others omit the word 'rule', yet
others omit 'let us mind the same thing'. Griesbach simply
cancels the whole passage and many critics take it for
granted that the reference to the 'rule' has crept in from
Galatians 6:16, which is a gratuitous piece of criticism.
The *kanon* 'rule' refers to 'the white line by which the
course in the stadium was marked out, including the whole
space between the starting-place and the goal; and that
those who ran out of that space did not contend lawfully.
The runners, in endeavouring to pass one another, were in
danger of going out of that space' (Hammond quoting
Julius Pollux, A.D. 180-238). Aquila uses the word *kanon*
in his Greek version of Job 38:5, so here in Philippians the
apostle says, 'I follow along the mark' *kata skopon dioko*,
'and as many as would be perfect' and obtain the prize,
they too will 'think this'. There are other things, such as

the observance of one day above another, or the eating or not eating of certain foods, in which there will be considerable differences of opinion, but provided that all press on in the right spirit, God will reveal these things to such. However much we may have outstript others and to whatever part of the course we may have arrived, let us go by the same rule, let us keep in mind what I have already told you of my own course. You are to be 'strivers together' for the faith, but not strivers with one another (Phil. 1:27; 2:3).

The apostle has, by his exhortation, thrown the believer back upon the example both of the Lord and of himself: he now proceeds to enforce the need for observing this example both positively, 'be followers together of me', and negatively, 'and mark them which walk so as ye have us for an ensample' (Phil. 3:17). The words of verses 18 and 19 are a parenthesis, the whole passage being constructed as follows :

Examples

A 17.   *Positive.*   Be followers together of me ...
                         us for an ensample.
B 17.   *Negative.*   Mark them which walk.
B 18,19.   *Negative.*   Their end — destruction.
A 20,21.   *Positive.*   Our citizenship is in heaven ...
                         we shall be changed.

Five things are enumerated by the apostle when speaking of those whose example was to be avoided.

(1) They were the enemies of the cross of Christ.
(2) Their end was destruction.
(3) Their god was their belly.
(4) Their glory was in their shame.
(5) They minded earthly things.

It is impossible to believe that a church of so high a spiritual standard as that of the Philippians could need a solemn warning not to follow a worldly crowd, yet at first sight such a list as that given above does not seem of possible application to a believer.

Let us examine them a little more closely, and let us start with the last named 'who mind earthly things'. It will be conceded after a moment's thought, that the unsaved man of the world has no option, *he can mind nothing else*.

Philippians 3:4-19 is a section complete in itself, and the word *phroneo* 'mind' occurs in it as follows :

A 3:15-.   As many as would be perfect (one thing, to hen verse 13) be thus minded.
B 3:-15.   Otherwise (*heteros*) minded.
A 3:16.   Whereto ... outstripped others ... mind the same thing (*to auto*).
B 3:19.   Who mind earthly things (*ta epigeia*).

It will be seen that those who mind earthly things are in correspondence with those who think differently from the apostle in his single eyed effort to attain the prize. 'Earthly things' therefore need not mean things positively sinful, but things that come in between the runner and his goal; 'every weight' as Hebrews 12 suggests. 'Earthly things' are in the original *ta epigeia* (Phil. 3:19). 'Things on the earth' are *ta epi tes ges* (Col. 3:2). 'Earthly things' are spoken of in John 3:12; James 3:15; 1 Corinthians 15:40; 2 Corinthians 5:1 and in Philippians 2:10 and 3:19. In each case, 'earthly things' are set over against 'heavenly', 'from above' and 'celestial'.

Those therefore who mind earthly things, are those who do not act in accordance with their heavenly citizenship (Phil. 3:20) and whose example must be shunned by all who seek the prize of the high calling. The example of Abraham, as set out in Hebrews 11:8-16, who desired a better country, 'that is, an heavenly', can be added to that of the apostle here. If the last of the list can describe those who are believers, let us return to the head of the list and ponder again the dreadful words 'the enemies of the cross of Christ'. James declares that friendship with the world makes one the enemy of God (Jas. 4:4), and it will not be denied that such friendship is possible to a child of God. One may become an enemy in the eyes of another by telling him unpalatable truth (Gal. 4:16), and enmity can be exhibited and maintained by a middle wall of partition (Eph. 2:15). One may therefore by adopting some attitude make oneself an enemy of the truth for which the cross of Christ stands. To many, the cross of Christ is seen only in an evangelical light, the central testimony to *unsaved* sinners. To those who see no further than this aspect of the cross, those referred to in Philippians 3:18, cannot possibly be believers. To those who have examined the place which the cross occupies in Paul's testimony and have seen its essential message to the believer who is already saved, the warnings of these verses will present no problem. We have demonstrated elsewhere the many ways in which the epistle to the Hebrews runs parallel with that to the Philippians, and the only reference to the cross in that epistle is found in Hebrews 12:2, in direct connection with 'running the race which is set before us'. This is the last reference to the cross in the New Testament, the earliest references (Matt. 10:38; 16:24) relate to the cross, also to discipleship and future reward. Paul uses the doctrine of the cross to counter the fleshly wisdom of the Corinthians (1 Cor. 1:17,18; 2:2), he teaches the Galatians that by the cross the world and its boasting are repudiated (Gal. 5:11; 6:12,14), and that the emancipation of the believer together with the complete reconciliation of the one body, are accomplished by the Cross of Christ (Eph. 2:16; Col. 1:20; 2:14).

Those who are 'otherwise minded' and whose associations with the world and the flesh run in opposition to the 'one thing' that characterized the apostle's testimony, such would be, though believers, 'enemies' of all that the cross of Christ stood for, and so become examples for the Philippians to shun.

The citizenship that persists, and its abiding influence

Those who enter the lists and who run for the prize, have a course to pursue, and a goal to attain that make demands upon their integrity and a whole hearted surrender to the grace of Christ. The apostle not only places before them his own example but warns them to mark those who deviate from the standard he has set. First note that the apostle does not say 'be followers OF me', but 'be followers TOGETHER of me', and the emphasis upon fellowship that so characterizes this epistle is a feature that must not be passed by without comment. These believers enjoyed a good deal of fellowship in their endeavour to press toward the mark. They were called *sunathleo* 'strivers together', 'labourers together' (Phil. 1:27; Phil. 4:3); they were *sunergoi* 'fellow labourers' or 'companions in labour' (Phil. 2:25; 4:3).

The companion epistle (2 Timothy) is marked by an absence of this fellowship, and in its place there is an emphasis upon an individual and lonely stand. These things should be kept in mind today, as we compare ourselves with the high standing of Philippians. The Lord knows our 'handicap' and is not unrighteous or without mercy.

The evil example against which the apostle warned the Philippians is summed up by the word 'walk'. 'Mark them which walk'; 'for many walk'. The Lord alone can read the heart, man must be guided by the walk, and whatever the ultimate judgment may be upon those whose example was to be shunned, their walk, as we have already seen, constituted them 'enemies' to the very truth which the Cross of Christ established. Trite sayings may not always be true, but a Proverb has been explained as 'the wisdom of many, in the wit of one' and the saying 'no cross – no crown' seems a just epitome of the teaching of this part of Scripture. In the section which deals with Prize and Crown, it is therefore important to notice that the Cross comes first.

The items that follow are expansions and applications of this enmity to the doctrine of the cross.

It has an 'end', namely destruction; it has a 'god,' namely the belly; it has a 'glory', namely in the things of shame; it sets its mind on earthly things. Its end is said to be *destruction*. We have already seen that Hebrews sheds light upon the relationship of the Cross to the Crown (Heb. 12:1,2), we shall now see that Hebrews illuminates this word 'destruction'. The word so translated comes in Hebrews 10:39, where it is translated 'perdition', and the whole epistle is written round the two ideas:

'Let us GO ON unto perfection' (Heb. 6:1).
Let us not 'DRAW BACK unto perdition' (Heb. 10:39).

In like manner could these self-same headings be written over Philippians 3. The word translated 'destruction' and 'perdition' occurs in Matthew 26:8, where it is used in its primitive, non-doctrinal sense of 'waste'.

While no believer could ever draw back to ultimate and utter destruction he could, like Israel in the wilderness, fail of perfection and so draw back to 'waste'. This was the unhappy goal of those who for any reason avoided the offence of the cross, or who side stepped the mark in their running for the prize. They themselves would not be 'lost', but they would 'suffer loss', being saved indeed, but 'saved; yet so as by fire (saved as through fire)' (1 Cor. 3:10-15).

Let us see whether we can get further light upon the next feature, 'whose god is their belly'. Seneca uses a similar expression *alius abdomini servit*, and the word is often used in attacks upon Epicureans who were prone to gratify their sensual appetite. We shall miss the point of the apostle's warning, however, if we allow ourselves to wander into the by-paths of Classical usage. Mere gluttony is not here in view, but something deeper, something that bears directly upon the running and the perfecting of the believer, and once again the parallel teaching of Hebrews helps us.

In the sixth chapter of Hebrews we have the exhortation to 'go on unto perfection' which is followed in verses 4 to 8 by references to Israel and Hebrew Christians, concerning whom it is said 'if they shall fall away', it is impossible 'to renew them again unto repentance'. These words are structurally balanced by Hebrews 12:17, where Esau is said to have 'found no place of repentance'. Hebrews 12 speaks of the heavenly Jerusalem, the city of the living God and of the spirits of just men 'made perfect', and in this context comes the example of Esau, 'who for one morsel of meat sold his birthright', he made a god of his belly and forfeited a place in the Church of the Firstborn (*protokia* 'birthright', *protokos* 'firstborn'). Esau's end is 'waste' and those concerning whom the apostle warned the Philippians were following in the steps of Esau, who for a little ease and worldly benefit were forfeiting the prize of their high calling.

'Whose glory is their shame'.

Hebrews 12:2, which has already helped us, tells us that the Saviour, for the joy that was set before Him endured the cross, and despised 'the shame'. To glory in one's shame is at the other extreme. The apostle's own testimony is also helpful:

'That in nothing I shall be ashamed, but that with all boldness, as always, so now also Christ shall be magnified in my body, whether it be by life or by death' (Phil. 1:20).

The reverse of this was to make a god of one's belly and to glory in one's shame. We have already considered the meaning of the words 'who mind earthly things'. Let us now turn to the positive teaching of the apostle, and putting verses 18 and 19 into brackets, observe the connection of thought between verses 17 and 20, 21.

'Brethren, be followers together of me, and mark them which walk
so as ye have us for an example (...) for our conversation is in
heaven, from whence also we look for the Saviour, the Lord Jesus
Christ : Who shall change our vile body, that it may be fashioned
like unto His glorious body, according to the working whereby He
is able even to subdue all things unto Himself'.

The first, positive and outstanding incentive which the
apostle places before those 'who would be perfect' is
related to citizenship. The word 'conversation' is the
translation of the Greek *politeuma*, which in Greek
writings means the administration of civil affairs, a
commonwealth. *Polis* is used in Hebrews 11:10 'he
looked for a city', which in Hebrews 12:22 is called 'the
city of the living God'. From this word comes *politeia*
'freedom' (i.e. Roman citizenship, Acts 22:28), and
'commonwealth' (Eph. 2:12), *polites*, 'a citizen' (Acts
21:39), and *politeuomai* 'to live' or 'to have one's
conversation', to act in harmony with one's calling or
citizenship.

We learn from Acts 16:12 that Philippi was a 'colony',
its full Roman name being *Colonia Augusta Julia
Philippensis*, as a coin in the British Museum shows. A
Roman colony was a miniature resemblance of Rome, and
it was at Philippi that Paul claimed the privilege that
attached to Roman citizenship. Rome divided the world
into two classes, 'citizens' and 'strangers', those who lived
in Italy being citizens.

'The City of Rome might be transplanted, as it were, into various
parts of the empire, and reproduced as a *Colonia*; or an alien city
might be adopted, under the title of a *municipium*. The privilege of
a *colonia* was transplanted citizenship, that of a *municipium* was
engrafted citizenship'.

'The colonists went out with all the pride of Roman citizens, to
represent and reproduce the city in the midst of an alien population.
Every traveller who passed thereby a *colonia* saw there the insignia
of Rome. He heard the Latin language, and was amenable, in the
strictest sense, to the Roman law' (Conybeare and Howson).

Every believer in Philippi when he read the words 'our
politeuma is in heaven' would realize the apostle's

intention. Just as the Philippian citizen, though miles away from Rome, yet lived as far as possible as a Roman, so the believer far from his heavenly city, lives here below as 'a citizen of no mean city'. The Revised Version has placed 'citizenship' in the text here, and 'commonwealth' in the margin.

This citizenship, says the apostle, 'is' in heaven. The verb *eimi* 'to be' is not used here, but a richer, fuller word is employed, namely *huparcho*. We have given a fairly full examination of *huparcho* in pp. 97-100, and have seen that it means the persistence of an original possession, in spite of extreme changes in circumstance. The two occurrences of *huparcho* in Philippians should be read together.

> Concerning Christ, Who passed through all the changes from glory to the utmost humiliation of the death of the Cross, yet never at any time did He lose that which was persistently His original possession 'Being in the form of God' (Phil. 2:6).

> Concerning the Believer; who was originally chosen to this high estate as a citizen of heaven itself, which citizenship persists as an unalterable fact, even though for the time being he may be in the flesh, in the world and encompassed by infirmity. His citizenship is as truly in heaven, even though he may not be there, as the Philippian citizenship existed in Rome, even though miles of sea and land intervened.

From whence we look for the Saviour. We realize that it is impossible to 'mind earthly things' and at the same time earnestly and eagerly to 'look for the Saviour from heaven', one or the other point of view will be out of focus.

The title Saviour applies to Christ not only with reference to salvation that is past, but also looks to the future completion of salvation 'the redemption of our body' (Rom. 8:23). We are therefore 'saved by hope' and if by hope we 'wait for it' (Rom. 8:24,25).

This redemption of the body is expressed in Philippians 3 in the words of verse 21, 'who shall change our vile body that it may be fashioned like unto His glorious body'. The Revised Version reads : 'Who shall fashion anew the body of our humiliation, that it may be conformed to the body of His glory', and in so revising the passage, they preserve the distinctive meaning of *metaschematizo* 'to fashion anew', and *summorphos* 'conform', which words are an echo of those found in Philippians 2:6-8 where the 'form' of God is the Greek *morphe*, and the 'fashion' as a man is the Greek *schema*. We are to be 'refashioned' and 'conformed', but this refashioning and conforming has to do particularly with the body. 'Our vile body' – 'His glorious body'. Once again we are turned back to Philippians 2. The word 'vile' which the Revisers render 'humiliation' is the Greek *tapeinosis*, which in the form *tapeinoo* is used in Philippians 2:8, where it reads 'He humbled Himself'. The word 'vile' could be used in earlier days without bringing into the mind moral depravity, for example the Authorized Version speaks of a poor man in 'vile' raiment (Jas. 2:2) and it originally meant anything small, cheap or of little worth. These bodies of ours are bodies associated with our humiliation. However 'fearfully and wonderfully made' they may be, life's processes bring with them many times a sense of shame. These will all pass away when we attain to the likeness of His resurrection, and receive a body that conforms with His body of glory. While this blessed likeness is the goal before every believer, it is not every believer that intelligently and willingly seeks 'conformity' *summorphoo*, to His death, and it is this character that is in mind in Philippians 3:21. Not every believer consciously realizes 'the body of this humiliation' and it is that body which is to be transfigured and transformed.

It will be seen therefore that there is an intended parallel between Philippians 3:20,21 and 2:6-8 which is indicated by the use of the words 'being', 'form', 'fashion' and 'humble'.

Christ was originally in the form of God, the citizenship of the believer abides from the beginning in heaven. This persistent state is expressed by *huparcho*. Christ was in the 'form' of God and took upon Him the 'form' of a servant. The believer desires to be conformable unto His death and looks forward to a body that shall be conformed unto His glorious body. This conformity and form is expressed by *morphe* and its variants. Christ was found 'in fashion' as a man, the transfiguration of the believer 'fashions him anew'. This is expressed by the Greek *schema*. Christ 'humbled' Himself, the believer who is made conformable unto His death will realize that he has now a body of 'humiliation', this is expressed by the Greek word *tapeinosis*. Like Him in humiliation, like Him in glory. This is the fulfilment of the apostle's desire that he might attain unto the out-resurrection and obtain the prize.

This transformation is brought about by 'power', even as nothing but the 'power' of His resurrection could enable the apostle to contemplate conformity unto His death. The change revealed in verse 21 therefore, is to be understood as an amplification of the 'out-resurrection' of verse 11. The whole wondrous change is according to the working whereby He is able to subdue all things unto Himself. This looks to 1 Corinthians 15:27,28 where 'the end' is foreshadowed. Just as the Church of the One Body is called 'the fulness of Him that filleth all in all' and so anticipates 'the end', so the resurrection and transfiguration of the believer, anticipates that day of glory. Our citizenship persistently remains unaltered since the choice was made before the overthrow of the world, its influence can be felt in every moment and circumstance of our earthly pilgrimage, and the hope of its realization turns our eyes away from earthly things to 'wait for the Saviour'.

CHAPTER 9

Reckon These Things

Philippians 4:1-23

Although we are commencing a new chapter in this book, and a new chapter in the epistle, we are still considering the section which commences with chapter 3:20. Its place in this structure and its corresponding section can be seen if we lift out the following details from the structure which appears on page 8.

C	1:27 to 2:5.	Conversation *here*.	Stand fast. Mind of Christ.
	* * * *		
C	3:20 to 4:10.	Conversation *there*.	Stand fast. Body of Christ.

We have examined the word translated 'conversation' and seen that it means a manner of life worthy of citizenship, this citizenship being 'in heaven'.

There are a number of features which were opened by the apostle in chapter 1, to which he now returns and carries to a completion.

These are the exhortations to 'stand fast' (1:27 and 4:1).
Oneness of spirit, soul and mind (1:27 and 4:2).
Striving together *sunathleo* (1:27 and 4:3) and
Neither being terrified nor anxious (1:28 and 4:4-7).
Other features will appear as we proceed.

'Therefore, my brethren dearly beloved and longed for, my joy and crown, so stand fast in the Lord, my dearly beloved' (Phil. 4:1).

The English 'therefore' while always indicating a logical process, translates a number of small Greek connections, each of which have their own special value and place. In Philippians the English word 'therefore' occurs in six places, and translates *oun* (Phil. 2:1,28,29; 3:15), *oun ... men* (Phil. 2:23) and *hoste* (Phil. 4:1). In Philippians 2:1, 'therefore' marks the logical inference, in verse 23 the *men* answers to the *de* in verse 24, placing Timothy over against Paul. In chapter 4:1 *hoste* expresses the result. This is seen in the sixteen passages where *hoste* is translated 'insomuch', as for example Matthew 8:24 and Galatians 2:13.

To the apostle it appeared to be a logical result that any who enjoyed so priceless a privilege as a heavenly citizenship, should be characterized by the quality of stedfastness. This word *steko* is used by Paul seven times and occurs but once outside of his epistles, namely in Mark 11:25, where it is employed in a slightly different sense. To encourage these believers the apostle not only addresses them twice as 'dearly beloved', but adds 'and longed for, my joy and crown'. The way in which the apostle used these words 'my joy and crown' in 1 Thessalonians 2:19, shows that he had 'the day of Christ' in view, as in Philippians 1:6,10. These very moving words appear to have been employed by the apostle to soften and extenuate the mild reproach that follows :

> 'I beseech Euodias, and beseech Syntyche, that they be of the same mind in the Lord' (Phil. 4:2).

Both of these names are found in the inscriptions and the feminine *autais* 'help them', i.e. these women, show that two sisters in the Lord are indicated by these names. It will be remembered that women figure prominently in the beginning of the Gospel at Philippi. 'We spoke to the women that were gathered together' (Acts 16:13). Women were held in higher esteem in this part of the world than elsewhere and not only at Philippi, but at Thessalonica and Berea, women of rank were numbered among those that believed (Acts 17:4,12).

> 'The active zeal of the women in this country is a remarkable fact, without a parallel in the Apostle's history elsewhere and only to be compared with their prominence at an earlier date in the personal ministry of our Lord' (Bishop Lightfoot).

We gathered from Philippians 3:1,2, that there were some differences that divided believers at Philippi, and here in his appeal to these two women, the apostle seems to indicate that Euodias and Syntyche were partly responsible and pleads for unity among them.

Who it was that the apostle called my 'true yokefellow' will never be known until 'that day'. Conjectures range from Epaphroditus, the bearer of the letter, to the wife of Paul himself. Some have taken the word *sunzuge* 'yoke-fellow' as the actual name of the person addressed, the added word 'true' being Paul's comment, 'truly so called', even as in Philemon he makes a play upon the name of Onesimus 'profitable' (Philem. 10,11). The omission of the name, however, enforces a necessary lesson. In the same verse, Paul speaks of 'Clement also, and the rest of my fellow-workers, whose names are in the book of life' (Phil. 4:3 R.V.).

Some names are rendered famous because the Scripture records their good or their evil acts, some servants of the gospel will remain anonymous, until that day when the books shall be opened. It is wonderful to think that the names of fellow sinners like ourselves appear on the pages of Scripture, but it is even more wonderful to know that our 'names are written in heaven'. These 'fellow workers' in the gospel, were 'fellow strivers' engaged in a contest, *sunathleo* 'fellow athletes' running for the prize.

Who was 'Clement'? Ignatius and Polycarp are associated with the church at Philippi, but there is no ground for believing that the Clement spoken of here, in Philippians 4, is the Bishop of Rome, 'the central figure in the church of the succeeding generation'. Clement was a very common name and it is quite arbitrary to assume that Paul here addresses the future Bishop of Rome.

'Crown, Joy, Book of Life', these words indicate that the apostle at least had his mind on 'things above', his heavenly citizenship was to him an intense reality. After a reiterated exhortation to rejoice, the apostle passes to a further exposition of 'the mind' that should be 'in them' whose citizenship is indeed in heaven, whose names, indeed are in the book of life.

> 'Let your forbearing spirit be known to every one – the Lord is near. Do not be over-anxious about anything, but by prayer and earnest pleading, together with thanksgiving, let your request be unreservedly made known in the presence of God. And then the peace of God, which transcends all our powers of thought, will be a garrison to guard your hearts and minds in union with Christ Jesus' (Phil. 4:5-7, Weymouth)

The apostle had exhorted the believer to 'stand fast', but there is always the possibility that inflexibility may be mistaken for integrity, and obstinacy be substituted for strength of mind. *Steko* 'stand fast' here may mean 'do not yield', but *epieikes* 'moderation' (Phil. 4:5) means 'yieldingness'. Grace alone can enable the believer to exhibit at the same time inflexible tenacity, infinite gentleness, incorruptible loyalty, and a willingness to yield to every legitimate claim made by others.

The word *epieikes* is derived from *eiko* 'to yield', which is found in Galatians 2:5, where the apostle said that where the truth of the gospel was concerned he yielded subjection, 'no, not for an hour'. This passage shows that the 'yieldingness' which he indicates in Philippians 4, is no weak-kneed compliance at the expense of loyalty, it is a gracious readiness to give up personal rights for the sake of the truth. *Eikos* is used in logic for a 'probable proposition' as opposed to a positive fact, in ordinary language, something reasonable, fair and equitable. Trench defines *epieikes* as 'that moderation which recognizes the impossibility cleaving to formal law, of anticipating and providing for all those cases that will emerge, and present themselves to it for its decision; which, with this, recognizes the danger that ever waits upon the assertion of *legal* rights, lest they should be pushed into *moral* wrongs'.

A poet has expressed the meaning of this 'moderation' as ' ... the *soul* of law, the *life* of justice, and the *spirit* of right' (Daniel). Aristotle sets the man who stands up for the utmost tittle of his rights, over against the *epieikes*.

Ellicott says of this grace that it is 'not only passively noncontentious, but actively considerate, waiving even just legal redress'.

It is this spirit that the apostle says goes with heavenly citizenship, the mind of Christ, and the running for the prize. To exercise it in any measure of fulness and freeness is beyond the power of man unaided by abundant grace. It needs the mind that was in Christ Jesus.

'The Lord is near'. This is given as a reason for and an encouragement to exhibit this moderation and gentleness. Many expositors interpret this as though it read 'the *coming* of the Lord is near'. In James 5:8, we certainly read 'be ye also patient; stablish your hearts: for the coming of the Lord draweth nigh', but the word *parousia* 'coming' is added. Here, in Philippians 4, it would have to be supplied. That the words *engizo* and *engus* do not of themselves speak of the coming of the Lord, James 4:8 '*draw nigh* to God and He will *draw nigh* to you' makes clear, as also the reference in Philippians itself 'for the work of Christ he was *nigh unto* death' (Phil. 2:30). While the apostle had 'the day of Christ' ever in mind, he knew also the reality of His presence. In Ephesians the doctrinal basis of this nearness is stated. 'Made nigh (*engus*) by the blood of Christ' (Eph. 2:13), but in Philippians the practical enjoyment of that nearness is intended, while we 'look for the Saviour' (Phil. 3:20).

'Be careful for nothing'. This word *merimnao* occurs in Matthew 6, six times, where it is translated 'take thought'. In the seven passages where it comes in Paul's epistles it is translated 'to care'. In Philippians itself it occurs in 2:20, where it says of Timothy, he 'will naturally care for your state'. The Greek word is derived from *merizein ton noun* 'dividing or distracting the mind' and is in exact opposition to that 'one mind' which is inculcated in chapter 1:27. Again, the mind of Christ is the power and the antidote.

'Nothing', 'everything'. No limitations are set to the subject of the believer's prayers. Some have felt that the passage here must be limited to spiritual things, but the sequel, verses 10-20, speaks very much of physical needs over which the apostle might have been exceeding anxious had he not realized the nearness of the Lord. Prayer mingled with thanksgiving places the whole of life's concerns before the Lord, and is assured of one answer, the answer of peace. Whether every request will be granted is another matter, the peace of God is guaranteed. This peace of God is said to pass all understanding, and the word *nous* 'understanding' glances back to *merimnao*, 'divided understanding or mind'. Again, and yet again, 'the mind that was in Christ Jesus' is seen to be the main spring of the believer's life.

This peace of God 'surpassing every device or council of man, i.e., which is far better, which produces a higher satisfaction, than all punctilious self assertion, all anxious forethought' (Bishop Lightfoot), 'keeps as a garrison'.

The word translated 'keep' is *phroureo*. It is composed of *pro* 'before' and *ouros* a 'keeper', and properly means a military guard as in 2 Corinthians 11:32. Peace enters into the armour of Ephesians 6, and peace is likened to a garrison or military guard here in Philippians.   In Colossians peace is said to act as an umpire (Col. 3:15), while it is the God of peace Who shall bruise Satan under our feet shortly (Rom. 16:20).   Peace is by no means conceived of as a passive or negative state, it is active.

In the course of our ministry we meet with misunderstandings, slights, rebuffs and underhanded methods, and we are tempted at times to take direct action – what a blessing therefore to 'stand still and see the salvation of God', to stand encircled with this blessed garrison, to be kept in perfect peace, with no anxiety, and see all opposition fade, even as Hezekiah who spread out his trouble before the Lord, saw the Assyrian menace vanish like breath into the wind.

The mind which was in Christ Jesus seen in operation

We have already dealt with the presence of 'finally' in chapter 3:1 and 4:8 on page 150, and will not repeat what we have said there.

'Finally, brethren, whatsoever things are true ... think on these things' (Phil. 4:8).

In this concluding exhortation we have eight 'virtues' which fall into the following groups.

'Things true, honest, pure and just, describe the character of the actions themselves, the two former, being absolute, the two latter being relative; the fifth and sixth, lovely and of good report, point to the moral approbation which they conciliate; while the seventh and eighth, virtue and praise are thrown in as an afterthought, that no motive may be omitted' (Bishop Lightfoot).

'To the six Greek adjectives used in this verse we have in English no six corresponding adjectives covering just the same ground' (Weymouth.)

As 'these things' flow out of the 'peace of God' and lead on to the 'God of Peace' no effort must be spared to understand their import. Macknight observes 'the Greek philosophers were as keen as the moderns, in their disputes concerning the foundations of virtue. These disputes the apostle did not think fit to settle ... he mentioned in this exhortation all the different foundations on which virtue has been placed ... to show that its amiableness and obligation result from the union of the whole'.

The apostle Peter was moved by the same inspiration to give a list of virtues that the believer should add to his faith, saying, 'if these things be in you, and abound, they make you that ye shall neither be barren nor unfruitful in the knowledge of our Lord Jesus Christ' (2 Pet. 1:5-8). Paul also was concerned for the fruitfulness of the Philippian believers (Phil. 1:10,11; 4:17).

Alethes 'true', heads the list. We see that the word *alethes* is made up of *a* the negative, and *letho* 'to be hid'. The mythical waters of Lethe blotted out all memory, both of joy and grief. It is the essential character of truth that it loves the light and scorns the ways of darkness. While *aletheia* 'truth' is of frequent occurrence in Paul's epistles the adjective 'true' is found but four times, namely, in Romans 3:4, 2 Corinthians 6:8, Titus 1:13 and Philippians 4:8. It will be seen that it is placed in contrast either with a liar, or a deceiver.

Semnos 'honest'. This together with *semnotes* occurs seven times, and all references are confined to Philippians, 1 Timothy and Titus. In the majority of passages the words are translated 'grave' and 'gravity'. Modern usage has limited the English word 'honest' to trustworthiness in business and conduct, as opposed to fraud and cheating, but this is a derived meaning of the word. The Latin *honestus* is from *honos* 'honour'. Many occurrences in Shakespeare limit the meaning of 'honest' to sexual purity. Today we could hardly say with Ben Jonson 'you have honested my lodging with your presence'. In classical Greek *semnos* was used originally only of gods and divine things. The word is derived, according to Parkhurst and Schrevelius, from *sebomai* to worship, and so when applied to persons or things, means venerable, grave, serious, decent. It has been our complaint on more than one occasion, that certain Christian brethren have not acted with ordinary common decency and surely, any who are running for the prize of the high calling cannot excuse any lack of such 'honesty' in their dealings with others. Because we belong to Christ, and are ministering in holy things, truth, honesty, honourable intentions, unquestionable methods are alone permissible.

Dikaios 'just'. In Philippians 1:7 this word is translated 'meet' and in Ephesians 6:1, 'right', while in Colossians 4:1 it is synonymous with that which is 'equal'. The word is mostly translated 'righteous'. The Authorized Version choice of 'just' here is however to be commended, for while the word 'righteous' contains all that the word 'just' conveys, it covers a wider area. The word just has been defined as 'acting according to what is right and fair; giving and willing to give all their due, fair and impartial'.

Agnos 'pure'.   In Philippians 1:16 this word as an adverb is translated 'sincerely'. The Corinthians were said to have made themselves 'clear', through repentance and carefulness, of the charges laid against them (2 Cor. 7:11) and the moral character of the word can be seen in the same epistle, where in 11:2 it is used of 'a chaste virgin'. These are the four virtues classed together as absolute and relative actions.   The next couple point to moral approbation.

Prosphiles 'lovely'.   This obviously means an inclination towards love of friend, friendliness, being agreeable. The word does not occur elsewhere in the New Testament, but it was in common use and is found also in the Apocrypha. 'A wise man by his words maketh himself beloved', says Sirach and enjoins his reader to 'get thyself the love of the congregation' (Ecclesiasticus 4:7; 20:13). 'Whatsoever is endearing' is the translation of Conybeare and Howson. Alas, there exists in the minds of some who have a zeal for the truth, that to be ruthless, abrupt, and superior to any attempt to endear oneself with those who hear the Word, is to be avoided as sure marks of weakness or apostasy.   The great apostle did not think so.   He ever inculcates gentleness, patience, meekness and a willingness to concede all possible points, together with an incorruptible loyalty, an unchallenged integrity, and a complete fulfilment of the requirements of a faithful stewardship.

A teacher who inspires reciprocal love, may not necessarily be a preacher of unadulterated truth, neither is a teacher whose manner is repellent necessarily to be regarded as unfaithful to the message entrusted, but neither of these teachers approaches the ideal – Paul would have us speak the truth, yes, but speak the truth in love.

Euphemos 'good report'. This word in classical Greek meant a word of good omen and so in time came to be synonymous with uttering a blessing. The word *euphemia*, 'good report' is used over against *dusphemia* 'evil report' in 2 Corinthians 6:8, where the apostle gives a list of what he had endured for Christ and His truth. The word has come over into English as *euphemism*, and one speaks euphemistically when asking a guest if he wishes to 'wash his hands'. He is a discourteous and ill mannered bore who misinterprets the intention behind this softening of crude terms. Euphemy is a recognized figure of speech. 'To cover one's feet' (Judges 3:24 and 1 Sam. 24:3) is an example of this delicacy of reference in the Bible itself.

We all know the man who calls himself 'John Blunt', who boasts that 'he calls a spade a spade'; he is usually an arrogant and offensive person, who hopes that his 'bluntness' will be mistaken for honesty and directness. The apostle had no room for such. To have an honest or good report from without is expressed by the Greek word *martureo*, and the fact that Paul has chosen the rare word *euphemos* shows that he has something else in mind.

Lightfoot, discussing the word used by Paul, says, 'not "well spoken of", "well reputed", for the word seems never to have this passive meaning, but with its usual active sense "fair speaking" and so "winning" "attractive"'.

'If there be any virtue, and if there be any praise'.

Does the apostle in these two expressions sum up or recapitulate the previous list? Some expositors think so. There is, however, another point of view. The Greek conception of 'virtue' *arete*, held little in common with Christian graces and the apostle never uses the word elsewhere. Virtue today stands for moral excellence, few if any use it with a consciousness that it is derived from the Latin *vir* a man, and so *virile*. Different ages have held different ideas of what is or is not virile and manly. In days gone by an addiction to book learning was scorned by the nobility, art and medicine being likewise held to be beneath the notice of a true man. The Greek word *arete* is derived from *Ares* 'Mars' the god of war (see Areopagus, or Mar's Hill, Acts 17:19,22), and in Homer this virtue is generally limited to military service. 'Valour' rather than 'virtue' approaches nearer to the meaning in modern terms. With these facts in mind, Lightfoot's suggestion sounds reasonable :

'Whatever value may reside in your old heathen conception of virtue, whatever consideration is due to the praise of men; as if the apostle were anxious not to omit any possible ground of appeal'.

'Think on these things', 'on these things meditate', 'cherish the thought of these things'. There is no word for 'on' in the original, and the margin of the Revised Version reads 'Gk. take account of'. *Logizomai* which is here translated 'think on' occurs in the Greek New Testament forty times, in ten references the Authorized Version reads 'think', in the other thirty references 'account', 'impute', 'conclude', 'reason', 'reckon', 'number' and 'suppose'. Had the apostle intended the idea of meditation or thinking on, he had well established words at his disposal. *Logizomai* is the great word of Romans 4, where it is rendered 'count', 'reckon' and 'impute', but never could be translated there, 'meditate' or 'think on'. In Philippians itself *logizomai* is translated 'count' in the phrase 'I count not myself to have apprehended' (Phil. 3:13).

The last reference of the apostle is in 2 Timothy 4:16, 'I pray God that it may not be laid to their charge', or, as the Revised Version puts it, 'may it not be laid to their account'. Instead therefore of reading 'think on these things', read 'if there be any virtue, and if there be any praise, *reckon these things*, lay it to the account, give credit or impute them'. It is far too easy to break a bruised reed or to quench a smoking flax, but so did not the Lord we serve. Most of us have an eye for the faults of others, and where loyalty to the truth is at stake, much so-called 'Christian charity' is but compromise or worse, but 'in many things we all offend' and even though the magnifying glass of grace and love be needed, let us, as we look on our brethren in the faith, 'IF' there be any virtue, 'IF' there be any praise, let us 'reckon' these things, for such an attitude of mind, 'the mind of Christ', yet once again indeed leads to fellowship with the God of Peace, a prize to be enjoyed here and now.

There is no need to assume that in verse 9 the apostle turns from mere 'thinking' to 'practising', rather his thought is 'reckon these things' and these things indeed ye have learned, received, heard or seen in me, for Paul did indeed 'practise what he preached'.

How closely the apostle associated his doctrine and his practice, how needful that all who follow his steps should have a tender conscience regarding the relationship of the things taught and the life lived. What a comprehensive inquisition into his own life the apostle narrates in this fourfold reference 'learned, received, heard and seen'. In connection with the race and the prize, he had said elsewhere that he disciplined himself :

> 'lest in any way after acting as herald to others, he himself should be rejected from the lists' (1 Cor. 9:27 Farrar).

The mind which was in Christ Jesus and spiritual independence

'The Lord is near', 'the peace of God ... shall keep', 'the God of peace shall be with you'. The believer who can enter into these relationships is blessed indeed, and is rendered independent of circumstance, raised above human antagonism or assistance, and kept as with a garrison. It may be that this consciousness of complete dependence upon the Lord and complete independence of all that man could do, made the apostle commence his next section with a 'but'.

> 'But I rejoiced in the Lord greatly, that now at the last your care of me hath flourished again; wherein ye were also careful, but ye lacked opportunity' (Phil. 4:10).

With these words Paul opens the closing section of the epistle, a section that balances the opening section of the first chapter:

B 1:3-26.   Fellowship in gospel from the first day.

          *   *   *   *

B 4:-10-20.   Fellowship in beginning of Gospel.

The 'but' 'arrests a subject which is in danger of escaping ... it is as if the apostle said "I must not forget to thank you for your gift"'. On more than one occasion we ourselves have set out to thank a believer for financial help, but have occupied the bulk of the letter with other important matters and apologetically slipped the recognition of financial help in at the end under a 'P.S.'. However much we may work under pressure, or place spiritual things foremost, there is need to watch so that we give none offence. It is easily done.

The words 'hath flourished again' translate the Greek *anathallo*, a word that occurs in the LXX in Ezekiel 17:24, 'cause the dry tree to flourish'. The words 'care', 'careful' or 'carefully', occur in several passages in Philippians but they do not all translate the same Greek word. There is the care that borders on distraction (Phil. 4:6), and which is used of the extreme care manifested by the apostle and Timothy for the believer's state (Phil. 2:20); there is the care associated with the sending of a messenger (Phil. 2:28), which implied a measure of haste to know the result of the enquiry; and there is the care of the Church at Philippi for the apostle (Phil. 4:10), where the two occurrences in this verse translate the Greek word *phroneo* 'to think'. This word does not occur in Ephesians and once only in Colossians where it is translated 'affection' (Col. 3:2).

Phroneo 'to think', in Scripture applies commonly to the will and affections and occurs in Philippians more times than any other epistle.

The 'care' of the Philippians and 'the mind' that was in Christ Jesus employ *the same word* (Phil. 2:5; 4:10). The mind that should characterize the 'perfect' and the mind that was devoted to 'earthly things' or to 'things above' (Phil. 3:19; Col. 3:2) further indicate the range of this word.

The care for the apostle by the Philippians is likened to the periods of active life and quiescence in a tree, the cessation not being the result of indifference on their part but that of inability and of seasonable opportunity. This he hastens to add lest they should misinterpret his reference to indicate either a mild censure or a reminder.

'Not that I speak in respect of want', I do not want you to misinterpret me here, says the apostle, 'for I have learned in whatsoever state I am, therewith to be content' (Phil. 4:11).

'I have learned'. There is one kind of 'learning' that is bookish, this is represented by the word *gramma* in Acts 26:24. There is another kind of learning that is the result of teaching or instruction, *didaskalia* (Rom. 15:4), but the 'learning' intended by Paul here in Philippians 4 is experimental, *manthano* and used in Hebrews 5:8 of Christ Himself, Who 'learned' obedience by the things which He suffered. *Mathetes* is translated 'disciple' throughout the New Testament. This conception of discipleship is never entirely absent from the verb 'to learn'. For example, 'take my yoke upon you and learn of Me' is a learning by experience rather than by a book. 'Ye have not so learned Christ' (Eph. 4:20) is likewise experimental rather than doctrinal. The apostle had not 'learned' in whatsoever state he may find himself to be, therewith to be content, by merely book knowledge or even by sitting at the feet of a Gamaliel, but in the great school of discipline and experience. The English reader is likely, however, to miss the point of the apostle's statement here. Our version reads 'therewith to be content' but the word 'therewith' is an intruder and is misleading. Paul was NOT content WITH his lot, but IN SPITE of it. The word 'therewith' should be omitted. Again, the translation of *autarkes* by 'content' is too tame. The root of the word is *arkeo* 'to suffice', as in the passage 'my grace is sufficient for thee', or, 'shew us the Father and it sufficeth us'. Words such as 'contentment', 'comfort' and the like tend to take on themselves an easier and less robust meaning than they had at the start. *Autarkeia* is translated 'sufficiency' in 2 Corinthians 9:8 and 'contentment' in 1 Timothy 6:6; the prefix *autos* makes the word mean 'self-sufficiency'. Self-sufficiency, however, scarcely fits a believer, and is certainly out of place on the lips of Paul. We find that in ordinary Greek usage the word might be used of a country that needed no imports, and the meaning given by Liddell and Scott to *autarkeia* is 'to be independent'.

If the apostle had uttered these words in a different context he might have laid himself open to the charge of foolish boasting; he does not say, however, that he was 'independent' either of the grace of God or of the fellowship of His people, but he had learned by experience that his joy and his peace, his fruitfulness and his service, were *independent of circumstances*.

'I have learned by discipleship, in whatever state or circumstance I might be found, to be independent'.

In extension and in part explanation of this thought, he continued – saying, in effect :

'I know the two extremes, the extreme of deep abasement and the extreme of overflowing abundance. In all places, experiences and times, I have been initiated into a secret, I know what it is both to be full and to be hungry, I know what it is both to labour and suffer need. I am strong enough to meet and triumph over all life's experiences in Him Who empowers me'.

Let us examine this rich and promising passage. For we observe that the apostle changes the word 'I have learned as a disciple' (11), for 'I have been initiated' (12). The word *mueo* primarily meant 'to initiate into the mysteries'. Throughout the Roman world, and especially in the region of Greece and Asia Minor, pagan mysteries were flourishing, and only by initiation could one attain unto the secret wisdom that they enshrined. The initiate into the pagan mysteries passed through a series of disciplinary experiences, involving fasting, washings and endurance. So, said the apostle, I have not only been initiated into the fellowship of the Saviour's sufferings but by virtue of the faith that links me to the Risen Christ, I am strong enough to meet all things, rejoice in spite of them, and triumph over them.

The words 'I can do' which the Authorized Version employs to translate *ischuo* are scarcely full enough, neither do they reveal the connection that is intended between this initiated ability and the resurrection of Christ.

Ischus means strength or might. It is found in Ephesians 1:19 and 6:10, 'His *mighty* power', 'the power of His *might*'. In Ephesians 3:18, the compound *exischuo* is associated with the necessary empowering of the believer that he might 'comprehend' that which, in reality, passes knowledge. Such 'might' and 'enabling' had the apostle, and because of this he was 'independent'. It would have been easy for the apostle in this plenitude of power and in the independence in which he rejoiced to turn aside the fellowship of his brethren, but such would have been most ungracious and un-Christlike. Consequently we find him once again assuring the Philippians that his claim to independence must not be misinterpreted. Strong though he was, initiated as he had been, independent as he had become, he immediately added 'notwithstanding, ye have done well, that ye did communicate with my affliction', and once again he refers with loving pride to the fact that the Philippians were the only Church that had fellowship with him when he departed from Macedonia.

'For even in Thessalonica ye sent once and again unto my necessity' (Phil. 4:16).

Under this word 'necessity' Paul gathered together all his needs, his wants, his losses, his endurance – *chreia*.

He uses the word in Philippians 2:25 where he speaks of the loving ministry of Epaphroditus to his 'wants' and in the conclusion of the passage before us, he employs it in the glorious exultation 'my God shall supply all your *need*' (Phil. 4:19).

'Again the apostle's nervous anxiety to clear himself interposes. By this enlarging on the past liberality of the Philippians, he might be thought to covet their gifts. This possible misapprehension he at once corrects' (Bishop Lightfoot).

'Not because I desire a gift: but I desire fruit that may abound to your account' (Phil. 4:17).

The repetition of the verb 'desire' is emphatic.

'I *do not* want the gift, I *do* want the fruit'.

The word thus repeated is *epizeteo* 'to seek earnestly'. In a less emphatic form he uses it in Philippians 2:21, when he says 'all seek their own'. Remembering this, he says therefore 'I do not seek a gift from you, but I do nevertheless seek most earnestly that there should be fruit abounding to your account'.

It appears that the apostle uses in this passage two favourite Stoic words, namely *autarkeia* 'independence' and *apecho* 'I am full'. Not only am I full, but says the apostle 'I am overflowing' *perisseuo*. This word is used in Philippians five times, in Ephesians and Colossians once each, making seven occurrences in the prison epistles. The references are Ephesians 1:8, Colossians 2:7, and Philippians 1:9,26; 4:12 (twice), 18 :

'I have all, and abound, I am full'.

Such words speak of a completion and an overflowing that we might well reserve for the gifts of God alone. It comes almost as an anti-climax to read in explanation, that they refer to his having received of Epaphroditus 'the things' which were sent from them. When we consider the extreme difficulty and danger of travel in the days of the apostles, and the great difficulty that Epaphroditus would have had to convey and deliver a parcel of any magnitude, we realize that 'the things' sent by the Philippians could not have amounted to much, in themselves.

We know that the apostle in his second imprisonment wished for a cloak that he had left behind, and we can imagine that 'the things' brought by Epaphroditus would be small personal comforts provided by the loving care of the Philippians, many of whom were women. The apostle saw in their gifts something that resembled 'the mind that was in Christ Jesus'.

He says 'the things' that Epaphroditus had brought from the Philippians were :

'An odour of a sweet smell, a sacrifice acceptable, well pleasing to God' (Phil. 4:18).

Most believers reading these blessed words immediately recognize that the apostle is using identical terms with those which he had employed of the sacrifice of Christ in Ephesians 5:2, but what is not so immediately apparent is the play upon the name *Euodias* in Philippians 4:2, for the sister who together with Syntyche had been enjoined to unity, bore the name which meant 'sweet smell'.

Paul himself had likened his own devoted service to the pouring out of the drink offering on the sacrifice and service of the faith (Phil. 2:17), he now looks upon the service rendered by the Philippians in the same light. Perhaps it is not too extreme to say that all true service will be touched with sacrifice, which Romans 12:1 calls our 'reasonable' service. The last word, however, is with God.

Even though the Philippians had been the first to have fellowship, even though they had resumed that fellowship at the first opportunity, and even though their fellowship took on the character of a sacrifice and an offering of a sweet smell, Paul had one more word to say :

'But my God shall supply all your need, according to His riches in glory by Christ Jesus' (Phil. 4:19).

'The pronoun is especially expressive here "You have supplied all *my* wants (16,18). God *on my behalf* shall supply all *yours*"' (Bishop Lightfoot).

We have met with Christians who confessed that they had not found Philippians 4:19 to work. The reason, however, is plain. The promise of verse 19 is conditional. The believer who is self seeking, who knows nothing of sacrificial giving, has no place in the work or the promise of this verse. What the apostle teaches is that where there is this loving giving on the part of any believer, he can be well assured that God will be no man's debtor. Philippians 4:19 when read in its context is but another way of saying :

'Let him that is taught in the word communicate unto him that teacheth in all good things. Be not deceived; God is not mocked: for whatsoever a man soweth, that shall he also reap' (Gal. 6:6,7).

'But this I say, He which soweth sparingly shall reap also sparingly; and he which soweth bountifully shall reap also bountifully. ... and God is able to make all grace abound toward you; that ye, always having all sufficiency in all things, may abound to every good work' (2 Cor. 9:6-8).

If we are in the running with the apostle for the prize of the high calling of God in Christ Jesus 'this mind' will be most evident among us.

The epistle ends with the benediction at verse 20. To this the apostle adds salutations to every saint in Christ Jesus, and sends the salutations of 'they of Cæsar's household' which is surely a note of triumph; and so with his 'sign manual' (2 Thess. 3:17,18) the apostle Paul brings his epistle to a conclusion.

'The grace of our Lord Jesus Christ be with you all. Amen'.

Thus ends our attempt to open up the epistle of the prize, the epistle of the out-resurrection, the epistle of the mind that was in Christ Jesus.

Ephesian grace and glory is here balanced with experimental truth. The salvation so freely given is here 'worked out', and so becomes 'the salvation which is in Christ Jesus WITH age-abiding glory' (2 Tim. 2:10). May we heed the exhortation to 'press toward the mark' and run with patience the race that is set before us. May we, like the apostle, be able to say :

'I have fought a good fight ... henceforth ... a crown'.

INDEX TO SCRIPTURE REFERENCES

INDEX TO GREEK WORDS

G

Genetai	165	Huper	123, 134
Genomenos	96, 122	Huperairomai	123
Genos	158	Huperupsoo	123
Ginomai	115	Hupo	97
Ginosko	177	Hupomnesis	17
Gnorizo	61, 62	Hupsoo	123
Gongusmos	135		
Gonguzo	135	**I**	
Gramma	220	Iesou	72
		Iesous	172
H		Ioudaious	55
Hades	58	Isa	96, 105, 107, 108
Harpage	106, 167	Isa Theo	ii
Harpagmon	ii, 105, 106	Ischuo	222
Harpagmos	96, 167	Ischus	222
Harpax	106	Isopsuchon	80, 146
Harpazo	106	Isos	107
Heauton	96, 119		
Hegeomai	108, 163	**K**	
Hegesato	105	Kai	122, 138
Hemeras	20	Kaleo	85
Heteros	198	Kanon	196
Heuretheis	96	Kara	41
Hina	23, 55	Karadokeo	41
Ho brabeus	192	Kata	186, 196
Homoioma	ii, 118	Kata to loipon	150
Homoiomati	96	Katabrabeuo	186, 192
Homoioo	118	Kataischuno	42
Hon	122	Kataluo	66
Honestus	214	Katantao	184
Honos	214	Katantesantes	181
Hos	96, 108	Katanteso	181
Hosoi	195	Katatome	153
Hoste	129, 208	Katergazomai	130, 131
Hoti	38, 70, 71	Kauchaomai	150, 151, 155
Humas	26	Kauchaomoi	155
Huparcho	5, 97, 98, 115, 204, 206	Keimai	82
		Kenodoxia	110
Huparchon	ii, 95, 96, 97, 98, 99, 127	Kenoo	ii, 109, 110
		Kenos	109
Huparchonta	97	Kenosis	8, 112, 118, 142, 144
Huparchontes	99	Kerdaino	54
Huparchonton	97	Kerdeso	55
Huparxin	97	Kerdos	54
Huparxis	5, 97		

INDEX TO HEBREW WORDS

CHALDEE WORD

INDEX OF CHARTS

INDEX OF STRUCTURES